THE LOSS DEVASTATED ME. Never before had I felt so singularly responsible for a defeat. Despite the efforts of several teammates who tried to assure me that there was blame enough for everyone, I sat in front of my locker replaying the horrifying moment of the fumble over and over in my head.

Finally, I looked up to see Al Davis standing over me, his face burning crimson, lips pursed. He just stared angrily at me for what seemed like an eternity before finally spitting out what was on his mind. "I shoulda traded ya," he said. And with that he turned and stormed away, never to speak kindly of me again.

In a post-game report, network sports announcer Jim Gray made an observation that I might well have played my final game in the Coliseum as a member of the Los Angeles Raiders.

MARCUS

THE AUTOBIOGRAPHY OF
MARCUS ALLEN
with Carlton Stowers

By Marcus Allen
and Carlton Stowers

St. Martin's Paperbacks

MARCUS

Copyright © 1997 by Marcus Allen with Carlton Stowers.
Postscript copyright © 1998 by Marcus Allen with Carlton Stowers.

Cover photograph of Marcus Allen by Lynn Goldsmith.
Action photograph on cover by David Liam Kyle.

All rights reserved. No part of this book may be used or reproduced in any manner whatsoever without written permission except in the case of brief quotations embodied in critical articles or reviews. For information address St. Martin's Press, 175 Fifth Avenue, New York, N.Y. 10010.

Library of Congress Catalog Card Number: 97-16522

ISBN: 0-312-96623-7

Printed in the United States of America

St. Martin's Press hardcover edition / September 1997
St. Martin's Paperbacks edition / October 1998

10 9 8 7 6 5 4 3 2 1

To Mom and Dad—
I can't imagine where
I'd be without you.

CONTENTS

ACKNOWLEDGMENTS

The task of setting your life and thoughts to written form is not an easy one. Like many other realizations that have come to me over the years, I've learned another lesson the hard way. I can honestly say that the book now in your hands would never have become a reality without a generous amount of help and support from others.

Where do you start when passing out nods of gratitude? It begins with my family—mom and dad, brothers and sister, wonderful grandparents—who you will meet in these pages; and with Kathryn, my wife and best friend, who not only lent her support but served as a valued critic along the way.

Jillian Manus went above and beyond the duties of a literary agent as she helped turn an idea into a reality and became a friend in the process. My thanks also to Janet Wilkens Manus for not only teaching her daughter well, but for the vital role she played in this project. And to St. Martin's Neal Bascomb for his thoughtful and patient editorial guidance. The interest and encouragement of John Sargent and John Murphy of St. Martin's is also greatly appreciated.

Ed Hookstratten has been with me throughout my professional career, sharing sound advice and wisdom. More important, he's been a wonderful friend. Sincere thanks also to Jon Hookstratten.

As an athlete, I've been blessed with coaches from whom I not only received a remarkable education in the X's and O's but a great deal more: Vic Player and Roy Reed at Lincoln High; John Robinson, John Jackson, and Hudson Houck at

USC; Terry Robiskie, Ray Woolsey, and Tom Flores of the Raiders; Jimmy Raye and Marty Schottenheimer of the Chiefs.

My days as a member of the Kansas City Chiefs have been made special by people too numerous to list, but I would be remiss if I did not mention owner Lamar Hunt and general manager Carl Peterson and their families. Valued friends, they made me feel welcome, breathed new life into my career, and restored my faith in those who oversee the game I play.

I have always felt that the most overlooked ingredient in the growth of popularity of professional football are the announcers who bring its drama into millions of homes each weekend. Al Michaels, Dick Enberg, Paul Maguire, Frank Gifford, Bob Trumpy, Charlie Jones, Pat Summerall, and John Madden lend added excitement to what we do. Without them, our games would be far too much like the old silent movies. And to Jim Hill, my appreciation for your friendship, insight, and professionalism.

To Bryant Gumbel, Ahmad Rashad, and Lynn Swann—know that you have all been an inspiration to me.

And to Ronnie Lott, Dennis Smith, and Kenny Easley, who showed me early on the importance of playing the game at the highest level possible. I like to think we brought out the best in one another.

Mike Ornstein, Howie Long, Mike Haynes, Steve Smith, Todd Christensen, and Junior Seau can't be overlooked. Nor can Wayne Hughes, George Athan, Louis Marx, Roy Green, and my friends at Logo—Tom, Eddie, and Heather.

Bob Moore, Duane Lindberg, and Tim Tessalone have been unsung heroes whose unselfish efforts I admire and appreciate.

And here I should offer an apology to those whose names do not appear in these pages for a variety of reasons. You know who you are and that I thank you sincerely for your efforts, your input, and your friendship.

To a couple of courageous little guys named Anthony, I must say that you have taught me that real heroes sometimes come in very small packages. By coming into my life you have not only enriched it more than you know but have helped me to put things into proper perspective.

Finally, I should note that the most treasured and lasting thing I will take from my career in football is the camaraderie I've enjoyed along the way. To my teammates, past and present, one and all, I say thank you.

Marcus Allen
May 27, 1997

PREFACE

I suppose there are those times that people in virtually every profession can point to as examples of why they have enjoyed what they do. For the teacher, I would guess, it is seeing that first spark of understanding in the eye of a student who finally grasps the mystery of long division. To a scientist, the instant comes when he succeeds in proving a theory few others have embraced. And a minister will surely remember that moment when he first realized that his sermon was not only being heard but heeded.

We all have our touchstone moments.

I've been a football player for all of my adult life, fortunate enough to have enjoyed more than my share of recognition and reward. From the playgrounds of my youth to NFL stadiums across the country, I've seen the good and bad, highs and lows, and the just and unjust attached to the game I play.

That is what this book is about. By definition it is an autobiography, but its real purpose is to share with you my feelings about the game, its people, its pressures and pleasures.

The world in which I've lived is both unique and imperfect—which is to say it is not that different from your own. I've long contended that the game of football is something far more than a sixty-minute celebration of athletic prowess; something that goes well beyond the euphoric rush that accompanies victory or the numbing disappointment of defeat. To me, football has been a microcosm of life, filled with ups and downs, problems begging instant resolution, and constant challenges demanding to be addressed. The game has offered me a great classroom in which to learn valuable lessons about myself and my fellow man.

As I've reflected on my career, I've spent no small amount of time searching for that anecdote I felt best explains the feelings I have about sports; that single moment that neatly capsules the determination and teamwork necessary for success.

For me it came in the twelfth year of my professional career, in the 1993 play-offs during my first season as a member of the Kansas City Chiefs. We were playing the favored Houston Oilers in the Astrodome for the Divisional championship and leading by a single point with only a couple of minutes remaining in the game.

It had been one of those dogfight days during which every player—offense, defense, special teams—had given everything he had. We were all running on empty yet doing what we could to summon something extra to hold on to the win that would advance us—a team given little chance before the season had begun—to the AFC championship.

It was essential that the offense retain possession of the ball, keeping it away from the ever-dangerous Oilers attack.

And as we'd done so often during the game, we came to a third-down situation that was critical. Deep in the Oilers' end of the field, we needed one more first down to assure that we could run out the clock and cheat Houston of any chance for a comeback victory.

As we huddled, it was not quarterback Joe Montana who first spoke. Nor me. Instead it was Tim Grunhard, our six-two, three-hundred-pound center. Bruised and exhausted, his uniform spotted with blood, he looked at us through the bars of his scarred helmet, tears in his eyes. ''Dammit, guys!'' he began yelling. ''I'm just a big fat white guy from Chicago! I'm no star and I've never won anything in my whole fucking life. I want this so bad. *Let's go, guys . . . Help me out here . . . Let's do what we've gotta do.*''

That I broke for a 20-yard touchdown on the following play to seal our 28–20 victory that afternoon is not my reason for bringing up the anecdote. Rather, it is the raw emotion and incredible intensity that Tim verbalized in the huddle that afternoon. What he said was what everyone who has ever seriously competed in team sports has felt. There is absolutely nothing that compares with winning. And once in the heat of battle, with the roar of the crowd blocked out and your entire world reduced to a 100-yard war, no personal sacrifice is too great to ask.

Tim Grunhard is not a household name in professional sports. Few offensive linemen are. Yet the quest for victory is every bit as important to him as it is for the MVP quarterback or the All-Pro running back. And if a team is to succeed, it must have Tim's spirit spread from one end of the roster to the other.

Of all the qualities that go into the making of the game—speed, strength, strategy, field conditions, weather, you name it—the most important is emotion. It was true on the hardscrabble fields the Lincoln High Hornets competed on in my teenage days, in the giant college stadiums visited during my years at the University of Southern California, and on the playing fields of the NFL, where I've spent my Sundays for the past fifteen years.

That, too, is what this book is about.

Can't is the worst word that is written or spoken:
Doing more harm here than slander and lies;
On it is many a strong spirit broken,
And with it many a good purpose dies.

—Edgar Guest

PART I

A boy's will is the wind's will
And the thoughts of youth
are long, long thoughts . . .

—Longfellow

one

Family Values

When I was a kid, my father was always talking to us about his travels and experiences and how they had provided him with the rules of life in which he so firmly believed.

If a person was to be successful, if he was to be a responsible citizen and make a worthwhile contribution to society, he had to be certain that he was properly prepared to make the right decisions, have a clear grasp of right and wrong, and an appreciation for the rights of others. He would tell us quick judgments were the folly of those too lazy to take time to understand the world around them.

In time we could recite his lectures word for word, even as he gave them.

To the best of my knowledge, his philosophy was not borrowed from any book he'd read or speech he'd heard. Rather, it was his own, fashioned from a life of hard work and hard times.

Then—and now—my dad has always seemed bigger than life. He grew up as a country boy in Denison, Texas, and at age eleven became head of the family when his father died, leaving him to help his mother with his younger brothers and sisters. In a manner of speaking, my dad's been raising kids all his life.

And if he ever viewed it as an unwanted burden, I've never seen the slightest hint of it.

Then there is the lady he first met at a church picnic and eventually married. My mother shared his deep appreciation for family, faith, and the fruits of hard work. And I learned, at a very young age, to admire her courage. I was ten years old when a car went out of control on Winston Drive and swerved into our neighbor's front yard, striking a small child. Standing on our front porch, I watched as my mother bent over the badly injured little boy, frantically trying to resuscitate him. The child died, but she did everything she could. I remember her walking slowly back to the house, blood all over her, crying as if she had lost a child of her own. I recognized the sadness of the moment, but at the same time felt an immense pride in the effort she had made.

Together, my parents formed a rock-solid foundation for their children, teaching, advising, guiding, and always supporting.

They saw to it that each of us understood the importance of education and discipline. We sang in the Calvary Baptist Church choir, went to Boy Scout meetings, were taught to do homework before we played, and learned quickly that if rules were broken, discipline would quickly follow. My father was a firm believer in the ''spare the rod, spoil the child'' principle.

So, if you're anticipating one of those stories of an athlete who overcame insurmountable odds, who survived the brutalities of a broken home and somehow managed to make his way without direction or role model, mine isn't what you're looking for. I grew up in a loving environment, watched over and encouraged by both of my parents, learning their lessons of right and wrong. And, most important, the value of family.

Which is to say I am among the lucky ones. And for that I shall forever be thankful.

Sports were always a big thing to us. Not because my father urged us to be athletes but, rather, because of the enjoyment we found in the neighborhood games we played. And like all youngsters, we did our best to emulate the star players we watched on television. In baseball season we would draw chalk baselines in the backyard and do our six- and seven-year-old best to re-create the games we'd watched, each taking on the identity of a favorite player. Most often, I would be Roberto Clemente. If we watched an NFL game that was played in the mud, we would water down the backyard before getting our version of the game under way so we would be certain to get as wet and dirty as our heroes. I was Leroy Kelley of the Cleveland Browns. When the season changed to basketball, I was Walt Frazier of the New York Knicks or Jerry West of the Lakers, driving the lane in the driveway.

It's funny the things you remember about your childhood. While I had no real grasp of its significance at the time, I still can recall sitting in front of the black-and-white television in our San Diego home, watching the funeral of President Kennedy with my parents. I remember the casket with the American flag draped over it and little John-John saluting. I was only three. It was that same year that I got hit in the face with a baseball while playing catch with my brother Harold in the backyard.

And I remember when Martin Luther King died shortly after I'd turned eight. I knew by the reaction of my mother and father that the deaths of Kennedy and King were important and had a great impact on them.

It would be years, however, before I would begin to gain a real appreciation for the historical importance of such tragedies. At the time, my world was one of innocent fun and games. My dad, having never given up his rural Texas upbringing, bought us Shetland ponies to ride and kept them in a small barn he'd built in a canyon behind the house. As soon as we were old enough, he purchased shotguns for each of us and took us squirrel and rabbit hunting. And despite my father's careful teachings of firearm safety, there was a time when we were out hunting and Harold tripped and his gun accidentally fired. I felt the shot breeze past my head and angrily looked in his direction, yelling a safety tip of my own: "Harold," I said, "watch what you're doing." Ignoring city codes, my dad also raised pigs, assigning us the task of feeding, cleaning their pens, and, on occasion, joining him in the garage as he cleaned and dressed one, then cooked it in a pit he'd dug in the front yard. That, frankly, was a lesson I could have done without.

I much preferred it when my dad would take us to Balboa

Stadium on a Sunday afternoon to watch the San Diego Chargers play. I memorized the names of the Chargers players: John Hadl, Jerry LeVias, Keith Lincoln, Speedy Duncan.

History has always been important to me, whether it is in politics, social reform, or sports. It amazes me today that so few of my teammates have any recollection of those who played the game before them.

HAROLD (RED) ALLEN: *I've been a big sports fan all my life. Back when I was a kid, I did it all—football, basketball, baseball—until I joined the navy when I was seventeen. But I made it a point never to push my kids into organized sports. That was a decision I left to them.*

Actually, when Harold and Marcus got old enough to play Little League baseball, neither expressed much interest. They'd rather play pickup games in the neighborhood with the older kids like Monte Jackson and Terry Jackson, who were in high school at the time. Monte later went on to play football for San Diego State and the Oakland Raiders. Terry played for the Jets and the Giants.

It was a kid named Roy Kuykendall who got Harold and Marcus interested in organized sports. He came by the house one day, wearing his fancy Little League uniform, and that did it. The boys came running to me, asking that I sign them up.

The next thing I knew, I was sponsoring and coaching a team called the Encanto Braves. Then, when Pop Warner football season rolled around, I found myself helping to coach the Southeast Lions.

I remember figuring up how much it would cost for bats and balls and equipment and telling Gwen, "Well, there goes my beer money."

My first real hero was my older brother. Harold was not only an outstanding pitcher and a tough linebacker, but one of those kids who was an outstanding student and got involved in every school and church activity available to him. And in time I became more than a little jealous of the attention he received.

So I decided that the best way to get the family to take more notice of me was to run away from home. I slipped away and hid in a small boat my dad had docked nearby, certain there would be all manner of frantic concern and search. But I waited and waited and nobody came. Disappointed and a little frightened as darkness approached, I returned home in time for dinner. Nothing was said and it would be years before I learned that my parents had known where I was all along.

Which is to say we did all the normal kid stuff: hiding in the trunk of someone's car to sneak into the nearby Rancho Drive-In, or running across the freeway despite stern instructions never to do so. A friend and I once hid in the canyon and tried smoking. On my first attempt to inhale I choked and tossed the cigarette away, setting a grass fire that required the attention of a couple of fire trucks.

It was not the only time they came calling. My first encounter with the incredible powers of an adrenaline rush came when I was ten years old and got word at school that our house was on fire. I sprinted all the way home, almost a mile, never feeling even slightly tired, and learned that the twins—Michael and Michelle were five at the time—had found some fireplace matches and taken them into one of the bedrooms to play with them. When they realized that the curtains were on fire, they simply left the room and closed the door. By the time my mother discovered what had happened, most of the bedroom had been destroyed, and my dad was faced with a sizable remodeling job on the house he'd originally built.

Everything we did, everything we were involved in, Dad saw as a learning experience. If some lesson was not taken from each new adventure, it was judged worthless in his eyes. When he would travel throughout San Diego County to various job sites, loading us into his truck to join him, there was a purpose. He wanted us to become familiar with the world beyond our predominately black neighborhood. When he coached our teams, he emphasized the importance of fair play and sportsmanship as much as he did the fundamentals.

When he came home with a drug-identification kit and he and Mom sat us at the kitchen table, carefully describing what marijuana, cocaine, and heroin looked like and the dangerous effects they had, we were really still too young to even be aware that there were drugs in our community. He wanted to be sure we knew the dangers before we ever faced them. "If," he told us, "any of you decide that you have to try alcohol or drugs, I want you to do it here at home. That way I can kick your ass right away." His message was clear: He didn't want us using drugs or alcohol at all.

If there was drinking or drugs at a party, we were told to leave and come home. Don't even drink the punch; someone may have spiked it. Stay out of the bathrooms; that's where a lot of people hide to smoke a joint or snort cocaine.

My parents had a remarkable knack for taking a proactive approach, of dealing with problems before they occurred. A touch of paranoia, Dad explained, was not a bad thing to have.

And certainly we kept them on their toes, rebelliously testing their authority. More often than not, I was the leader in that respect. For instance, there was the Great Team Boycott that I organized and orchestrated.

As our Little League coach, my dad was convinced that my abilities as a shortstop were most beneficial to our team. I was determined to play center field. I repeatedly asked him to move me to that position, only to be told that it was a selfish wish that did not take into consideration the overall good of the team.

Finally, I devised another plan of attack, summoning the help of my teammates. Playing the clubhouse lawyer, I solicited their support, not only convincing them that I should play center field, but to refuse to play any more games unless the coach allowed me do so.

Once I had the backing of my teammates, I boldly issued the ultimatum to my dad. With the team gathered around, he listened patiently to my demand and the threat of a peewee players' strike, then just nodded. "Well," he said, "I guess the season's over, then."

The support of my fellow players collapsed like a house of cards. And I returned to my spot at shortstop—and was named to the all-star team at the end of the season.

• • •

Looking back, I marvel at the energy my parents had. While both worked, they always seemed to get everyone to practice and games on time and to be there when we played. For every hour my father put in as a Little League or Pop Warner coach, my mother matched it in the role of team mother.

GWEN ALLEN: *Marcus was always the last kid out the door, except when it came time to go to practice or a game. On Sundays, when we were getting ready for church, he had every excuse in the world not to go. He'd lost his shoes. He wasn't feeling good. What he wanted to do was stay home and watch football on television. He knew he wasn't going to fool me, but he never stopped trying.*

I think at a very early age he knew he was going to do something special as an athlete; as if he knew it was his calling. Even when he was little, he seemed much more co-ordinated than the other kids, so much more focused. I can remember him telling me that he would dream about his games the night before he was to play them. And in his dreams he always won. It was fun for him, but it also seemed to be more important to him than it was to his friends. Back in Little League and peewee football, Marcus was the only one I ever remember crying if they lost. Winning was impor-tant to him, even then.

Participating in our athletic endeavors, however, was but a small part of the job they did as parents. They were also our protectors.

Despite the efforts of many who lived in our part of town, the neighborhood had fallen victim to the same problems that were affecting urban areas throughout the country. As my father constantly warned, drugs were becoming increasingly prevalent. And gang activity was on the upswing.

At Lincoln High there were almost one thousand students enrolled, yet the average daily attendance had fallen to some-thing like five hundred. Student discipline had become such a problem that school officials at first decreed that all sports events would be played during daylight hours in an effort to better control the crowds. Then, when that failed to solve the problem, they were forced to move all games away from the campus to a safer, neutral site.

And though still in junior high at the time, I was fast becoming aware of the dangers that had invaded our streets. It was not at all unusual to be confronted by some high school student while walking home from school. One afternoon I found myself in a fight with this older guy. We were going at it in the middle of the street, and as I began to get the best of him, two of his buddies jumped in. Then a couple of my friends joined in. Finally, when it was clear we were not going to back down, the fight ended as quickly as it had begun. But as I was walking away, I heard one of my classmates yell out that the guy I'd been fighting had a gun. I immediately ran to a neighbor's house, where I phoned home. No one was there, so I eventually started walking on toward our house. And soon got my second lesson in the magic of adrenaline.

As I neared the house, the guys I'd encountered earlier jumped from behind some bushes, wielding boards with nails in them. I again began running, this time into the street, where I narrowly escaped being hit by a car. Then I hurdled a fence in stride and returned to the house of the neighbor, who volunteered to give me a ride home.

When I got there, I ran inside and got one of my dad's guns, then sat on the front porch with it on my lap until my parents arrived.

As I waited, a throbbing pain developed in my right wrist. It was broken.

When my parents got home, I explained to my dad what had happened and told him there was a good chance that I would be involved in another fight the next day.

That, he said assuringly, would not happen. For the next two weeks, Dad drove me to school and was waiting in his pickup outside every day when class let out. He made certain that the shotgun he had with him in his truck was visible to anyone who passed by.

So I didn't grow up in Mayberry RFD. Nor, on the other hand, was it a ghetto by any means. It was a neighborhood populated by far more good people than bad. And my parents and those like them refused to give in to that element that seemed dead-set on turning it into a combat zone.

In time there was a fragile standoff. The gangs didn't go away but stayed more to themselves, marking off their turf, where we learned not to trespass. The drug sellers and users moved in their own circles, rarely trying to invade ours.

Though Lincoln High School labored under the reputation of one of San Diego's "rough schools," it fought to survive, with teachers and concerned parents determined to keep a wholesome academic atmosphere alive.

It would ultimately be the scholastic home of all the Allen children. And the good times and fond memories would far outweigh the bad.

It troubles me at times that so much public attention has been focused on me during my athletic career when everyone in my family has accomplished so much. For my money, seeing five children through college is every bit as noteworthy as winning a Heisman. Touching lives in the way my mother has for so many years as a licensed vocational nurse is considerably more important than the Sunday NFL scores.

And it should be noted that I was hardly the only Allen family member who enjoyed success in athletics.

Had it not been for a stroke of fate, Harold would probably be playing major-league baseball today instead of selling pharmaceuticals. While he was in high school, the Cincinnati Reds were interested in signing him as a catcher. But in his junior year at Lincoln High, he visited Australia as a foreign-exchange student and returned home with troubling pain in his ankle. Doctors found a tumor and a small hole in one of his bones and an operation was necessary. And while the tumor was benign, the ankle problem reduced his mobility.

Damon, my younger brother, has been matching or bettering me all his life. While I quarterbacked Lincoln High to the CIF championship, he did it twice. While I was on a national championship football team in my freshman year at USC, he pitched Cal State Fullerton to the 1984 College World Series championship. And though the Los Angeles Rams expressed interest in drafting him as a running back, he made it clear he would play football professionally as a quarterback or not at all. He went to the Canadian Football League, where he is now in his thirteenth season, starting for the British Columbia Lions. He's proud of the fact that I played on a Super Bowl championship team and was named the game's Most Valuable Player, but quick to point out that he quarterbacked the Edmonton Eskimos to *two* Gray Cup titles and was voted the MVP in *both* games.

The twins also made their athletic marks. Michael had the ability to be a great center fielder—a cannon for an arm—and went to Cal State Fullerton on a scholarship. And Michelle, who played basketball, softball, and volleyball, was Lincoln High School's Most Outstanding Female Athlete in her senior year.

Michael now works for a subsidiary of McDonnell-Douglas and Michelle is raising two children of her own.

And there's the youngest, Darius, now twenty and in his third year at Southern Cal. A soft spot discovered in his lumbar vertebrae shortly after he was born prevented him from being involved in sports.

I can honestly say that my parents are proud of all their children. They have spread their love equally, and that, to me, is an incredible accomplishment. I find myself wondering at times if they realize the remarkable job they have done; if they know what shining examples they have been, not only for me, but for us all.

I tried a few years ago to say some things to my father that were long overdue. I bought a video camera and for Father's Day made a tape that I sent to him. I had Whitney Houston's "The Greatest Love of All" playing in the background, and I tried to tell my father how much he meant to me.

I said, "Granted, there are times when we don't see eye to eye. I attribute that to the way you raised me. At a young age you instilled in us the importance, the significance, of being an individual. To depend on no one. To be a proud, dignified, and confident individual. To carry ourselves as winners at all times. We tend now to depend on you less and less. Don't feel hurt or unappreciated. Understand, you created these little monsters. We are a reflection of you. I may be stubborn and hard-headed and think at times that I'm invincible. But that's not true. I need you, Daddy. I love you with all my heart. And I thank you for being my friend.''

Later Mom told me that he hadn't been able to make it all the way through the tape the first time he watched it. She said he turned it off and sat crying for quite some time.

HAROLD ALLEN: *I was always looking for anything that would keep the kids out of trouble. So, when he was young, I signed Marcus up for piano lessons. For two or three months, I'd drop him off at the teacher's house, then go pick him up a couple of hours later. Then one day the teacher called me and said, "Mr. Allen, I just got your check in the mail . . . and I don't think it's right for you to be paying me for lessons your son isn't taking."*

When I asked Marcus about it, he admitted that what he'd been doing was waiting until I turned the corner, then sneaking off to play ball with some of his buddies until it was time for me to come back and pick him up.

GWEN ALLEN: *After he signed his contract with the Raiders, you know what he did? He bought himself a baby grand piano and hired a teacher. Marcus has always been one of those who felt there was a right time for everything, that God gives you everything you need to get you where you're going.*

Of all the wonderful things that have happened to me, my parents are far and away the best. I grew up in a family rich with love, and my role models weren't celebrated athletes or high-profile stars from the entertainment world. They were the construction worker and vocational nurse who sat across the dinner table from me as I grew up.

I couldn't have asked for more.

two

"Dammit, Just Score"

In the years before court-ordered school integration and busing of students, Lincoln High School was predominately white, with one of the largest enrollments in the San Diego school system. But by the time I arrived, in the fall of 1975, there was only one white among the one thousand students. Thus we were referred to as a "predominately black school." With a very heavy emphasis on *predominately*.

The school's once-rich athletic tradition—which I'd first become aware of as a little kid when my dad would take me out to Lincoln's football and basketball games—was taking a beating. The days of producing such great players as Art Powell, who later played for the Raiders; Wally Henry, who went on to the Philadelphia Eagles; and Dave Lewis, later a Tampa Bay Buccaneer, were gone. Other programs throughout the city and county had as many as three thousand students from which to select members of its teams. Once, virtually every able-bodied kid in school had participated in sports, eager to be a part of the Hornets' championship tradition. But by the time I moved from junior high to the Lincoln campus, a sizable portion of the student body had other interests. For the first time, I began to see the drug problem my father had so long lectured against.

No weekend party, it seemed, was complete without alcohol and marijuana. And it was not at all difficult to pick out those who were experimenting with angel dust, a hallucinogenic drug that was growing in popularity. They walked the halls like zombies, their brains apparently fried to a crisp.

Why they would endanger their minds and bodies in such a manner was a mystery to me. Seeing someone so out of control, having no real idea what he was doing or what was going on around him, bothered me greatly. I could not understand it any more than I'm able to today. All my life I've felt this need to be aware of my surroundings, to be in control of my emotions and actions. Getting high or drunk, it was easy to see, made such control impossible and I wanted no part of it.

Vic Player, a smallish history teacher who also served as Lincoln's football and track coach, had no tolerance for drug and alcohol abuse. If you were to participate in his programs, the rules were simple and strictly enforced: Miss a practice without written permission from your parents or the family doctor and you weren't allowed to play in the next week's game. If you smoked, drank, or used drugs, you shouldn't bother checking out a uniform. He would find out and you would be quickly dismissed. There was no second-chance clause written into any of his rules. The ability to block, tackle, run, and jump played no part in his decision.

"I love what I do," he would tell us, "but I'm damned if I'm going to waste my time on somebody not willing to make a one-hundred-percent commitment to what we're trying to do."

None who reported for football practice my sophomore year doubted his sincerity.

It has been my good fortune during the course of my career to play for a sizable number of excellent coaches. Some have been better tacticians than others, some better at relating to the players, making game-day decisions, or determining the best way to use available personnel. It is my opinion that no coach deals better with the myriad responsibilities of the job than those at the high school level. Many manage to achieve success in spite of tight budgets, low salaries, limited time, and talent pools from which to draw that would make a college or pro coach throw up his hands in surrender.

Vic Player was such a coach. He'd come to Lincoln in 1968 to coach the track team, then was given the job of head football coach six years later when the program was at one of its lowest points. He not only brought to the task a reputation for discipline but a drill-sergeant work ethic. And he was, first and foremost, a teacher of what he called ''life lessons.'' If you played for Coach Player, you were expected to learn the benefits of fair play and sportsmanship, academic excellence, and team effort.

''If you play for me,'' he would tell us, ''I become your surrogate father and I treat you like you're my own. I make the rules.''

His entire staff consisted of assistant Gary Flisher, a former San Diego State player who coached the offensive and defensive lines, and Roy Reed, who coached the junior varsity squad. Reed, in fact, had been something of a second father to my brothers and me, involved in our athletic pursuits from Pop Warner days through high school, teaching and encouraging us every step of the way.

I had watched my brother Harold play middle linebacker for the Hornets, admiring the aggressive play he brought to the game despite the fact that he weighed only 155 pounds. I made it clear to Coach Player that my goal was to uphold the Allen tradition as a hard-hitting defensive player. During my sophomore year I got my wish, when he put me into the starting lineup at free safety.

And even through most of my junior season, there was little mention of my spending much time on offense. On the depth chart I was listed as the backup quarterback but seldom played the position unless we had a game well in hand and the coaches wanted to give the starters a breather. Which was fine with me. Compared to the action on defense, the quarterback's role was pretty boring stuff.

Our defense was getting more attention in the press than our offense. Against Madison High, a school with three times the enrollment of Lincoln, we played to a 0–0 tie in a game that a number of people said was one of the best they'd ever seen. That afternoon I made something like forty tackles and got my picture in the paper for the first time.

I was feeling pretty good about myself until Coach Player

called me into his office, pointed to the newspaper, and gave me his speech about how he tolerated no "stars" on his teams. He congratulated me on my play and even admitted that he was pleased to see that I was getting some recognition, but his primary message was clear: No individual, regardless of how many tackles he might make, was more important to the team than anyone else.

For the first time in years, Lincoln made it into the playoffs, matched against traditional powerhouse Morse High.

It, too, developed into a defensive struggle until early in the third quarter when our offense moved the ball to the Morse one-yard line. With a first-and-goal, we were confident that we could power the ball into the end zone and take the lead.

To help out with the blocking, I was sent in to play at the wingback position. From a foot away, our fullback dove into the line and was met by a big Morse tackle who jarred the ball loose. Their middle linebacker picked it up and was running toward our goal line before I realized what had occurred. Picking myself up off the ground, I took off in pursuit, having no real chance of catching him. Instead, I did one of the most stupid things I've ever done as a player.

Catching up to one of the Morse players who was trailing behind the ball carrier, I vented my frustration by hitting him in the head with a forearm. The referee immediately threw his flag, said I'd committed an act of unsportsman-like conduct, and told me I was ejected from the game.

Not only were we down 6–0, but I had been banished to watch the remainder of the game from the sidelines. After the coach chewed me out for my senseless behavior, I took a seat on the bench while our offense tried to mount a comeback.

We failed to move the ball and were forced to punt. When I heard the coaches yelling for the defense to get ready to go back out, I pulled on my helmet and quietly slipped into the group waiting to take the field. I had not seen the official come to our bench and inform anyone that he'd ejected me, so maybe Coach Player was under the impression that my punishment had only been the 15-yard penalty I'd received. I knew that in all likelihood the referee would turn me around and send me back to the bench, reminding me that he'd thrown me out. But what the hell? I figured it was worth a shot.

To my surprise, nothing was said as I lined up at my safety position. I played the remainder of the game.

And though we would lose by that one fluke touchdown, we left the field optimistic about our team's future. Most of our starters would be back the next season.

One of the few key players we would lose to graduation, however, was our quarterback. Coach Player began talking about me taking his place the following fall. It was not an idea for which I had even the slightest degree of enthusiasm. I was a defensive back—had, in fact, been picked to the All-CIF team after my junior year—and it was there I wanted to stay.

Coach Player met me halfway. "You're now a two-way starter," he announced.

VIC PLAYER: *Despite all his talent, Marcus was never a prima donna. He worked hard, always trying to improve himself. But that's not to say he didn't need to be disciplined at times. He was a prankster. He'd hide over by the pole-vault pit when it came time to do wind sprints, just waiting until we discovered that he was missing. Then he'd appear with this mischievous grin on his face and get back to work. From the first time I met him, I could see that football was fun for Marcus. Before I really got to know him, I wondered if maybe it was too much fun for him; if he'd be even better if he took things more seriously. But I learned pretty quickly that he knew when to end the fun and get serious.*

The idea of becoming the starting quarterback is the dream of the majority of kids who play high school football. But not me. I was a defensive player and that's all I wanted to be. And so, during spring training, I set out to convince Coach Player that I wasn't the man for the job. I fumbled snaps, I took my time getting back to set up to throw passes, threw interceptions, and often loafed during drills. I pouted and constantly begged to be allowed to go to the other end of the field where the defense was practicing.

"Look, we have a chance to be the best team Lincoln High has had in a long time," Coach Player said, "but only if we come up with a quarterback who can move the ball. You're that person. That's going to be your job."

I continued to argue.

He threw me off the team, sending me to the locker room in the middle of practice. His words are just as clear to me now as they were on that afternoon two decades ago: "If you're not going to try, then get the hell out of here."

I rushed home, expecting some sympathy, maybe even some manner of intervention from my dad, only to learn that the coach had already called to explain his reason for dismissing me from the team. Surely my father would be outraged. After all, I'd been All-CIF and the team needed me at safety, right?

To my dismay, Dad was quite nonchalant about the whole matter. Finally, I asked what he had said to Coach Player. "I told him that the problem was between him and you," Dad said with a disinterested shrug. "Now, don't you have some homework you need to do?"

Such were his lessons on priorities.

Later that evening, I approached him again. "Do you think the coach would let me back on the team if I promised to try hard to be a quarterback?" Again I secretly hoped that my father might feel inclined to put in a good word for me, to rescue me from the hole I'd dug for myself.

"I suppose that would be up to your coach," he said.

The following morning, hat in hand, I went directly to the coach's office and apologized, promising I'd do everything I could to become the best quarterback I could be. I was allowed to return to the team that afternoon, feeling greatly relieved that my athletic career was still intact.

And Coach Player's prediction came true. During my senior season we scored over five hundred points, establishing a new county record. And our defense set new marks for the most shutouts by a team and the fewest points allowed opponents.

We went into the play-offs only a 0–0 tie short of a perfect season. And while I should admit that my abilities as a passer were nothing that would have caused Joe Montana concern, I found myself enjoying being a two-way player.

The offense that the coaches had designed for us was bottom-line simple. Our basic play was what we called a flood option, which called for putting three receivers on one side of the field. A fourth receiver would go deep from the opposite side. On each play I had four receivers. And if none of them were open, I was supposed to run the ball. With limited confidence in my ability to throw deep, I ran a great deal.

Once in the play-offs, we were faced with a situation all too familiar to Lincoln High. Every other school was much larger than ours—and they were all undefeated.

There were also some whose fans were well out on the fringe. Our first play-off opponent was Granite Hills High School of El Cajon, a part of the county where, rumor had it, redneck ways and Ku Klux Klan activities were still part of the lifestyle. In the week leading up to the game, anonymous calls and letters came to our school regularly. "If you bring that quarterback with you," one letter suggested, "he won't get his black ass home alive."

If it was meant to upset or frighten me, it was a waste of someone's time and postage stamp. As my dad observed, if a guy doesn't even have the courage to sign his name, it is unlikely that he has the courage to follow through on any kind of threat. "Don't give an asshole like that the satisfaction of a reaction," Dad suggested. I took his advice and made up my mind to focus my attention on playing as well as I possibly could.

Still, I was relieved when we defeated them in a close game.

The following week against Sweetwater, we jumped out to a 21–0 halftime lead and thought we were well on our way to another of our shutouts and an easy victory, but with a couple of long runs and deep completions, they came alive and soon were ahead by a field goal.

The score remained that way until late in the game, when we faced a fourth-and-15 situation at midfield with just forty-five seconds remaining. We advanced the ball to the 35 with a halfback pass, then, behind great blocking, I ran it in for a touchdown on the final play of the game.

Our next opponent was Patrick Henry High, a team whose uniforms looked just like those worn by the Green Bay Packers. And they looked to be almost as big. Again, it was a game that went down to the wire. Trailing 3–0 with just a minute left to play, we got the ball at our own 48-yard line.

Throughout the season, Coach Player had rarely sent in a play from the sidelines. But at that particular moment, with the season hanging in the balance, I was eager for any advice he might have to offer. I called time-out and jogged to the bench area. Even before I reached him, I could tell that the coach was not happy.

"What do you want me to do?" I asked.

Coach Player glared at me. "Young man," he said, "I think it is pretty obvious. Dammit, just score!"

We moved downfield and on fourth down from the one, I faked a handoff to our fullback and threw a touchdown pass to the tight end. We'd cut it pretty close. Only three seconds had remained in the game.

The win over Patrick Henry put us into the county championship game against Kearny High School in San Diego Stadium. Early in the week we began hearing reports that a crowd in excess of twenty-five thousand was expected to be on hand.

Kearny, unbeaten, had advanced through its bracket of the play-offs in much easier fashion, winning each of its games by sizable margins. I don't have to tell you who was favored. The newspapers were billing the game as something of a David vs. Goliath kind of matchup.

We beat them 34–6. Everything we did seemed to work perfectly. Early in the game I got loose down the sidelines and went 85 yards to score on my longest run of the season. I later had runs of 30, 20, and 10 for touchdowns. And, finally, I intercepted a Kearny pass and returned it 60 yards for my fifth touchdown of the night.

I couldn't believe it later when someone told me I had accounted for 317 yards of offense.

Looking back, I'm not sure I've ever been more thrilled over a victory. Fans were cheering, bands playing, the cheerleaders crying.

We did something that night that went far beyond a championship trophy, letter jackets, and newspaper clippings for scrapbooks. Before that year, people had looked down on Lincoln High. In the minds of many, we were just another urban school that was steadily going to hell in a handbasket. And unfortunately there were those on our own campus who had begun to believe such an image was justified.

But that championship changed things. It provided the foundation for a change of attitude, the rebirth of a pride that was desperately needed.

I was neither old enough nor smart enough to realize it at the time, but what was proven in that championship season of 1977 was that sports can work wonders.

As we stood on the field, celebrating our triumph, I saw my father climbing down the retaining wall near the stands. I began jogging toward him just as a security guard stopped him and informed him that no one was allowed on the field except players and coaches.

I heard Dad yell to the guard as he pointed in my direction, "That's my son!" The guard smiled, nodded, and urged him in my direction.

As we embraced he was crying and told me how proud he was of me. I've never felt better in my life.

VIC PLAYER: *In thirty-eight years of coaching, I've had one parent give me an award. After we won the 1977 CIF championship, Marcus Allen's dad presented me an engraved pen-and-pencil set. That meant a great deal to me.*

Red Allen never interfered, never criticized. He told me, "You're the coach." But he also warned me, "If Marcus's grades ever fall below a B, I'm pulling him off the team."

I've never seen anybody take over a team the way Marcus did that year. He was one of those kids with that special gift for rallying everyone around him. When he had something to say, all the other kids listened. If he thought something could be done, everyone else soon believed.

Was he a great quarterback? Nah. Most of the passes he threw that year looked like wounded ducks. But he did throw for 1,434 yards and nine touchdowns that year. Was he fast? He never even came close to making any of our relay teams during track season, but in his senior year he ran for 1,098 yards and scored twelve touchdowns. On defense he was even more incredible, intercepting eleven passes and returning four of them for touchdowns. And he had almost one hundred unassisted tackles. He was a winner, and that's the kind of person we had to have if we were to accomplish our goal. Marcus never saw himself as the star, but the truth is he was the reason we won the championship that season.

I was so pleased when he was named the CIF Player of the Year and selected to three schoolboy All-American teams—Parade magazine, Scholastic Coach magazine, and the National High School Coaches Squad. The awards were all well deserved. Before he graduated we did something that we'd never done for any Hornets player: We retired his jersey and placed it in the trophy case.

Truth? Back then, I had no idea Marcus was going to develop into the great athlete he has become. But I did have the strong feeling that he was going to do something special with his life; that he would grow up to be someone who made a difference.

The remainder of my senior year sped by with basketball season and a steady stream of calls from college recruiters. Not surprisingly, little was mentioned about me one day becoming a great college quarterback. They were all looking for someone who could play in the defensive secondary. Finally, I felt confident that there would be no argument about what position I was best suited to play. My offensive days, I felt sure, were over.

Toward the end of the year, the *San Diego Tribune* named me its Schoolboy Athlete of the Year, an honor that surprised me since I'd participated in only two sports. Generally, the award went to someone who excelled in football, basketball, and one of the spring sports. But because of the visits I'd planned to make to some of the college campuses, I'd decided Coach Player would have to look elsewhere for another six-two high jumper. I knew my absence would do absolutely no harm to the track team's chances of winning another championship.

I would be lying if I said that the awards and the attention I'd begun to receive weren't flattering. But it did nothing to really change who I was. There still were a lot of pretty girls at Lincoln High who weren't that interested in going out with a guy whose only transportation was his dad's old work pickup. When I went to parties, I always made it a point to park several blocks away so my friends wouldn't see what I was driving.

One spring evening soon after, my mother came into my room and asked if I'd ever heard of the Waldorf Astoria Hotel in New York. ''You're going to be visiting there soon,'' she said, beaming.

The Hertz Corporation had instituted what it was calling the Number One Award and announced that a selection committee had picked what it considered the most impressive performance by high school athletes in each state.

My five touchdowns in the CIF championship game had been selected as the top performance by a California athlete. She explained that the banquet would be held at the Waldorf.

Handing out the awards, Mom told me, would be O.J. Simpson, a man I viewed as one of the greatest football players in history. For years I had followed his career with the Buffalo Bills on television, admiring the grace and power he brought to the game, at times fantasizing of one day playing at his level.

What I didn't anticipate was that in the years to come we would become close friends.

three

Higher Learning

My father had this routine that he put each of his sons through. First it was my older brother Harold, then me, and later Damon. Dad would pick the hottest day of the summer and take us to whatever construction site he was working on and assign us the most difficult task he could find. From sunrise to sundown we labored to keep pace with him and the other crew members. The job was backbreaking and thankless.

Then, at the end of the day, when we were dog-tired, thirsty, and hungry, Dad would give his speech. "You've got a choice," he'd say. "You can do this every day for the rest of your life. Or you can go to college and learn to use your brain instead of busting your ass."

For as long as I could remember, there was never any doubt about my going to college. The only question was where. And when the recruiters began to show an interest, my parents made it clear that the decision would be mine.

Their only advice was that I understand the greatest value of an athletic scholarship was the educational opportunity it offered.

It was flattering and exciting to receive calls, letters, and visits from coaches from all over the country, all inviting me to come look over their campuses. My first inclination was to take advantage of the offers and do some traveling. It sounded like fun to visit places like Hawaii and the famous Notre Dame campus, to see the stadiums where Washington,

Nebraska, Arizona State, and the University of Michigan played their games.

But as time neared for the visits, I began to question my reasons for making them. I knew Notre Dame was an excellent school but I had no interest in going there. The more I heard about the winters in Nebraska and Michigan, the less enthusiasm I had for their schools.

I did travel to Norman, Oklahoma, though, to look at the University of Oklahoma and get better acquainted with its coach, Barry Switzer. He was a likable, laid-back kind of person with a reputation not only as an excellent coach, but as one who genuinely cared about his players. And, of course, the Sooners were among the best college football teams in the country. What intrigued me most, however, was the fact that Coach Switzer had been the only one to recruit me as an offensive player. He said I would be his next triple-option quarterback.

While I still felt the real excitement of the game was on defense, I have to admit that during my final year at Lincoln High I had enjoyed playing offense. A solid tackle or an interception is one thing, but I learned that the rush from scoring a touchdown is something special. I didn't mind at all the idea of doing it at the collegiate level.

Thus I returned home from Oklahoma, excited over the possibility of playing for the Sooners. And concerned about how my parents would feel about my attending a school so far away. From Little League and Pop Warner days, they had never missed one of my games. "Don't worry about that," Dad assured me. "If that's where you want to go, it's fine with us. I might have to rob a bank now and then, but we'll be there to see you play."

In time it occurred to me that my interest in Oklahoma had more to do with the challenge of playing there than it did with Barry Switzer and his program. He was apparently the only one who felt I had the talent to make it as a college quarterback. And I liked the idea of proving that I could.

There were some friends who urged me to stay at home and attend San Diego State, a smaller university with a fine reputation and a good football team. They hinted I would get lost among the superstar players at a major university. Such suggestions were subtle and rarely made to me directly, but the message was clear: There were those who doubted that I had the ability to make it on a big-time team.

In Southern California there have historically been two legendary athletic programs. The UCLA Bruins had one of the finest basketball teams in the nation, while across town the USC Trojans could always be counted on to be among the best in college football.

From the moment USC expressed interest in me, I knew where I would go to school. I had watched them on television as a kid, memorizing the names of their great players, trying to imagine what it would be like to wear one of those cardinal-and-gold uniforms and play in front of eighty thousand people in the Los Angeles Coliseum.

Going out of the way to show interest, Hudson Houck, one of the Trojans' assistant coaches, attended every game I played my senior year. He never pressured me, didn't criticize other schools, never hinted that USC might be willing to bend the rules and offer some kind of illegal incentive should I agree to come there. He just made it clear that they wanted me and would give me every opportunity to prove myself.

HUDSON HOUCK: *When you're trying to convince an athlete of Marcus's caliber to come to your school, the recruiting process becomes very similar to dating. I did everything within the NCAA rules to make him aware that USC was keenly interested in him.*

Every Friday during the season, I'd leave Los Angeles just as soon as our practice was over and drive to San Diego to watch him play. Lincoln High was a small school in a pretty rough neighborhood. There was such concern about the dangers people faced after dark that school officials had decided against playing games on their campus. So, in effect, Lincoln played an away game every Friday.

It was remarkable to me that in the midst of all those problems, the Allen family was so upbeat and positive. Marcus's parents were determined to raise their kids in the right way, and doing a helluva job at it. I've never met a more solid family. And that was one of the things we coaches looked for when we were out recruiting. You wanted to know where a kid's from, what kind of value system he's been exposed to.

There was no doubt that Marcus's life was in order. He was a polite, happy-go-lucky kid with remarkable athletic ability. You didn't have to be around him long to pick up on his character and determination to succeed.

I saw it every Friday night during his senior year. I saw it when I attended his basketball games. I saw it every time I went down to watch him receive some new award. I even saw it in the way he walked across the school grounds.

Barry Switzer, the coach at the University of Oklahoma, wanted him in the worst way and was our main competition. He was talking to Marcus about being an option quarterback in college, and for most kids that would have sounded far more glamorous than playing defensive back. But I shot straight with him. USC wanted him in its secondary.

Gwen Allen was a delightful lady. I ate quite a few of her home-cooked meals that year. And Red and I got along great. We'd go out now and then and shoot pool or have a few beers. A lot of times we'd talk very little about Marcus. Red Allen was just someone who I enjoyed being around and getting to know.

I had no doubt that Marcus could play at the college level, but it was that Kearny game that made me realize he was going to be something very special.

O.J. Simpson helped us in recruiting Marcus. It was standard procedure for us to occasionally call on some of our high-profile alumni to put in a good word, write a letter or make a phone call. I don't recall ever specifically asking O.J. to contact Marcus. He did it on his own. They'd met during the Hertz Number One Award banquet, and from that time on, O.J. took a special interest in Marcus.

By the time John Robinson, the USC head coach, paid a visit to our home, I was ready to sign. It was a thrill just to meet the man I'd grown up greatly admiring, to have him sitting in our living room. It was one of the few times in my life that I can remember feeling really awestruck. And a little embarrassed. During his visit, there was a storm and the electricity went out and for much of the evening we sat talking in the light of the candles Mother had lit.

Coach Robinson was not only likable, he was a straight-shooter. There was no talk of my one day becoming a great quarterback for the Trojans. "We want you," he said, "in our defensive secondary."

That sounded fine to me.

The transition from high school to college is a hazardous venture for anyone. One day you're eighteen years old, living in the comfortable routine of your own home, familiar with everything and everyone around you. The next day you're in a new world, walking among a sea of strangers on a campus that is larger than your old neighborhood.

I was immediately appreciative of the fact that my father had seen to it that my brothers and I were introduced to a world beyond our all-black neighborhood as we grew up. His purpose in seeing that we were exposed to a wide variety of people and places became evident—and a valuable asset as I made my way into college life.

In addition to its well-earned academic and athletic reputation, the University of Southern California is a school whose enrollment is dominated by affluence. It is a "rich kids" school; new cars and designer clothes are the rule rather than the exception. Most of its students arrive from upscale high schools with excellent academic reputations.

Lincoln High lacked such credentials. Though I had graduated with a 3.3 grade point average, I quickly realized I was less prepared for college-level courses than many of my classmates. I could see immediately that I was starting out behind. Fortunately, I'd never had any problems with studying and schoolwork and was able to get over that hurdle with a minimum of difficulty. For most, the greatest adjustment is more social than academic.

Some of the black players who were cast into a mixed-race environment for the first time in their lives admitted concern over the fact that they had no idea how to interact with white classmates. My advice was far from original, coming instead from my father: You treat everyone equally and as a friend until you're given some good reason not to.

Then there was the economic reality of life as a college athlete. There are those who insist that a scholarship athlete—getting a free education in exchange for simply playing a game—has absolutely nothing to complain about. And while it was true that many of my teammates would not have been able to attend college without their scholarships, it hardly meant that they were totally free of financial concerns.

Not until this year did the NCAA finally recognize one of the biggest social problems faced by collegiate athletes throughout the country. Under the terms of a scholarship, an athlete is provided tuition, books, fees, and room and board. Financially, then, we did have a free ride.

But what about those times when an athlete wants to ask a coed out on a date and doesn't have the money for a movie or dinner? What does an athlete from a poor family do when he's in need of a new pair of shoes or bus fare home and has no money in his pocket?

In my first year, I can remember how badly I felt for some of my teammates who, after we had won a game played before a sold-out stadium, would return to the dorm rather than go out for dinner or on a date to celebrate, because they didn't have any money. Something was drastically wrong with that picture.

The NCAA rules said that athletes on scholarship could not work, even at a part-time job. At the same time, the coaches could accept lucrative contracts from manufacturers just for the assurance that the players would wear a particular shoe or line of jerseys. A football program like the one at Notre Dame could make a multimillion-dollar deal with a TV network for exclusive rights to broadcast its games. Everyone's pockets were being filled—except the athletes'.

There were stadiums filled with season-ticket holders coming to see us play, and all the while, too many of those who the fans came to cheer couldn't even afford to send out for a pizza after the game. While the economic problem was more generally prevalent among the black players, it affected everyone.

And it created a confusing contradiction. The football players, generally among the most widely known members of the campus community, felt a sense of isolation from the mainstream. All because they were constantly broke and embarrassed to admit it.

In January of 1997, almost two decades after I first stepped onto a college campus, the NCAA narrowly approved a rule change that would allow their athletes to hold a part-time job and earn as much as $2,500 during the course of a school year. There were even a few of the governing body's members who suggested that the time had come for athletes to be paid some small amount directly by the school. But, as usual, they were too much in the minority. It'll probably not happen in my lifetime.

And all the while college coaches and administrators wonder publicly why more and more athletes, finally tired of being exploited and broke, are prematurely giving up their eligibility and signing professional contracts.

The NCAA's new ruling does not solve the problem. Okay, so they're saying an athlete can get a part-time job and earn $2,500 during the school year. When is he going to do it? He's got classes to attend, studying to do, daily practices, team meetings, travel to away games. That doesn't leave a lot of time to do much else.

The unfairness still exists. And as long as it does, it is going to be very difficult to argue with an athlete who decides to give up his last year of eligibility and sign a high-dollar professional contract. While I did complete my four years at USC, I made the decision to go on to pro ball without first getting my degree. It was purely an economic choice. And though I still don't have one, I know that a college diploma is a valuable thing. But when measured against a million-dollar signing bonus, it becomes something you can go back and get later, when you can better afford it.

The Trojans' recruiting class of 1978 was considered one of the best in the country. There were my dormitory roommates Chip Banks and Riki Gray, both outstanding high school linebackers. We had defensive linemen Dennis Edwards and

Charles Ussery, fullbacks Arthur Hemmingway and Paul DiLulo, and quarterbacks Scott Tinsley and Timmy White.

All of us secretly wondered how we would be able to convince the coaches that we deserved playing time in our first seasons, what with the impressive upper-class talent that was available. I had trained harder in the summer months than ever before, running for hours along the beach in a heavy pair of combat boots I'd bought at an Army-Navy store for fifteen dollars. Even with that, I was concerned over whether I would be in good enough shape to compete with the kind of athletes I knew USC had. To me, the starting lineup looked more like an all-star team than a college squad, with people like Ronnie Lott and Dennis Smith at defensive safeties, Charles White at running back, and Brad Budde, Anthony Munoz, and Keith Van Horne in the offensive line.

Whatever questions I had would only be answered when two-a-day practices got under way, and I couldn't wait to learn the difference between high school and college workouts. What I had not considered was the possibility that my entire athletic future would quickly take a dramatic and unexpected turn before I'd even suited up for my first college game.

We were still in the first week of practice and I was playing defensive back behind Larry Braziel when Coach Robinson approached me. "I've got something I want you to think about," he told me. A couple of our tailbacks who were expected to be backups to starter Charles White had been injured, causing an unexpected depth problem at the position. "What do you think about moving over to offense and working behind Charles and Dwight Ford?"

I'd never taken a handoff in my life, had no real grasp of the demands of the position, and had come to USC convinced that my ever playing offense again was a dead issue.

Naturally, I told the coach that I was ready to give it a try. If memory serves me correctly, I even made some flip remark about not being able to win the Heisman Trophy playing defense.

• • •

Aside from my weekly trips downfield as a member of our specialty teams, I played sparingly my freshman year. But I learned a great deal, much of it from watching Charles White. In practices or games, I'd never seen anyone tougher. At five-ten, 180, he was small by tailback standards but ran with the authority and aggressiveness of someone who thought he was seven feet tall and weighed three hundred pounds. Despite quickness, speed, and moves that left defenders grasping at air, he seemed to delight in the opportunity to run over people.

And he quickly taught me a lesson I continue to use today. It has been a long-standing tradition among USC tailbacks to run the ball 40 to 50 yards downfield on every practice play. The Mike Garretts and O. J. Simpsons and Anthony Davises had done it before Charlie. I immediately fell into the routine.

But with White having an All-America season and the team in the running for the national championship, I rarely got much chance to show what I was learning on game days.

Still, the excitement of college football Saturdays exceeded my wildest imagination. The bands, the giant stadiums filled with people, the television cameras, and the travel to places I knew little or nothing about was fast becoming an education in itself.

For instance, I had never been to the Deep South, and like most black men had heard of its history of racial injustice, marches, riots, and Ku Klux Klan mentality. I knew that by 1978 giant strides had been made in equality and integration but, like most of the blacks on our team, still felt some apprehension over a scheduled trip to Birmingham to play Alabama in the third game of the season.

As the week approached, good-natured jokes—mostly aimed at the younger and less traveled members of the team—filled the dressing room. Teammates mockingly wondered what "two" hotels we would be staying at since it wasn't altogether certain that Birmingham's better hotels would allow blacks to stay. Somebody mentioned that Alabama was one of the few schools in the U.S. that still routinely burned a cross during its pre-game pep rallies.

I knew that my chain was being yanked. But on the nig

we checked into our Birmingham hotel, I had a moment of doubt. There was a knock at my door well after curfew, and when I opened it there were several figures clad in white sheets standing in the hall. The look on my face must have been something as my visitors—pranksters on our team— were laughing their asses off as they ran down the hallway, back to their beds from which they'd robbed their disguises.

I wasn't offended. I knew my teammates well enough to be certain there was no cruel intent to what they'd done. It was what it was: a harmless college boys' prank. What it did, actually, was poke fun at an old mind-set that was finally giving way to more enlightened thinking.

There is an often-told story that suggests it was the University of Southern California and an outstanding black fullback named Sam Cunningham who actually did more for integration in the South than all the civil-rights workers combined. It was in his first varsity game that Cunningham ran for 135 yards on just a dozen carries, scoring two touchdowns in a 42–21 upset victory over an all-white Alabama team in 1970. Legend has it that immediately after the game ended that afternoon in Birmingham's Legion Field, the Crimson Tide coaches received instructions to begin recruiting black players in earnest.

I have no such heroics to report from my first year with the Trojans. My playing time on offense came late in games, after Charles had done his damage and we had big leads. There were a couple of times against Michigan State when I very nearly broke loose for a touchdown, only to lose my footing on the damp Coliseum turf when I tried to cut too sharply. Afterward, Coach Robinson told reporters that I "wanted to go places my body wouldn't take me."

But I was making progress and enjoying being part of a team that was proving itself better than the pre-season pollsters had predicted. We had opened the year with wins over Texas Tech and Oregon, then scored a big upset against Alabama as White had one of those afternoons that is a ~~ight-reel maker's dream. He ran for 199 yards, through, ~~d around the Crimson Tide defense.

~~st as everyone was beginning to feel we were on

a big-time roll, Arizona State defeated us, 20–7. And while
the loss was disappointing, it provided a jolt we needed. We
rebounded to win our next seven games, including a real nail-
biter against Notre Dame.

Our quarterback, Paul McDonald, had a hot hand that day,
and when we led by 24–6 after three quarters, I began enter-
taining the hope I might get in for a few plays at tailback
before it was over. But then Notre Dame quarterback Joe
Montana put on one of the displays that would become his
trademark in years to come. With forty-six seconds left in the
game, he had led his team into a 25–24 lead.

But with the final seconds ticking away, a long pass from
McDonald to our tight end Calvin Sweeney moved us downfield, and with only two seconds remaining, Frank Jordan
kicked a 37-yard field goal that gave us a 27–25 victory.

We ended the season at 11–1 and were headed to the Rose
Bowl, ranked third in the nation behind Penn State and the
Alabama team we had already defeated. You figure that one.

While the nation's press was billing the Sugar Bowl matchup of undefeated Penn State and Alabama as the battle for
the national championship, we defeated Michigan, 17–10, in
the Rose Bowl. And being a part of it was one of the greatest
thrills of my athletic life. It was a time when the Rose Bowl
was not only the ''granddaddy of all the bowl games,'' but
the most prestigious to play in. Add the fact that we were
playing for the national championship, and it became college
football's version of the Super Bowl.

I felt strongly that we deserved to be number one, particularly in light of the fact that Alabama had knocked Penn
State from the unbeaten ranks.

The Associated Press would award the national title to Alabama while United Press International's poll picked USC. I
don't think it's necessary to tell you which one I agreed with.

My introduction to college life went far beyond those things
I had dreamed of. It was more than warm, colorful autumn
Saturdays and winning games. More than late-night dorm
room bull sessions, Rose Bowls, and a run for the national
championship. It was a time in which I began to get my fi-

real look at the adult world; a time when I began to learn new lessons about priorities and started to realize that some of the most important things in life are never reflected on a stadium scoreboard.

A friend of mine, Arthur Hemmingway, had arrived at USC at the same time I did. A highly recruited fullback, he, too, looked forward to making his place on the team, but just weeks after his arrival, he stepped from a curb near campus and was hit by a car. For several weeks he lay in a coma. When he finally woke, he was told that he would survive and ultimately recover from his head injuries, but his days as an athlete were over.

It had never occurred to me that things could end so swiftly, so unexpectedly. Nor had I thought about how much we take for granted in our daily lives.

Months later, on a Friday night before we were to play Stanford, my mom phoned to tell me that my grandfather had died after a lengthy battle with cancer. I had known for some time that his health was failing, but had never really considered that he would soon be gone.

As I'd grown up, loving him, looking up to him, I was certain he would be a part of my life forever. Like my father, he had been a man so kind and generous that every kid in the neighborhood knew they could go to him for help and guidance. There were times when I was jealous of the fact that so many of my friends greatly admired my grandfather. I remember thinking, Why don't you guys get your own grandfathers?

His death had a profound effect on me, just as Arthur Hemmingway's accident had. And as I pondered the events, measuring them against concern over playing time, won-lost records, and national polls, I learned something of the importance of priorities.

Change, it occurred to me, was something over which none of us have a great deal of control.

wo-a-day practice sessions that preceded my sophomore had just begun when our sports information director aside to say that I was to meet Alan Greenberg, a sportswriter for the *Los Angeles Times,* in Heritage Hall immediately following the morning workout. Greenberg wanted to interview me and get my reaction to being moved to yet another position.

With Charles White entering his senior year as the odds-on favorite to win the Heisman Trophy, there wasn't much chance that I was going to see a lot of playing time at tailback. "But we need for you to be part of the offense," Coach Robinson had explained. To do so, I would need to play fullback, where my primary job would be to again do something at which I had little experience. There would be an occasional opportunity to carry the ball or run a pass pattern, but first and foremost I would serve as Charles's lead blocker.

Eager to play, I assured the coach that I could handle the job, giving little thought to the size and strength of linemen and linebackers who I would be required to block.

Keeping my appointment with Greenberg, I gulped down cups of apple juice as he asked his questions. He wanted to know how I was adapting to the shift to fullback.

"Sookay. Ahn' kinna likin' it, really."

I'm sure he must have wondered how I ever expected to earn a degree in speech and communication as he strained to understand my mumbled responses.

Looking back, I probably should have explained to him that during the morning practice I'd collided with linebacker Larry McGrew, who was roughly the size of the building in which we were sitting, and my nose had been broken and was swelling even as we spoke. I should have let him know that at the moment I was having one helluva time even breathing, much less enunciating properly.

In his article, Greenberg kindly made no mention of my garbled answers and wrote his forecast for our upcoming season. Charles White, he pointed out, would serve as the thoroughbred of the USC backfield.

My role would be that of the plow horse. And while I preferred it to sitting on the bench, waiting to go in on special teams or for a few offensive plays late in the game, there were times when I wondered about the wisdom of volunteering to become a human punching bag. I lost track of ''stingers'' I experienced after shoving a shoulder against some defensive tackle who outweighed me by a hundred pounds or so. Upon impact there would always be this sudden burning sensation that began at the base of my neck and went all the way to the tip of my fingers. Then for a few seconds there would be a feeling of numbness. After each game there wasn't a muscle in my body that didn't ache. Before one bruise healed I had another one on top of it. My shoulders felt like exposed nerve endings. Most nights I couldn't even find a comfortable position that would allow a really restful sleep.

From the experience I gained a new respect for backs who spend their entire athletic careers blocking for others. And I looked eagerly toward the day when I could hand the job off to someone else.

RONNIE LOTT: *There are few more thankless jobs than the one Marcus had in his sophomore year. Mind you, he wasn't some 250-pound linebacker-type the coaches decided to put into the backfield to open holes. This was a guy of average size who had come to school determined to be a great defensive back. And before he could even get settled in, he was being moved all over the field. First to tailback, which he'd never played. Then to blocking back.*

During his sophomore year I saw him endure pain that would have caused a lot of players to walk away, saying it just wasn't worth it. Some of us had moved into an off-campus apartment that fall and invited Marcus to live with us, so I got a firsthand look at what he was going through.

There would be times when he'd come home after a game and his hands would be so swollen from hitting the shoulder pads and helmets of big defensive linemen all afternoon, that he couldn't even pick up a fork. I wondered how he kept doing it.

When I give talks to high school players, I tell them about ~~s~~ Allen. Not the guy who won the Heisman or was the ~~~uable~~ Player in the NFL, but Marcus Allen, the col-~~~~ore who blocked his ass off to help someone else ~~~~. I've always said that the real team player is

the guy who willingly steps up and does something no one
else wants to do. That's the Marcus Allen I tell the kids about.

I'm sure Ronnie doesn't tell them what a lousy cook he was.

He and fellow defensive backs Dennis Smith and Eric
Scoggins—they called themselves "The Three Blind Mice"—
had this apartment in the Hancock Park area and invited me
to move in with them. They didn't bother telling me until I
arrived that there were only three bedrooms—each taken, of
course—and I would be sleeping in the living room, where
any hint of privacy was nonexistent. All traffic to the kitchen,
the bathroom, or the front door went directly past my bed.

Ronnie, I quickly learned, fancied himself something of a
gourmet despite the fact that the only recipes he ever learned
were those printed on the back of Hamburger Helper packages. He'd make this elaborate production of preparing dinner
for the four of us, always promising a treat unlike anything
we'd ever experienced. Then he'd bring out another Hamburger Helper dish.

The excitement that preceded the '79 season was electric. On
the basis of our showing the year before, just about everybody
was picking us as the favorite to win the national championship. With so many starters returning, several sportswriters
and broadcasters were even suggesting that we might be the
best USC team ever.

And Charles, already the leading rusher in Pac-10 history,
was ready to make his run for the Heisman.

It was all pretty heady stuff, and the chance to be a part of
it quickly dulled the aches and pains that accompanied my
new job.

Early in the year, I even got an opportunity few Trojan
fullbacks receive. In our season opener against Texas Tech,
White suffered a shoulder injury early in the game. With him
on the sidelines, we became a fullback offense for the remainder of the afternoon, and I carried the ball for over 100
yards and scored my first collegiate touchdown as we won.

Looking back, it was probably one of the most important
games of my career. No matter how confident and well pre-

pared one is, there is always that whisper of doubt that you can actually get the job done until you've actually had a chance to prove it. Scoring the touchdown was not so much a thrill as it was a relief. Playing well against Texas Tech was a great confidence-builder for me. I left the field that day fully convinced that I was going to be able to compete at the big-time college level.

But I didn't break out in any wild celebrations. I knew that getting to carry the ball that often would hardly be the norm. A week later White was back and off to the races. Against Oregon State and Minnesota, we had scored thirty-five points by halftime and by the fourth quarter the starters were already through for the day.

Still, the coaches constantly reminded us of the danger that is attached to believing our press clippings, pointing out that the tough part of the schedule lay ahead.

It was hard not to think highly of yourself when you read that someone like Charley McLendon, the legendary LSU coach, was saying you were "the best team in the country—right after the Pittsburgh Steelers and the Dallas Cowboys."

Coach McLendon's praise was clearly a psychological ploy. His Tigers gave us a large and much-needed dose of reality when we played them in Baton Rouge. Though Charles would gain 185 yards rushing, we had trouble getting the ball into the end zone and after three quarters were trailing 12–3. Everything Coach Robinson had warned us about Tiger Stadium was true. The LSU band played so loudly that we had difficulty hearing our signals, and the roar of the crowd never seemed to stop. It was like trying to play football in an insane asylum.

Finally, we managed to score twice in the final quarter and win the game, 17–12. Everyone was glad to leave Baton Rouge behind. My ears were still ringing when we got home, our number-one ranking a bit tarnished but still intact.

The following Saturday, in the comfort of the L.A. Coliseum, we beat Washington State, 50–21. Then things went south.

Stanford was our homecoming opponent and, despite their

being a better than average team, came into the game as a decided underdog. Their defense was vulnerable and we took full advantage of it in the first half, building up a 21–0 lead. Our running game was working like clockwork and the defense was stopping Stanford cold.

But in the second half the wheels came off. The Cardinals' quarterback, Turk Schonert, came out throwing in the third quarter and couldn't miss. Picking at our defense, he moved his team on long drives that kept our offense standing on the sidelines, wondering if we would ever get back on the field.

Before all was said and done, Schonert had directed his team to three touchdowns. The game ended in a 21–21 tie. And I couldn't imagine a loss feeling any worse.

Though still unbeaten, we were no longer the front-runner in the polls—and the toughest part of our schedule remained ahead of us.

There are those who insist that the shock of a near-loss to a team you felt you should have beaten is just the kind of wake-up call needed to make a team realize its full potential. Since I've never been much of a fan of losing or ties, I'm not sure I totally agree with the philosophy, but the fact remains that once our winning streak ended and we'd dropped in the polls, we turned into one helluva football team.

White ran wild the next weekend against Notre Dame, gaining 261 yards on forty-four carries. McDonald threw for 311 yards and a couple of touchdowns. And we won it, 42–23. Aside from a couple of times when I was almost certain that I'd knocked a shoulder out of place or broken my hand blocking against the gigantic Notre Dame defenders, it was an ideal day.

Played before a national television audience, the game was the showcase that Charles needed to convince the Heisman voters that he was the premier running back in the United States, not Oklahoma's Billy Sims.

From that point on we never faltered, beating California, Arizona, and Washington before closing out the regular season against UCLA.

• • •

Of all the great crosstown rivalries that once appeared on the NCAA schedule, only Southern Cal vs. UCLA remains. Gone are the days when Fordham against NYU shut down Madison Avenue and caused great swarms of New Yorkers to break out in frenzied renditions of their favorite fight song. It's ancient history now. Same with the once-legendary Battle of Boston that annually matched Holy Cross and Boston College.

Today, only USC-UCLA can split a city into divided loyalties without benefit of an election year. Alums come out of the woodwork; the game is the topic of discussion in boardrooms and at the noon Rotary meetings; the campuses turn into Mardi Gras West.

Traditionally, it is the USC student body that shows the greatest enthusiasm as Troy Week is declared in the days leading up to the big game. Decorations go up all along the Row, where the school's fraternities and sororities are housed; there are street dances, pep rallies, and bonfires. Students take turns keeping day-and-night watch over the statue affectionately known as Tommy Trojan, a campus landmark that on occasion has been stolen or painted UCLA blue-and-gold by midnight raiders from the Westwood side of town.

Around the clock, the Victory Bell, the prize that annually goes to the winner of the game, rings across whatever campus has most recently claimed it.

Which is to say, it is far and away the most fun game of the year. It is the excitement of college football at its very best.

And in his final game in the Coliseum, Charles White gave the USC fans something to celebrate, scoring four touchdowns as we won, 49–14. We were 10–0–1 and headed back to the Rose Bowl, this time to face an Ohio State team that was undefeated and ranked number one in the nation in the Associated Press poll.

First, however, there would be the moment we'd all waited for since the first day of practice. Charles White's season had been remarkable. He'd led the nation in rushing, averaging 186.4 yards per game. When the votes were tabulated, he was the runaway winner of the Heisman Trophy.

And while White was being honored as the best college player in the country, guard Brad Budde was named winner of the Lombardi Trophy as the nation's top lineman.

In the Rose Bowl, Charles made a dramatic farewell statement to college football. With just five minutes and twenty-one seconds remaining in the game, Ohio State led 16–10, and we had the ball on our own 17-yard line.

Under normal circumstances, a team attempting a last-quarter comeback against the top-ranked team in the country would go quickly to its passing game. However, Coach Robinson believed the most certain way for us to get the job done was to put the ball in the hands of Charles White.

It was a drive that people would talk about for years to come: White bursting off right guard for a 32-yard gain. Then a sweep to the left for 28. Michael Hayes came in to pick up seven, then I ran for five to the Ohio State 11. Then, with time ticking away, Charles did the rest: up the middle for three, off tackle for five, a sweep to the one. And finally over the top for the touchdown. Charles had gained 71 of the 83 yards we needed to get into the end zone. Voters for the Heisman who watched had to be feeling very good about their choice.

Eric Hipp's conversion gave us the 17–16 victory.

By beating the number-one team, we felt we were rightful claimants to the national championship. But the Stanford tie came back to haunt us once more as both the Associated Press and United Press International moved undefeated Alabama, winner of the Sugar Bowl, to the top of their lists. We were number two in both polls.

For me, it was a season of satisfactions I'd never before experienced, despite all the bumps and bruises. While the spotlight had focused on White and his bid for the Heisman, it felt good to know that I had helped his cause along. And, as I said, I gained heightened respect for the role of those whose job it is to open the holes and clear the way.

I also gained a new appreciation for our backfield coach, John Jackson. From the day I stepped into the fullback position, he had stayed on my ass. No matter how much I complained or tried to find a way to get out of a practice, he kept pushing. I wasn't too crazy about it at the time, but as I look back, I realize what a huge favor he did for me. Coach Jackson pushed me beyond where I thought I could go.

I liked the fact that I'd proved to myself and my teammates that I could do the job. Not only had I developed a new and valuable skill, but I had gotten the opportunity to show that I could do something once the ball was in my hands. I'd gained 649 yards rushing, caught passes for 314, and scored eight touchdowns.

My apprenticeship had been served. And I immediately began looking to a new year—and, once more, a new position. With Charles White's magnificent college run complete, the tailback position would be mine.

four

The Year 2,000

It is no secret to anyone familiar with the history of USC football that the role of starting tailback for the Trojans is one that is certain to command a great amount of attention. Charles White had only added to a rich legacy, taking his place alongside the likes of Jon Arnett, Frank Gifford, Anthony Davis, Ricky Bell, Mike Garrett, and O.J. Simpson.

And now it was my turn.

There were those who doubted that I could successfully fill the shoes of my predecessors. The coaching staff made no secret of the fact that it had tried hard to recruit two of the nation's premier high school running backs—Herschel Walker of Wrightsville, Georgia, and Huntington Beach's Kerwin Bell—but Walker and Bell had chosen to go with the Georgia Bulldogs and Kansas Jayhawks respectively. And while Coach Robinson insisted to the media that, even if either had agreed to attend USC, I would still have been his choice to start at tailback, I had to wonder. So, too, did some of the alumni.

Though we went through the first eight games of the 1980 season undefeated and I led the nation in rushing and was second in all-purpose yardage, it was clear that I wasn't getting high marks from the critics. Even the sports editor of the campus paper was asking if the grand tradition of Trojan running backs had come to an end. He wondered in print where the 60-yard breakaway touchdown runs USC fans were accustomed to seeing had gone. He suggested in print that the offense might be better served by my moving back to fullback and allowing Mike Harper, my backup, to take over as tail-back.

The dissatisfaction caught me by surprise. Maybe I wasn't exactly setting the world on fire, but I damn sure felt I was getting the job done.

Actually, it was not just my performance that gave rise to the fan frustration. A pall had fallen over the football program when it was discovered that several players had received credit for a speech class they had not actually attended, and the Pac-10 ruled that we would not be allowed to participate in any bowl games at the end of the 1980 season. Our Rose Bowl string was ended even before the year got underway. In a manner of speaking, we were a team that was dressed up but with no place to go. And, admittedly, our offense had not been as exciting as it had been the year before with Charles at tailback and Paul McDonald quarterbacking.

Stepping in for Paul was Gordon Adams, a fifth-year senior with very little playing experience, and he was suffering the same comparisons as I was. I told him at least the guy they were comparing him to hadn't won the Heisman Trophy in a walk.

I tried to block out the pressures and concentrate on the adjustments necessary to become the kind of tailback I was confident I could be. I was learning in every practice, every game, and making progress. And we were winning. Still, I would be lying if I said that I wasn't stung by the criticism. I'd never before heard boos directed at me. Looking back on it all, I have gained a new appreciation for the pressures a college player endures. In the pros, if you have a bad game and people are down on you, the solution is pretty simple: You stay at home, take the phone off the hook, and avoid going anywhere but to practice. But, as a collegian, you have to daily face your critics, on the campus, in the classroom. You aren't afforded the luxury of hiding and licking your wounds.

The truth of the matter was that it angered me—and made me even more determined to prove myself.

If those who doubted my abilities had known at the time

the course I'd begun to plan for myself, their eyes would have rolled. Almost daily I would drop by Heritage Hall and spend a few minutes in the lobby, looking at the glass-encased Heisman Trophies that had been won by previous USC running backs: Mike Garrett in 1965, O. J. Simpson in '68, and Charles White in '79.

I wanted my name added to that list.

By the time we lost back-to-back games late in the season to Washington and UCLA, ending our string of twenty-eight games without a defeat, I'm sure there were those who would have laughed out loud at the goal I'd set for myself. Though I ended my first year as a starting tailback with 1,563 yards rushing—second only to South Carolina's George Rogers— it was cause for little applause.

That should tell you something about the standards people set for the USC tailback.

I was not without my supporters, however. Coach John Robinson, whom I still consider one of the greatest teachers, psychologists, and motivators I've ever been associated with, urged me to ignore the critics. He had seen the progress I'd made and assured me he felt my senior year would be something special.

Coach Jackson agreed. But he had reservations when I confided to him what I had in mind.

Each summer, players would traditionally meet with coaches to discuss individual goals for the upcoming season. When it came my turn to visit Coach Jackson in his office, I was eager to share with him the plans I had for my senior year.

"I want to gain two thousand yards," I told him.

He smiled but quickly dismissed the idea. "It's never been done," he pointed out. The closest anyone had ever come was Tony Dorsett, the four-time All-American at the University of Pittsburgh who had rushed for 1,948 back in 1976.

"That's why I want to do it."

He continued to smile. "I like that kind of thinking," he said, "but let's talk about something more realistic."

"To me, two thousand yards *is* realistic." Not only did I

think I had the ability to do it, but I knew our offensive line was going to be the best in college football.

Looking back, I can understand his reluctance to share my optimism. For someone who would not even be selected to any of the pre-season All-America teams, making college football history had to sound like the impossible dream.

To make it come true, I determined to take preparation for my senior year to another level. I worked hard throughout the summer, focused on the goal I'd set for myself. In fact, I worked harder than had most of my predecessors. For years, it had been traditional for the USC tailback to work at Universal Studios in the summer prior to his senior year. He ran errands, worked as an extra on whatever movies were being filmed, and had the opportunity to meet some of the stars. Not exactly a backbreaking job. It was my luck that the studios were on strike that particular summer. So what I did for three months was dig ditches for Arco, reporting to a Long Beach job site at seven each morning. I would get off at three in the afternoon, giving me time to get home for a shower and a short nap before doing a late-afternoon workout.

It didn't exactly leave a great deal of time for much of a social life. Still, I should admit that I had no intention of living the life of a monk. I enjoyed going out, seeing people, and attending parties as much as the next guy.

The difference was that I seemed to get credit for doing a lot more than I really did. I've heard stories that suggested that I was quite the social animal, dating a new girl every night, always out on the town. Such was hardly the case.

I went out on dates and had a good time, but I was never interested in getting into a serious relationship. Yes, I enjoyed being invited to parties, but it wasn't exactly New Year's Eve seven nights a week. I had my fun, but never at the expense of my primary purpose for being at USC.

I didn't belong to a fraternity, primarily because I viewed the whole pledge-hazing scene as stupid. Like a lot of other students, I didn't have the money to finance a four-star dating life even had I wanted to. Mine was a movie-and-a-burger budget. More often, it was a party at someone's apartment where everyone just hung out and listened to music. Once in a while we'd even cross the battle lines and socialize with students at UCLA or invite them to our side of town.

No doubt being a member of the Trojans football team offered a certain status, but if I was viewed as a Big Man on Campus, it was an honor not fairly won. In fact, aside from attending classes and practice, I spent very little time there.

To accomplish what I hoped to, I felt it important to maintain a single-minded focus. And for that, I needed a certain amount of privacy.

I suspect there were those on the team who might even have considered me something of a loner in my last couple of years in school. My best college friends—Ronnie, Eric, and Dennis—had all graduated ahead of me. And while I enjoyed the camaraderie of my other teammates and had a good relationship with everyone, I was no longer part of the hang-out crowd.

To avoid distractions, I moved into a guest house in the rear of my aunt's home in Inglewood, ten miles away from USC, for my senior year. It was an ideal place, with a ceiling so high that a cousin of mine who had lived there before me had installed a regulation-height basketball goal on one wall of the living room. Occasionally, when a buddy would come over to study, the best of academic intentions would give way to a quick indoor game of one-on-one.

But virtually everything I did—eating, sleeping, practicing—was done with my goal in mind. When we began pre-season practice, I continued the Trojan tradition of running downfield 40 or 50 yards on every play from scrimmage.

Among the valuable lessons Coach Robinson taught was that the thing that separates the good player from the great one is what he does when others aren't watching. Only those willing to put in the hard work and single-minded dedication can expect to rise to the next level. It was a philosophy I was eager to buy into.

JOHN ROBINSON: *I can only say that those who were critical of Marcus's performance in his junior year were not very knowledgeable of the game. On the other hand, he was still* *learning. He hadn't quite perfected the cutback that would eventually be his real trademark.*

In the summer between his junior and senior years we spent a lot of time looking at film, talking about the little things he needed to do to turn a short run into a long one. That, I think, is when I realized what a remarkably intelligent player he was. He not only picked up on things immediately but was able to go out on the field and do them at full speed.

I've seen running backs who were a little faster and maybe even a little stronger than Marcus Allen, but none who had his combination of intelligence and competitiveness. Those are the things that have set him apart from the rest. Add to them the God-given physical characteristics that a great back needs—balance and vision, ability to get into the holes quickly, explosion at the end of a run—and you've got the whole package.

I'd be lying if I said I expected something like the year he had as a senior, but I wasn't that surprised.

And I did know early on that he was going to be something special. I knew that the first week of two-a-day practices in his freshman year when we still had him working with the defensive backs.

I was coming out of my office one afternoon and met him in the lobby of Heritage Hall and we stood there near the display of Heisman Trophies. As we talked, he kept glancing over at them, then finally grinned and said, "I can't win one of those playing defensive back, can I?"

It was the next day that I moved him to tailback.

Through much of my junior year, my problem had been a failure to run under control. I would see an opening and cut to it so quickly that I'd slip while trying to make the break necessary to get the long gain. Patience, never one of my greatest strengths, was something I preached to myself. The mind and body, I knew, had to be in sync.

Such was the case when we opened the season against Tennessee. I ran for 210 yards, scored four touchdowns, and came out at the end of the third quarter. A week later, I gained 274 against Indiana and could have gone over 300 had I not spent most of the last quarter watching from the sidelines.

Our first real test of the season would come a week later, as we hosted the University of Oklahoma in the Coliseum. The polls had us ranked number one and the Sooners number two.

Twice during the game we trailed by ten points but continued to come back. In the fourth quarter I scored my second touchdown of the day on a short run to pull us to within 24–21. Then, with four and a half minutes left in the game, we got the ball at our own 22-yard line with one last chance to win.

John Mazur, our sophomore quarterback, went into a two-minute offense that was a thing of beauty. He connected with split end Jeff Simmons for a long gain, kept the drive alive at one point with a fourth-down quarterback sneak, then threw complete to Malcolm Moore to the Oklahoma seven. With little time remaining, there was a confident feeling in the huddle as John called another pass play that had me crossing in the end zone. "Do whatever you have to do," he told me, "but get open quick and I'll get it to you."

As I broke free in the back of the end zone, John threw in my direction. And just as I was preparing to make the reception, Fred Cornwell, our tight end, raced in front of me from the opposite side of the field and tipped the ball away.

With time for only one more play, Mazur called the same route I had just run. This time, a Sooner defender tackled me as I was running my pattern. The only receiver open was Cornwell, and Mazur quickly hit him for the touchdown.

The Coliseum went nuts as we pulled it out, 28–24, with only two seconds left to play.

In the dressing room afterward, Cornwell sought me out after learning from reporters that he had not been the intended receiver on the deflected pass. "Man, I'm sorry," he said. "I just saw it coming and . . ."

I couldn't help but laugh. All that concerned me was that we'd won.

The Sooners defense had been impressive, yet I managed to keep my 200-yard string going, getting 208 on thirty-nine carries. On that day, there would be no rest in the fourth quarter.

Later I learned that Barry Switzer, the OU coach who had once recruited me, had called me "the best back in the country" after the game. "He's got my vote for the Heisman," he told reporters.

That's what I wanted to hear. What it told me was that I was being viewed as a legitimate candidate.

There is a fine line in team sports that separates the importance of winning games and establishing personal records. It has always been my belief that one has little meaning without the other. Winning has to be the primary concern. If rushing for 200 yards and scoring a lot of touchdowns contributes to that, it is a worthwhile achievement. But records simply for records' sake have no lasting merit.

When I set my goal to rush for 2,000 yards, there was some personal ego involved. At the same time, I knew if I could be that productive our chances of having a great season would be dramatically enhanced. If I were to emerge as a Heisman candidate, it would surely mean that our team was having a great year. Rarely had the award gone to a player on a team that had a mediocre season.

I pursued my goals with no attempt to keep track of the accomplishments of others who were being considered candidates. Sure, I knew that Herschel Walker was having another great season at Georgia and that Jim McMahon was throwing for incredible yardage at Brigham Young, but I made up my mind that I would not concern myself with their weekly statistics.

My father's philosophy again came into play: I made up my mind to concentrate solely on what I was doing and not concern myself with things over which I had no control. Nothing I might have done would have reduced Walker's yardage or the number of touchdown passes McMahon was throwing.

In a manner of speaking, I tried to put the Heisman Trophy out of mind once convinced that I was being looked upon as a legitimate candidate.

And when I did so, the season became even more fun. A

week after defeating Oklahoma, we scored a 56–22 win over Oregon State and I maintained my string, getting 233 yards.

But if you're looking for proof that individual statistics are but a small part of football, you need look no further than our game against the University of Arizona. I carried only twenty-six times but gained 211 yards. I broke for a 74-yard touchdown that was the longest of my career at USC.

And we lost the game, 13–10.

However, we bounced back quickly, winning our next four. But increasingly teams were stacking their defenses to stop our running game. Against Stanford, I was held to 153 and Notre Dame allowed even less—143 yards. But we won both.

I made up some ground against Washington State, carrying for 289 yards, then got 243 against California despite the fact that I literally got knocked silly and had to sit out several offensive series. For the first time in my career I had to be helped to the sidelines as bells rang in my head and my knees wobbled. Teammates later told me that I sat on the bench for several minutes, laughing for no apparent reason and repeatedly asking, "What happened?"

With two games remaining, I knew I was going to get the 2,000.

By the time we traveled to Washington I needed only 32 more yards and got them in my first four carries on a day when just about everyone on the field was more concerned with not drowning than playing football. A freezing rain came down in sheets, and the wind roared off Lake Washington, almost pushing you back at times. And the electrical power in the stadium went off.

It's interesting how there are some days etched in my memory while others are a faint blur. That mid-November game against Washington is one of those for which I have instant recall. Throughout the week there had been a great deal of attention focused on the fact that I was so near the goal I'd set for myself. I was eager to get it done and behind me.

And I did so early in the game. On my fourth carry I followed my blockers around right end, slogging for a 13-yard gain that put me exactly at the 2,000 mark. Three plays later I gained four and was home free.

It would have been great to reach the milestone in the Coliseum, before the home fans, but the Washington crowd was incredibly gracious, giving me a lengthy ovation when the public-address announcer informed them that I'd gone over the mark.

By day's end I'd slipped and slided for 155 yards in a game that everyone was glad to get behind them. We could score only a field goal, losing 13–3. The only touchdown of the day came when a Washington kickoff following its second field goal bounced off the hands of one of our return men and was recovered in the end zone by a Huskies special teams player.

In the locker room afterward there was a feeling unlike any I'd ever experienced following a defeat. Even Coach Robinson showed little disappointment over the loss. While quick not to take anything from Washington's efforts, he made it clear that on this particular day the elements had made it impossible for either team to put its best foot forward.

No one seemed happier about my accomplishment than he did. "Hell," he yelled out to the team, "we've done the two-thousand-yard thing. Let's go for three thousand."

With only UCLA remaining on our schedule, not even I had that kind of optimism.

It took another come-from-behind win, but we edged UCLA 22–21 in my final home game as a Trojan. In truth, I went into the game determined to do something memorable in my final home game as a collegian. All week I'd reflected on what it had meant for me to play at USC. I'd learned so much, been given such opportunities, and I wanted to somehow demonstrate my appreciation. So what did I do? I fumbled all over the place. Four times. I didn't realize it at the time, but I was trying too hard.

Finally, with two minutes left to play, I went around left end for a touchdown that finally put us into the lead. But for a time it looked as if that wasn't going to be enough. With the final seconds ticking away, UCLA drove into field-goal range, looking as if they might make it two in a row against us. It would not be Marcus Allen who saved the day, but, rather, George Achica. He reached high to block the Bruins' field-goal attempt and preserve our one-point victory.

I gained 219 yards to bring my season total to 2,342. The impossible dream had become a reality.

I felt a flood of emotion as I left the field that day. There is a long-standing USC tradition that I'd participated in during my undergraduate days and found most impressive. At the end of the final home game, the seniors return to the dressing room through a line near the sidelines, which is formed by the freshmen, sophomores, and juniors on the team. Fans crowd along the first rows to say their good-byes to each senior as his name is called out on the public-address system. It is an electric moment in the life of anyone who ends his playing career as a Trojan.

As I made the walk toward the tunnel, I realized that another chapter in my athletic career, my life, had come to an end. It was a bittersweet feeling.

five

Hello, Heisman

I had known of and fantasized about the Heisman Trophy since I was a little kid, aware that it was one of the most important and prestigious awards an athlete could receive, but as a youngster I wasn't quite sure how you went about winning it. See, I thought they gave it for any sport. When we'd play pickup baseball games in the backyard, I'd think to myself, Someday I'm going to win the Heisman Trophy. Same thing when we turned our attention to the basketball goal in the driveway.

The first time I realized that it was an award given annually to the best player in college football was when O.J. won it in 1968. I was eight years old at the time.

But by the end of my senior year at USC, I was well-versed on the history of the Heisman, what it was all about, who had won it—and the campaigning that went into the attempt to win it. It seemed to me I'd spent about as much time with Duane Lindberg, the university's sports information director, as I had with my coaches. His role was much like that of a political campaign manager. He would set up interviews and send out press releases, photos, and game film clips, keeping 1,050 members of the nation's press—who would ultimately cast ballots—up to date on every yard I gained, touchdown I made, and record I set.

Interviews became a part of my daily routine. And while I've known a lot of athletes who dislike the media's endless prying and barrage of questions, I generally enjoyed it. With an exception here and there, the press had always treated me kindly. And since I was majoring in speech and communications, I was learning something new with each interview.

By the end of the season it was generally felt that the leading candidates for the award were Walker and myself. Amazingly, Herschel had finished third in the balloting as a freshman. And as his sophomore year began, there had been those predicting that he would become the first second-year collegian ever to win the award. He'd dominated the preseason All-America team lists and then proceeded to live up to the expectations with an outstanding season. Using his power and 9.3 speed, he had finished the year with 1,891 yards rushing.

Frankly, I felt my record spoke for itself and that I deserved to win the award by a landslide. But throughout the season Lindberg had continually voiced his worry over the strength of what he called the "Southern vote." The sportswriters and sportscasters in the South were justifiably enamored of Walker and likely to cast a strong block vote for him.

As I mentioned, I just decided to quit worrying about it. With the season over, I'd done everything I could do.

I had flown to Phoenix for a weekend gathering of the Kodak All-America team, where a banquet was to be held and a team picture taken, when I received a long-distance call from Lindberg.

"Marcus," he said, "is there anyone there with you right now?" He sounded like something straight out of a spy movie.

"No."

"You've got to go to New York immediately," he said. A ticket would be waiting at the reservation counter and a representative from the Downtown Athletic Club would pick me up upon my arrival. "You can't say a word to anybody," he warned.

"Anything else?"

"Yeah," he said. "Congratulations."

The cloak-and-dagger routine continued upon my arrival in New York. Taken to a Manhattan hotel late on Friday evening, I was told to stay out of sight until someone came to pick me up the next day and escort me to the announcement ceremony.

Once in my room, the first thing I did was break my vow of silence, phoning my parents to tell them to be sure to watch TV the next afternoon.

Alone that night, I found myself in a reflective mood, feeling more a sense of relief than excitement over what would take place the following day. It began to sink in that I had actually won the award.

For all the thought I'd given to one day being added to the list of great USC running backs, it had never really occurred to me just how incredibly humbling it might feel to actually realize such a goal. All the practices, the bumps, bruises, and sacrifices that are a part of athletics suddenly seemed such a small price to pay. I began to realize that, regardless of what my future held, this would be a moment I would remember forever; an accomplishment that could never be taken away.

The next day, when I arrived at the Downtown Athletic Club, I was quickly ushered through a back entrance and into an elevator. The first familiar face I saw was that of my running-back coach. The minute the elevator door opened, Coach Jackson grabbed me and gave me a bear hug and began to cry. "I'm so damn proud of you," he said.

I'd never seen him so emotional.

Understand, this was before the announcement of the Heisman winner had become a major television production with a half-hour buildup; before it was decided to have the four or five top candidates seated in the audience to sweat out the agonizing procedure, then smile bravely and applaud when their name was not the one announced. I'm not sure I could have handled that kind of made-for-TV drama.

In 1981 the winner of the trophy was the only player on hand and, while the announcement was nationally televised, it was short and sweet, then back to the basketball game or Alpine skiing that had been interrupted for the news.

Once I was invited to New York, the only suspense left for me was to learn the margin by which I'd won. I had received 441 first-place votes and 1,797 points (based on a system that awarded a first-place vote with three points, second with two, and third, one). Walker got 152 first-place votes and 1,199 points.

I had led the voting in five of the six geographic regions while Walker, as predicted, had all but swept the South. He was, I felt certain, the odds-on favorite to win the award the following year.

The press release that would later be handed out to the media offered a breakdown of the voting:

Marcus Allen (441 first-place votes) . . . . 1,797 points

Herschel Walker (152) . . . . 1,199 points

Jim McMahon (91) . . . . 706 points

Dan Marino, Pittsburgh (16) . . . . 256 points

Art Schichter, Ohio State (21) . . . . 149 points

Darrin Nelson, Stanford (7) . . . . 48 points

Anthony Carter, Michigan (2) . . . . 42 points

Kenneth Sims, Texas (3) . . . . 34 points

Reggie Collier, So. Miss. (2) . . . . 30 points

Rich Diana, Yale (3) . . . . 23 points

I would have given anything to have been in two places at the same time on that day. Standing at the podium, the magnificent bronze statue before me and framed oil paintings of previous winners hanging on nearby walls, I first did what every Heisman winner before me had. I thanked my teammates, my coach, my parents, everyone who had helped me on my journey to this moment. I tried to explain how I wished that, instead of the one large trophy, there were many small ones so that I might share them with my teammates and coaches.

And even as I spoke, I found myself trying to imagine the scene in the living room of my parents' home back in San Diego. I would have loved being there, seeing their reaction.

Once the award ceremony was completed, I answered

"How does it feel?" questions of the press for almost an hour. Finally, someone—a writer from the South, I'll bet—wanted to know if I honestly felt that I deserved the trophy.

"At the risk of sounding self-centered," I answered, "if I'd had a vote, I would have voted for myself."

For the first time in the twenty-one years I'd known him, my father was speechless. I called home just as soon as the presentation and press conference was over and he answered the phone.

"Dad," I said, "we did it."

He made no reply.

"Dad? You there?"

Still no reply.

Finally, I heard my mother's voice. "Everyone here's so excited," she said. "We're so happy, so very proud of you."

"Is Dad okay?"

"Son, your father has never been better." She laughed, then explained that he had been so emotionally overcome since the announcement that he'd had difficulty talking.

At that moment, I was reminded of just how fortunate I was, not only to have parents who were encouraging and supportive—and proud—but to have had the opportunity to do something that offered tangible evidence that their love and hard work had paid off.

Earlier, as Dad and I discussed the upcoming NFL player draft, I'd told him that as soon as I signed my contract, he was going to retire. And that I was going to build him and my mother a new home.

He just laughed. "In the first place," he said, "I'm way too young to retire. Wouldn't want to even if I could. And in the second place, you don't owe your mother and me but one thing: respect."

In my heart, I knew I owed them far more than I could ever repay.

As I reflect on it today, that was what made winning so special. I flew home from New York with the trophy resting between my feet. People at the Downtown Athletic Club had offered to carefully box it so it could be placed in the baggage area, but I'd declined. I didn't want to let it out of my sight.

To this day, it is the one award that is displayed in my home. All the others are boxed away.

A few weeks later I was back in New York for the formal banquet the Downtown Athletic Club annually holds to honor the Heisman winner. Many of the past recipients were there in the grand ballroom of the Hilton Hotel and several made moving speeches.

One was delivered by O.J. Simpson. "Quite honestly," he told the audience, "I never expected Marcus to be the kind of player he has become. It just goes to show that with proper commitment and hard work, there is nothing one can't do. By the end of his senior season, Marcus was as fine a running back as I've ever seen at any level of football. I've never been around anyone who worked harder for this, or who is more deserving."

What he said meant a great deal to me. And as I listened to him, I thought back to those days when he was still playing for the Bills and the Sunday mornings when I would hide my dress shoes and insist to my mother that I couldn't find them. Without them, I reasoned, I'd just have to stay home from church and watch football on television. It never worked. But I'd spent a lot of time sitting in a pew next to my mom, worried more about how much yardage O.J. was getting than my own salvation.

And now, years later, we were not only fellow Heisman recipients but were becoming friends.

I had been told I could invite my parents and four other guests of my choosing. So, in addition to Mom and Dad, I asked the people who had been so responsible for clearing the way for me—literally—to join us on the trip: Trojan linemen Roy Foster, Don Mosebar, and Bruce Matthews, and fullback Todd Spencer.

It was my parents' first visit to New York and they made the most of it, seeing as many of the tourist sites as possible and having dinner at several nice restaurants. At the banquet they were recognized and received a round of applause.

If there was a moment during the trip that I had to judge as the most special, the one I felt certain would remain with them after all others had faded from memory, it came when we were shown into the Athletic Club's Heisman Room, where the original announcement had been made. The podium from which I'd spoken was gone; so were the rows of chairs where members of the media had been seated.

There was an almost reverent atmosphere in the softly lighted room with its polished floors and rich, dark paneling. Along the walls were oil portraits of every Heisman Trophy winner, dating back to Chicago's Jay Berwanger, who had received the initial award in 1935.

Each of the portraits had been painted by Tommy McDonald, a former University of Oklahoma All-American and NFL All-Pro who had himself narrowly missed winning the Heisman in 1956. That year he'd received the most first-place votes, but wound up third behind Notre Dame's Paul Hornung and Tennessee's Johnny Majors in the closest ballot in history.

After his retirement from football, McDonald had begun a new career as a portrait artist, and in 1968 he approached the Heisman committee with an oil painting he had done of O.J. after he'd won the trophy.

So impressed was the committee that it commissioned McDonald to do portraits of all past winners and then each honoree thereafter to be permanently displayed.

When we were directed to the spot where McDonald's painting of me had been hung, both my parents stopped as if frozen in place.

This time, it was not just my father who was speechless.

Before all was said and done, I would be named the College Player of the Year by Walter Camp, the Maxwell Club, and *Football News*. And while each new honor was thrilling, none would compare to the looks on my parents' faces that moment when they stood side by side in the Heisman Room, seeing that portrait for the first time.

That was my every dream come true.

six

"He's Your Guy . . ."

Depending on which NFL draft pundit you listened to, I (1) had a good chance of being the first player selected; (2) lacked the overall talents the pros were looking for and therefore would see a number of other running backs picked before I was; and (3) had won the Heisman simply because anyone with a modicum of ability could have rushed for the kind of yardage I did behind the USC line. Herschel Walker, according to one sportswriter, could have gained 3,000, maybe more, if he'd been playing for USC instead of Georgia.

Who were these people, these so-called authorities, who obviously didn't know me? I kept thinking back to my parents, who had brought me up to believe I could do anything I wanted to, as long as I worked hard enough. But now, suddenly, I was again being told that I couldn't, that I was destined to be average.

There was no way I could accept that. I knew there was no test or machine or questionnaire that could measure the size of a person's heart and will.

Actually, though, I hadn't done a great deal to enhance my cause in the days after our regular season had ended. The Fiesta Bowl, frankly, had been a letdown for a team whose annual goal was the Rose Bowl. We had played lethargically and were defeated by Penn State, 26–10. Not only had I fumbled to set up the Nittany Lions' first touchdown, but I gained only 85 yards in the worst game of my college career. On the other hand, I was invited to Honolulu to play in the Hula

Bowl all-star game and had a very good day, running the ball well and scoring a touchdown even after a defender had knocked my helmet off.

The business of being a Heisman winner had turned into a full-time job. Traveling here and there—I logged over twenty thousand air miles—I had very little chance to sleep, much less focus on football. When I'd received an invitation to play in the first—and, as history would later show, last—Olympia Gold Bowl, another post-season all-star game, I accepted only because it was going to be played in my hometown. San Diego had even planned a ticker-tape parade in my honor in the week prior to the game. It was the first such parade my hometown had staged since one it held to honor the legendary transcontinental flier Charles Lindbergh decades earlier.

Because of the wall-to-wall appearances that the USC publicity department had committed me to, I wasn't able to get to the Gold Bowl until Thursday, two days before the game. I participated in only one brief practice.

Tom Flores and his Raiders staff were in charge of the West all-star team I would play on and seemed to understand that I was exhausted. "Look," Flores told me when I reported, "you don't have anything to prove here, but people will want to see you play. We'll get you for a few plays here and there." That was fine with me.

In the limited time I was on the field, I made only one play of any note. Going down the sidelines on a pass route, I stretched until my body was horizontal to the ground and made a pretty dramatic catch. And with that I came out of the game, unaware at the time that the effort I'd extended to make that single reception would play an important role in my future.

Insurance salesmen and college recruiters, for all their persistence and powers of persuasion, have nothing on sports agents eager to sign up new clients. They seemed to be everywhere: on the phone, on the campus, on planes, in the hotel lobbies. I think they knew my travel plans before I did.

And, to the man, they all had nothing but my financial future in mind, each assuring me that I was the most valuable football player since Jim Brown, and that they were best suited to protect my interests. I couldn't help but feel their pitch was well rehearsed and that I hadn't been the first to hear it. Nor would I be the last.

The smoothest of the talkers was a man named Mike Trope, who in recent years had gained the reputation of being the representative of a lengthy list of number-one draft picks. Among his clients was Tony Dorsett, the University of Pittsburgh running back who had won the Heisman and was enjoying a great career with the Dallas Cowboys. When Trope said he would be happy to write me a check for five thousand dollars—seed money until the big bucks started rolling in— I did what most unemployed twenty-one-year-olds I knew would do. I signed with him.

I regretted taking the money almost immediately. Because I really wanted a different kind of agent, I returned the money and continued to look.

With his football days ended after playing out his career as a member of the San Francisco 49ers in 1978 and '79, O.J. had settled back in Los Angeles, tending his myriad business interests, doing movie roles, and re-establishing his ties with USC. As he began attending our games instead of preparing for one himself, I saw him regularly. It was O.J. who mentioned a Los Angeles attorney who had advised him in the days leading up to his signing with the Buffalo Bills. One of the city's most prominent and successful lawyers, Ed Hookstratten had a lengthy history in sports, both as a three-year letterman pitcher at USC and as general counsel for the Los Angeles Rams. He had even negotiated the contracts of a number of college and NFL coaches, but focused the bulk of his efforts on clients in the broadcast field. Among his clients were network luminaries like Johnny Carson, Vin Scully, Tom Brokaw, Phyllis George, Bryant Gumbel, Tom Snyder, Dick Enberg, and local sportscaster Jim Hill.

I was more than a little intimidated when I visited his office in Beverly Hills to ask if he might consider handling negotiations with whatever team drafted me.

Still very much the athlete, he prided himself on what he liked to describe as a "pretty wicked" left-handed tennis serve. Unlike most high-profile Beverly Hills lawyers, Hook-stratten preferred to report to work in slacks and a sport shirt instead of a three-piece suit. And despite his well-earned reputation as a tough negotiator, I would eventually learn that his bark was much worse than his bite. Most important, he was a straight shooter.

While he stopped short of an immediate agreement to serve as my agent during our first meeting, he made it clear that he'd already done some thinking on the matter. "I've talked with some of the Rams scouts I know," he said, "and the general concern about your making it in the NFL is your speed. So I've been thinking about some way we can deal with that problem."

I was amused. During one of the scouting combines I'd attended—a cattle-call gathering of college players eligible for the draft who go through a series of drills and physical exams for the benefit of coaches and scouts—my best time in the 40 had been 4.62. Carl Lewis had nothing to worry about.

"I called Jim Bush, the track coach out at UCLA," Ed continued, "and asked if he will work with you." Bush, I knew, was regarded as one of the premier track-and-field coaches in the world. He'd routinely produced Olympians and world-record setters during his brilliant career.

"What Jim tells me," Ed says, "is that it is very unlikely he can increase your speed measurably. But what he can do— if you're willing to work at the program he gives you—is improve your strength to a point where, by the midway point of your rookie season, you'll be running past people you could never beat in a hundred-yard dash."

Even as I was nodding in agreement, he was dialing Bush's number to set up my first session at the UCLA track.

JIM BUSH: *I was excited over the prospect of meeting Marcus. I'd watched him kick our football team around pretty good for two years and was anxious to see what made the guy tick. We met in my office and I outlined a program that I thought might benefit him, and he was ready to start that day.*

I made it clear that I couldn't turn him into an Olympic sprinter, but I'd make him think he was faster. I'd lectured to a group of track coaches in New Zealand a few years earlier and several of them had explained to me a training program they'd designed to improve the leg strength of their runners. What it amounted to, basically, was a lot of repetitive sprints up small hills, mixed with flat running, where the athlete concentrated on not only reaching maximum speed, but maintaining body control while doing it.

What I envisioned was Marcus improving his strength to where his leg muscles didn't tire late in a game like most football players' do. That, and being able to run under control at full speed while a defensive back trying to catch up to him was straining so that his coordination would break down.

We met five times a week, and on one day he would do seven 100-yard sprints up this hill near Sunset Boulevard, then the next he would do ten 100-yard dashes, always mindful of body control.

His work ethic, and the fluid motion of every muscle, were something to see. A coach's dream come true.

By the end of his rookie season, the television announcers were talking about how Marcus seemed to have gotten faster. That thrilled me.

That call from Ed Hookstratten really started something. The next year the Raiders sent Howie Long to me. Then, when I retired as track coach at UCLA, the Raiders hired me to work with all the players. I wound up with a Super Bowl ring before it was all over.

The NBA Clippers also wanted to give it a try so I started working with their players. Then the Dodgers jumped on the bandwagon. They were so pleased with what we were able to do that they presented me with a championship ring after they won the World Series.

But Marcus Allen was the first to buy into the idea. His willingness to try something new, in hopes that it might gain him even the slightest edge, opened the way for a lot of other people.

I liked Ed Hookstratten immediately. I admired his no-nonsense demeanor and, most important, his philosophy. So many professional athletes, he told me, get lost in all the fly-by-night financial propositions that come their way once they have money in their pockets and the NFL spotlight shining on them. "They get rich, then want to immediately get richer. And wind up going broke before they know what's happened," he explained.

As I sat in his office, surrounded by framed photographs of those whose careers he helped direct, he offered advice that even today I can't put a price tag on. "You're a football player," he said. "During the season, that's all you should concern yourself with. Don't go to practice worried about some deal you've been offered. Don't go into a game wondering if the investment you made the day before was a sound one. Play football the way you're capable of doing, and everything else will come in its proper time. If you want to take acting lessons or get into a business or serve as a spokesperson for some product, do it in the off-season. Keep football and everything else separate. That's how you insure your future."

I only wished he'd had a contract ready for me to sign at that moment. Finally, though, it was left to me to ask the question. Would he consider being my agent?

"Let's both think it over," he suggested.

If he did agree, I asked, what kind of "seed money" would he be willing to offer?

"Marcus," he said, smiling, "I don't pay anyone for the right to represent them."

Sweating out the draft is not unlike that first school dance where the boys are seated against one wall and the girls against the other, all in fear that he or she won't be quickly picked as a partner. It's worse than waiting for any kickoff I can remember. Why? Not so much because the higher you're picked, the bigger the numbers are likely to be on the contract you eventually sign. Not really even the knowledge that the higher round you're picked in, the better your chance of making the team will be. Any player who is honest will admit that it's an ego thing. I've always loved the remark of Darrell Royal, the former University of Texas coach, who was re-flecting on his team's chances of being ranked number one: "If they hold a beauty contest," he had said to reporters, "you damn sure want them to vote you pretty."

Though I did my best to hide it, that's the way I was feeling.

In the days leading up to the draft, my phone rang constantly. Scouts and coaches from various teams were asking if I would play for them if they selected me. Of course, I told each of them I would. The speculation I was hearing was that the teams most interested in me were Cleveland, the Los Angeles Rams, the Vikings, the Raiders, the Giants, Denver, Philadelphia, and Dallas. Gil Brandt, head of the Cowboys' scouting department, had been quoted in the papers, saying he felt I might well be the first player picked and he'd love to have me. I wondered about the statement at the time. What did Dallas need with another running back when they already had Dorsett?

And if Brandt thought I was such hot stuff, why hadn't he picked me for the pre-season *Playboy* All-America team that he'd helped select for years?

Among the more absurd rumors that got around to me was that some teams were concerned that I might be too much of a party guy. The reasoning went something like this: O.J. Simpson moved in L.A.'s fast lane and made no secret of his love for the nightlife and bright lights. O.J. and I had become friends. Therefore, I must be out on the town with a girl on each arm every night.

Once again I was getting far more social credit than I deserved.

I would hardly consider taking a date out to a movie or a nice dinner, or even attending an occasional barbecue that O.J. and his girlfriend, Nicole Brown, liked to host at his Brentwood home, as being "out on the town."

As O.J. and I became friends, I would occasionally drop by his house on weekends to watch a game on television or play some hoops in the backyard. He talked me into taking up tennis. It was fun to hang out with him and his best friend, Al Cowlings, doing very little, really.

But we were, at least by my definition, far removed from the "nightlife and bright lights."

By the time draft day finally arrived, I'd tried to block out all the speculation and just sit back and wait to see what happened.

It was the first year that the player draft was developed into a major event, televised nationally by ESPN. Instead of sitting by the phone, awaiting the call that would tell me what the future held, I did the same thing millions around the country were doing. I watched TV at the home of friend Allan Schwartz, a well-known clothier and big sports fan.

Jim Hill, a Los Angeles sportscaster, and his camera crew joined me, waiting to broadcast my reaction live. I'd admired Jim for years and felt comfortable with him sharing the wait with me. Not only was he a reliable, hardworking reporter, but he'd played with the Chargers and Packers and had a real understanding of the game. I told him I hoped he wouldn't have to wait around too long.

Ken Sims, a defensive end for the University of Texas, was the first player picked. So much for Gil Brandt's prediction.

It got exciting quickly when my roommate Chip Banks was announced as the second player selected. He was going to the Cleveland Browns. I gave him a call at his parents' house to congratulate him.

Then my phone began to ring. Bum Phillips, the head coach of the Houston Oilers, called and asked how I would like to block for Earl Campbell. I tried to be as diplomatic as possible, suggesting that I hoped maybe we could block for each other. The second call was the strangest. Someone from the Raiders wanted to know what I weighed. I thought of all I'd heard about how sophisticated and high tech the scouting departments of various teams had become in recent years. Supposedly, the touch of a computer button could tell every scout in the NFL the most minute detail about every prospect. And they wanted to know something they could have found out by buying a game program! I told him I still weighed 207. "Thanks," he said, then hung up.

Shortly, it came time for the Vikings to make their pick. I

put my head down and crossed my fingers. "Please don't let it be Minnesota," I said. I couldn't imagine living and playing in a part of the world where ice fishing was considered a major sport. To my relief, they selected Darren Nelson.

Nine picks would be made before I finally heard my name called. NFL Commissioner Pete Rozelle, announcing each of the picks, said, "With the tenth pick of the first round, the Raiders select Marcus Allen, running back from the University of Southern California."

I felt mixed emotions. As a longtime fan of the Raiders, I knew that theirs was a fullback-oriented offense. The primary function of the running back was to block. I had no reservation about that aspect of the game. But I thought of myself as a multidimensional player. I liked running the ball and going downfield as a pass receiver. The news that I would begin my professional career with the Raiders made me somewhat apprehensive. At the same time, I was excited about the prospect of being part of a team that had such a great tradition of winning—and would, by all reports, soon be leaving Oakland to play their games in the Los Angeles Coliseum.

So as soon as my name was announced, I was assured of forever being the answer to a sports trivia question: If nothing else, history would remember me as the first-ever draft selection of the Los Angeles Raiders.

It was a pick that clearly did not impress ESPN analyst Paul Maguire in the least. As soon as the Raiders' selection was announced, he began to shake his head. "I don't understand that one at all," he told his audience. "I have absolutely no idea why the Raiders would draft Marcus Allen. He doesn't have the speed to be an effective running back in the NFL. Maybe they're planning to move him to wide receiver or something. But there's no way he's going to fit into their scheme."

In one breath he was saying I wasn't fast enough to play running back, then suggesting that I might be tried as a wide receiver, where even greater speed is demanded.

Paul Maguire went to the top of my list of Least Favorite Sportscasters. Only later would I hear the same story from several people, who suggested he'd not been the only one displeased by the Raiders' choice.

At the time of the draft, I was told, Raiders president Al Davis was in Los Angeles federal court, preparing to testify in the trial that would ultimately determine whether he had the right to move his team from Oakland. Throughout the day he would slip away from the proceedings to phone the Raiders office and see how the draft was progressing.

Apparently there had been an ongoing battle between Davis and personnel director Ron Wolf over who the team should select. Wolf lobbied to pick me in the event I had not already gone to another team. Meanwhile, Davis reportedly favored a big, fast Baylor running back named Walter Abercrombie.

Even as the draft was under way, the heated debate continued, right up to the time the Raiders were to make their selection. From the phone, the frustrated Davis—forced into a position of juggling the importance of his lawsuit and the draft—had finally told Wolf that he was being summoned back into the courtroom and for them to make whatever pick they felt best. "But," he reportedly said, "I want you to remember one fuckin' thing: If you pick Allen, he's your guy, not mine."

And while Wolf would tell me years later that there had never been any disagreement in the Raiders front office over the decision to draft me, I couldn't help but wonder.

I was unaware of any such reservations when I arrived in Oakland the following day to attend a press conference at which I was to be introduced to members of the media that regularly covered the team. Mike Ornstein, the club's public relations director, had met me at the airport with a warm handshake, and a smiling Coach Flores was waiting as we entered the media room.

The idea of being a member of the Raiders was growing on me fast.

It would not be until well into the summer that I finally met Al Davis. His victory against the league won and plans under way to begin operation in Los Angeles, he invited Ed Hook-stratten—who had agreed to represent me in contract nego-tiations—and me to have dinner with him at the Sheraton Grand on Wilshire Boulevard.

It was a pleasant enough evening as we listened to our host extoll the remarkable history of the franchise that he'd built and talk of his grand plans for the future.

He was every bit the legendary figure I'd heard, read about, and seen on television for years. Dressed in all-white, he wore two Super Bowl rings, and dark glasses despite the dim light-ing of the dining room. His hair was combed back into a ducktail that I'd only seen in Fifties movies about rebellious teens. And the rapid clip of the boyhood Brooklyn accent he'd never lost had about it an almost hypnotic quality.

At some point during the conversation I told him that I was going to be unlike any player he'd ever had. What I'd been trying to do was assure him that I planned to be the best player he'd ever had. His only response was a rather puzzled look.

But if he secretly wished he was sitting across from Walter Abercrombie instead of me, he hid the fact quite well.

seven

Rookie Raider

Training camp, like war, is hell. It is a six-week time frame during which a hundred or so players come together to do everything in their power to make sure they get one of the forty-five spots on the roster. It is an odd mixture of established veterans, most of whom are certain to be around on opening day, and a few hoping desperately to hang on for one more season; some who have been released by other teams and are looking for new life as a Raider; and rookies of every size and shape from schools large and small, some drafted, many signed as free agents, with survival chances that are slim to none.

It is an atmosphere that a drill sergeant would love. Isolated from the rest of the world, players live in small rooms whose function is only to provide a place for a few hours' sleep before the next workout. There is practice morning and afternoon and the meetings are endless. Everyone eats in a communal dining room and football talk never stops. If you have some free time, the coaches warn, it would be best spent studying your playbook. Violation of the nightly curfew results in fines. Remember the movie *Groundhog Day*, in which Bill Murray wakes only to find that each new day is exactly the same as the one before? That's training camp.

It is an intense time during which football takes precedence over friends, family, and world events. Were a nuclear war to break out in late July and early August, the equipment manager would simply order up oxygen masks for everyone and practices would go on.

The Raiders' training camp was located in the small, quaint community of Santa Rosa, just north of San Francisco. We stayed at the El Tropicana, practicing on two football fields that had been built directly behind the hotel.

Eager to prove myself, I made every effort to fit in, participating in all the rites of passage a rookie is made to endure. In the dining hall during the evening meal, I stood to sing every time a veteran player demanded, belting out a medley of Stevie Wonder hits until someone would yell for me to ''shut the fuck up and sit down!''

I was very conscious of the fact that, in all likelihood, there were going to be those on the team who resented the fact that I had been the team's first-round draft selection and had signed a nice contract. I tried to deal with everything and everyone as diplomatically as possible. The last thing I needed was to have any of my future teammates thinking I was a cocky twenty-two-year-old rookie who was going to teach people a lesson or two about how the game should be played.

The only run-in I'd had with one of the veterans had come during an earlier minicamp when I'd gone out for a pass and collided with linebacker Matt Millen. We'd gotten into it for a minute or two but, fortunately, he seemed to have forgotten about it by the next time we saw each other.

I would quickly learn that fights on the practice field were a routine occurrence for the Raiders. Tempers would flare and guys would go at it like World War III was breaking out. Once it was over, they'd get back to the business of practice so they could go out and have a couple of beers.

Everything I'd heard about the odd mix of personalities on the team was true.

The day I reported to camp, my mind became a sponge, soaking up everything I heard and saw. As the winner of the Heisman and the team's number-one draft pick, I knew that every step I made was going to be judged harshly by coaches and teammates alike. While confident that I would make the team—I wasn't aware of a first-round pick ever sent packing by any team in the NFL—I made certain that no player worked harder than I did.

I not only wanted to make the roster, I wanted to start. And that meant that I had to convince the coaching staff that I was the best running back in camp; better than Mark van Eeghen, who had started the year before; better than my friend Greg Pruitt, who had been an exceptional player for the Cleveland Browns before being traded to the Raiders; better than any of the other rookie candidates.

There is an assumption by most fans that players battling for the same position are automatically enemies, immediately ready to do anything to advance their own cause while sinisterly looking for ways to undermine the efforts of the competition. Such may be the isolated case, but by and large, it is one of pro football's great myths.

No one of the Raiders helped me grasp what pro football was all about more generously than Greg Pruitt. I'd watched him on television when he'd been an All-American at the University of Oklahoma, then during his great years with the Browns. Few backs I'd seen had been better at eluding tacklers with dancelike moves or catching the ball out of the backfield. He may have lost a step by the time he came to the Raiders, but I still envied his speed.

And while he clearly wanted to make the team, it didn't prevent him from lending me advice. "I'm a short-timer here," he would admit. "You're the guy with a future." Greg, then, became my mentor.

During fifteen years in the league, my feelings about training camp have changed little since that rookie summer in Santa Rosa. I hate it. I hate the routine, the boredom, the isolation, the fact that grown men are given children's rules to abide by.

It *is* mind-numbing, but at the same time one of the most fascinating times of the season. Training camp is an endless sampling of human drama where the survival of the fittest comes together with pure luck; where one's whole outlook on life is dependent on how he feels about his performance in the last workout.

It is unrelentingly boring. Ted Hendricks, Dave Dalby, and Mark van Eeghen—real characters—were forever thinking up new ways to break the monotony. One afternoon, as everyone was dragging their tired butts out for yet another practice, Ted came up wearing shorts, sunglasses, and a baseball cap instead of his pads and helmet. Under one arm he had a beach umbrella and under the other a folding chair. Without so much as a word to anyone, he marched to the center of the practice field, set up his umbrella, and took a seat as if he were at Malibu instead of training camp. Ignoring the calisthenics and wind sprints going on all around him, Ted did his best imitation of *M*A*S*H*'s Hawkeye Pierce until one of the less than amused coaches suggested he had five minutes to slip into something more suited for blocking and tackling.

Before arriving, Dave and Mark had leased an old Cadillac convertible from something called Rent-a-Wreck. Each evening, shortly before curfew, they would go out to the car, rev the motor, turn up the radio, and for a few minutes do screeching circles in the parking lot. It helped, they said, blow off steam so they could sleep.

Veteran antics aside, it was the rookies who most fascinated me. Virtually every player invited had spent most of his athletic life in the comfortable knowledge that he was the best of the best. He'd been a standout in sandlot games and high school, then at the college level, constantly hearing a litany of praise since the day he made his first catch or run, his first block or tackle.

Then he steps to the next level, the pros. And for so many it is a bitter learning experience. Routinely, during the course of training camp, a call will come from one of the coaches or trainers, asking that a player collect his playbook and report to the hotel's makeshift office. There he will be told for the first time in his life that, for whatever reason, he is not good enough. He's given a plane ticket home and a good-luck handshake and that's the end of it, suddenly and abruptly.

It is one of the game's most cruel but necessary exercises. And it is a heartbreaking thing to watch. As a veteran, you come to learn not to let yourself become too personally attached to rookies who you know are fighting long, almost-impossible odds. By doing so, you spare yourself some of the pain they experience when the Turk—football's nickname for the messenger of the bad news that you've been released—comes calling.

Sad though it may be, it is interesting to watch the manner in which young players deal with the news. In my rookie year, a linebacker from Penn State who had worked his butt off only to be cut, calmly walked back to his hotel room and proceeded to go ballistic. He tore up the furniture, knocked holes in the wall, and ripped up carpet. Then quietly left camp.

To some, the embarrassment is so severe that they won't even say good-bye, choosing instead to sneak away. Others simply refuse to leave, even after being cut. No longer welcome in meetings or at practices, they'll hide away in their rooms, continuing to eat in the dining room, until a coach or member of the front office realizes their presence and escorts them out of camp.

On other teams I'd heard of one guy who, after being cut, rushed to the nearest bar, got blind drunk, and wound up married to the bartender before leaving town. One rookie with an unusual flair (and more money in his pocket than most) ordered up a stretch limo stocked with a magnum of champagne in which to make his grand exit. "If I gotta go," he yelled to teammates as he waved a champagne glass from the limo's open sunroof, "I'm going with some class!"

One of the most cruel episodes I ever witnessed came late in camp as we were boarding a chartered plane en route to a pre-season game. A free-agent defensive player, who had survived several weeks of cuts and was feeling increasingly confident that he would make the team, was told he was no longer a member of the squad only after he'd settled into his seat. The decision to release him had been made earlier that morning when a veteran player the Raiders had picked up arrived. There had been no time to inform the discarded rookie in the haste to prepare for the trip. Thus a team official was given the unenviable task of delivering the news just moments before we took off, telling the embarrassed player that he was no longer on the team and that his seat was needed for the newly arrived player.

I can still remember the look of utter dejection and embarrassment on the player's face as he slowly rose from his seat and walked from the plane.

In truth, there are times when neither lack of ability nor lack of effort is the cause of a player's departure. It is not at all uncommon to see a young guy who is clearly talented enough to play in the NFL not make the team because there is simply no spot available. It's a numbers game. At his particular position there are just too many experienced veterans. Thus there are those who arrive in camp knowing full well that their chances of earning a spot with the team that drafted them are slim. So they set their sights on a different goal. Through hard work and maybe an outstanding play or two in scrimmage or a pre-season game, they might catch the eye of some other team with a need for their particular talent.

It has always made me feel good to hear that someone who didn't make it at his first stop managed to find a job somewhere else in the league.

Finally, there is the luck factor that drives players to continue giving their best effort in practices, despite the fact that there is ample veteran talent on hand at their position. More than once I've watched young players work themselves to exhaustion, all the while wondering why they were doing it. No way were they going to beat out the two or three veterans, some of the All-Pros, who were ahead of them on the depth chart. Then, just when you thought their fifteen minutes of NFL fame had run its course and they could anticipate a call from the Turk, a veteran would go down with an injury, suddenly opening a position on the roster.

By the time all the morality plays had run their course and the pre-season was completed, we had a team that promised to be among the best in the league.

Though I hadn't started in any of the pre-season games, I'd played a good deal, and felt it was only a matter of time before I would be moved to the number-one offensive unit. That occurred in the week before the regular season began when van Eeghen was placed on waivers.

For the '82 season opener, veteran Kenny King would start at fullback and I would be at the running-back position. As we went through our warm-ups in the Los Angeles Coliseum, I recognized a number of former Raiders greats along the sidelines. Al Davis had long made it a custom to invite members of what he called the "family" to games, feeling their presence would serve as a reminder to current players of the proud tradition that had preceded them.

As one who had always had tremendous respect for great players of the past, I found it inspirational to have them on hand. Jack Tatum, the former cornerback who some even today judge the meanest and dirtiest player ever to wear a Raiders uniform, came up and welcomed me to the team. "I want you to go out there and kick 'em," he urged, "then spit on 'em."

While spitting and kicking seemed a bit extreme, I must admit that I admired Jack's attitude. Football is a game that should be played with an aggressive attitude.

We opened against the defending Super Bowl champion San Francisco 49ers and won. I had over 100 yards rushing and remember talking afterward with friends who had watched the game on television. Sportscaster Dick Enberg had—very prematurely, I should note—announced that "a new NFL star had been born."

Afterward, several sportswriters asked me to compare my first NFL game to college ball. It was a difficult question to answer. Certainly the overall caliber of professional players was obvious. But I had known that would be the case. What was important to me was to establish myself as quickly as possible. And I felt I had done that, not just in the first regular-season game but during practices against my own teammates and the pre-season games that had preceded the opener. As I said, I had a tremendous amount of respect for those I was playing with and against, but I knew I could not allow myself to be awed by anyone if I was to prove I belonged on the field with them.

The following week we looked sharp in defeating Atlanta. Then everything came to a sudden halt.

For months there had been talk among the veterans that unless the owners soon met a lengthy list of demands that had been presented by the NFL Players Association, a strike was certain. It was announced immediately after the second game.

And for the next eight weeks stadiums throughout the league stood empty. During the fifty-seven-day work stoppage—the longest in NFL history—I received a crash course in what a big business the game of professional football really was. And learned how little leverage the players really had.

Curious and with time on my hands, I even made a trip to New York to see firsthand what the negotiation process was all about. What I heard was nothing but rhetoric. And I realized quickly that I didn't like Ed Garvey, the negotiator for the players. We were together in the elevator of the hotel where meetings were being held when he gave me this puzzled look and said, "What are you worried about? You've already got your money."

Why would he say that to me? I had supported the strike. I hadn't crossed the picket line. I thought to myself, If this is our leader, we're in big trouble.

On the afternoon of November 16, Jack Donlan, executive director of the NFL Management Council, and Garvey announced that an agreement had been reached. I was thrilled. But once I learned the terms of the agreement, I was stunned. Though still relatively uneducated in the business aspect of pro football, I could not see that anything of substance had been accomplished for the players. All the promises and angry challenges had really meant nothing as the owners simply waited until players began to examine their bank accounts and realized how much money the strike was costing them in lost wages.

The players' union, I could see, had lacked the unity and resolve to make a legitimate fight of it. I couldn't help but wonder why we'd even bothered.

We'd missed eight games and the league's players had lost a collective $72 million. The league was tossing out figures that suggested each of its twenty-eight teams had lost between $18 million and $29 million. And for what? Small victories for our side.

The settlement did include higher salary minimums for players, slightly improved benefits that included a severance program, increased medical coverage, and immediate bonus payments to players who, the league had finally admitted, were underpaid. First-year players got an immediate bonus of $10,000, second-year players received $20,000, those who had been in the league for three years got $30,000, and everyone with four or more years' tenure received $60,000.

What Garvey had failed to get for the players was the 55 percent of the owners' gross revenues that the association had so long been seeking. Nor, as the negotiations wound down, was he able to convince the owners to play out the abbreviated season to its regulation sixteen games. What we would do was return and play for the remaining seven weeks left on the original season schedule.

One of the things that really troubled me during the strike was the public sentiment. With the daily spin from league management and a number of vocal owners, the players were painted as overpaid and greedy. We were trying to rob our bosses blind and it was our fault that there were no games on Sundays. If there was fan sympathy for the players' cause, I did not hear it on the streets or read about it in the newspapers.

The general public had no conception of the financial magnitude of the NFL, no real understanding of the fact we were not only asking for fairness in our own situation, but that we were fighting for a better future for players who would come into the league years after we were gone. Without a doubt, we were the bad guys.

All of which only added to the angry grumbles from players as they returned to practice in preparation for resuming the season. Young and inexperienced, I had mixed feelings. On one hand, I knew full well that we'd been shortchanged. On the other, I was anxious to get back to playing.

There wasn't much else to do. Since the Raiders still trained in Santa Rosa, flying into Los Angeles for our "home" games, I lived my rookie season in the Oakland Hilton. Even on the off-days following games when Howie Long and I would jump on a commuter flight and make a quick visit to L.A., my residence there was Allen Schwartz's guest house. I had bought a condo, but it wouldn't be ready to move into until the season was over.

I had received a $400,000 signing bonus and was to earn $150,000 in my rookie season. And I was living in a hotel room, hadn't gotten around to buying a car, and was wondering when we'd start playing games again. The glamorous life of pro football was something less than I had been led to think it would be.

During those first days that we were finally back together, I listened as veterans expressed their disappointment. At least on my team, many felt that Garvey had misled the players throughout the ordeal. A lot of players felt the next order of business of the Players Association was to send Garvey packing.

Almost to a man, my teammates and players throughout the league were saying the same thing: "What it boils down to is that I lost a half year's salary and we didn't accomplish a damn thing."

Though spokespeople from management's side modestly insisted to the media that there had been no real winners in the matter, it was clear they were once again playing to the emotions of the fans, and perhaps trying to appease the returning players.

The truth of the matter is, they kicked our butts.

Still, despite the disappointment and anger that lingered among the players, it was good to be back on the field.

The Oakland–turned–Los Angeles Raiders finally made their long-delayed home debut in the Coliseum on a November Monday night against the San Diego Chargers. And we were able to give the fans an interesting introduction to a brand of football that those in Oakland had long enjoyed. Few teams over the years have staged more dramatic comeback wins than the Raiders. And absolutely no one had won as regularly with a Monday-night audience looking on. Since ABC had first begun bringing the NFL into the nation's homes during prime time, the Raiders had won eighteen of the twenty-one *Monday Night Football* games in which they had appeared.

Our game against the Chargers would not only add to that legacy, but offer a textbook guide to what coming from behind to win is all about.

In the first half, San Diego quarterback Dan Fouts was unstoppable, putting on what amounted to a pass clinic as the Chargers jumped out to a 24–0 lead. Nowhere in the Raiders record book was there any notation of our ever having come from that far behind to win a game.

Even when we got our offense in gear late in the second quarter, there were precious few watching who entertained serious thought that we might make a game of it. With just forty-seven seconds remaining before intermission, Jim Plunkett finally got us on the scoreboard when he threw a short touchdown pass to tight end Todd Christensen.

In the dressing room Flores spent little time pointing out the myriad mistakes we'd made—including my near-disastrous fumble on our only scoring drive—and instead reminded us that every player and coach in the NFL was at home watching us embarrass ourselves. He talked of the Raiders' tradition of Monday-night success, noting that we had only thirty minutes of playing time to live up to our reputation.

As the third quarter got under way, our defense began to put pressure on Fouts. A sack by Ted Hendricks stymied the Chargers' first offensive series and provided us our chance to move to within striking range. Plunkett kept hitting Christensen for medium-range gains, and Kenny King and I helped to keep the drive alive by getting tough yardage up the middle. I scored from the three and we narrowed the margin to ten.

The defense came up with yet another big play when Odis McKinney forced a fumble by San Diego tight end Kellen Winslow and Ruben Vaughn fell on the loose ball.

Suddenly, we were playing Raiders football. Our offensive line began to dominate, opening holes through which King and I were able to pick up good yardage. As we moved into the Chargers' end of the field, Kenny broke loose for a 21-yard gain on a trap. Then, with just over two minutes left in the third quarter, I scored again, this time on a six-yard sweep.

Down by only a field goal and with momentum on our side, we began to feel the game was ours to win. And, with just under six minutes left to play, we finally took the lead.

Plunkett picked up first downs with completions to Christensen and Cliff Branch, my training camp roommate, as we moved into scoring range. A reverse to wide receiver Malcolm Barnwell caught the Chargers' defense by surprise and picked up 14 yards. Then fullback Frank Hawkins went in from the one to put us into the lead.

The problem was that 5:54 remained, ample time for the strong-armed Fouts to do a great deal of damage.

Along with the rest of the Raiders offense that was crowded on the sidelines, I yelled encouragement to the defensive unit, pleading for them to shut Fouts down one last time.

And finally they did when our left cornerback, Lester Hayes, batted away a Fouts pass intended for Charlie Joiner in the end zone.

As we left the field, guard Mickey Marvin placed a bloody and bruised arm around my shoulder and smiled. ''Welcome to Monday-night football,'' he said.

At 3–0, we were feeling pretty good about ourselves—until the following Sunday afternoon, when the Cincinnati Bengals knocked us from the ranks of the unbeaten with a 31–17 defeat.

It would be the only loss we would suffer over the course of the abbreviated regular season as we went on a five-game winning streak. The week before Christmas, it would take yet another miracle comeback to keep the string alive.

On something of a milestone NFL Sunday, the L.A. Raiders, the new team in town, was scheduled to play the L.A. Rams, the team local fans for decades had been cheering for. And while the Rams had begun playing their home games in nearby Anaheim, it was clear that the majority of those who visited the Coliseum that afternoon held tightly to old loyalties.

With our 5–1 record we were riding atop the NFL standings, a play-off spot already clinched. On the other hand, the Rams came into the game with only one victory. If they were to salvage anything from the strike-marred season, their coach Ray Malavasi—once a Raiders assistant—had told them, it would have to be accomplished with a victory over the Raiders.

They scored twice in the first nine minutes of the game and led 21–7 at halftime.

Then, in the third quarter, we awoke. In the second half alone our offense would account for 316 yards—and thirty points. Greg Pruitt flashed his old Browns form with long, weaving punt and kickoff returns. Plunkett was hot. And our running game went into a higher gear. I got our first touchdown of the second half with a one-yard slant off tackle. Then Chris Bahr hit on a 24-yard field goal to bring us to within four points as the third quarter ended.

In the fourth quarter I scored again on another short-yardage play to put us on top, 24–21. Later Plunkett connected with Pruitt on a six-yard touchdown pass to improve our lead.

The difficulty with comeback football, however, is that the job can't be judged as done until the final whistle blows.

The Rams continued to fight back and narrowed the margin to 30–28 when Vince Ferragamo scored on a quarterback sneak with only 2:25 left to play.

One good offensive drive was all we needed to assure our sixth win of the year. And we didn't get it.

We were forced to punt the ball away and, with only a minute and a half left, the Rams connected on a 36-yard field goal that gave them a one-point lead.

As the kick receiving unit ran onto the field, defensive linemen Lyle Alzado and Ted Hendricks were beating their helmets on the ground. "Goddammit!" Lyle screamed. "Somebody do something!"

Greg Pruitt did. He returned the kickoff 43 yards to put us in good field position. Then Plunkett went to work, putting the two-minute drill he'd spent long hours practicing into motion. He threw to me for 5, then hit Branch for 13 and Barnwell for 10. Then I broke around left end on a sweep that picked up 14, advancing the ball to the Rams' 11 with just thirty-five seconds left. With the Rams defense anticipating a pass, Plunkett gave me the ball on the same sweep and I had clear sailing until I neared the goal line. With one defender in my path I went airborne and landed in the end zone. Finally, the comeback was accomplished.

That 37–31 win is still remembered as one of the greatest come-from-behind victories in the franchise's history.

I was fast beginning to realize that pro football was not only fun but very nerve-racking.

We went on to end the shortened season at 8–1 and began thinking about winning it all.

A huge crowd turned out in the Coliseum for our first play-off game against Cleveland, proving that fans' memories are short-lived. Once angry at us over the strike, they now cheered wildly as we defeated the Browns, 27–10, and advanced into the semifinals.

Unlike the standard course of NFL play-offs, the revamped manner in which the league champions would be determined more resembled a basketball tournament bracket. Division winners automatically advanced, but there were no true wild card teams. Instead, those with the best won-lost records in each conference filled out the play-off field.

Our semifinal opponent would be the New York Jets, giving rise to recollections of the most famous encounter between the two teams. I remembered it well, watching the game on television with my dad in 1968. It had pitted the Jets' flamboyant quarterback Joe Namath against a great Raiders defensive team. With two minutes left in the game, New York led 32–29—and NBC pulled the plug. The game was running into the prime-time hour and network officials made the decision to forego showing the final two minutes so that the movie *Heidi* could be shown. What angered television viewers—myself included—was that they did not get to see a miraculous Raiders comeback that saw the team score twice in the final minutes to win, 43–32, in one of the most exciting games in NFL history. In time, league historians, recognizing the impact of the event, would give it a name of its own: the Heidi Bowl.

Which is to say there was no worry on anyone's part that the network might suddenly break away from the game this time around. In retrospect, it might have been to our advantage had they chosen to pull the plug a little early on this particular occasion.

With over ninety thousand watching in the Coliseum, the Jets took a 10–0 lead in a first half that had more fistfights and errors on our part than the previous nine games combined. We managed to come back in the third quarter and actually take the lead, 14–10, but then the wheels fell off. There would be no miracle that day. In the fourth quarter the Jets came back and won, 17–14, earning the right to advance to the AFC championship.

My first year as a Raider, then, had been a roller-coaster ride all too soon ended. In the nine games we played, I managed to rush for 697 yards and eleven touchdowns, and caught thirty-eight passes for 401 yards and three scores. I was named the NFL Rookie of the Year, picked to several All-Pro teams, and invited to play in the Pro Bowl.

All pretty heady stuff. Still, like my teammates, I felt a great disappointment over our missed opportunity to reach the goal we'd all begun working for months earlier in training camp.

In professional football, I'd quickly learned, the Super Bowl is the Holy Grail. As I watched the Washington Redskins defeat Miami in the championship game, I was convinced that we could have beaten either of them.

But it would be twelve long months before we could prove it.

eight

Super Sunday

For years the National Football League has perpetuated the myth of the 1,000-yard rushing season. It is the yardstick by which backs are measured, trumpeted as some superhuman achievement. *So-and-So, of Such-and-Such team, who rushed for 1,000 yards, established himself as one of the league's premier running backs. . . .* Players and agents use it as a negotiation tool, owners include it in the incentive-clause section of contracts, sportswriters make a big deal of it, and fans determine a player's true value to his team by it.

In truth, it is one of those ancient statistical accomplishments handed down from a time when there were only a dozen teams in the NFL and the season didn't stretch to sixteen games. Even in the old days, it was a yardstick borrowed from the college sport when a ten-game schedule was the norm. To reach the 1,000-yard mark in a season, a collegiate back then had to average 100 yards rushing per game. An impressive feat.

Put some math to what it takes to reach that milestone in today's NFL. To be included among the elite 1,000-yard rushers, today's back has to average only *62.5 yards per game.*

I've had seasons in which I rushed for over 1,000 yards, yet look back on them with some degree of disappointment. And there have been years when I didn't reach the so-called magic mark yet felt I made a valuable contribution to the offense.

In my second year with the Raiders, I ran for 1,014 yards

during the regular season—and rarely left the field with the feeling that I'd had an exceptional game. My timing seemed to always be off; I fumbled far too much. I was awful. The only 100-yard day I had, in fact, came in the third game of the season when we defeated the Dolphins. My most note-worthy statistic, as far as I was concerned, was the sixty-eight passes I caught for 590 yards.

Despite the fact that I'd never put much stock in the idea of a "sophomore jinx" that some teammates had warned me about, I just couldn't seem to get into any kind of rhythm. A hip pointer suffered against Denver in the fourth week of the season didn't help. For several days I couldn't even jog without feeling pain, and was looking at the very real possibility of sitting out my first game since turning pro.

A week later I was standing on the sidelines, watching as the Redskins beat us with a fourth-quarter comeback. Determined to keep my string of games played intact, I slipped onto the field briefly as a member of the receiving team on an on-side kick.

Still, '83 was a year of great expectations. There were those—Al Davis included—who were voicing the opinion that this Raiders team was potentially the best in the franchise's history. Only the strike had prevented our showing just how good we could be the year before.

We opened with four straight wins, but then lost three of our next five. I wasn't the only one having difficulty getting into a groove.

Jim Plunkett, one of the most courageous players I've ever been around, was nearing the end of his career and wanted to go out in a blaze of glory. He was not, however, having a great season. Marc Wilson, meanwhile, had become impatient waiting in the wings to advance to the starting quarterbacking job. So, early in the season he began to complain about his lack of playing time and talked of taking an offer that had been extended him by Donald Trump, owner of the New Jersey Generals of the newly established United States Football League.

Davis put a stop to those plans when he not only gave Marc a new five-year $4 million contract but told Flores to put him into the starting lineup against the Dallas Cowboys.

We were coming off a loss in Seattle and Wilson added a much-needed spark to our offense. Against the Cowboys he threw for 318 yards and we scored a season-high forty points. The Raiders' quarterback of the future had arrived—and lasted for another three games before suffering a shoulder injury.

In the meantime, the inactivity had added fire to Plunkett's determination to prove he was still the best quarterback on the team. The week he returned, we beat Kansas City and never looked back. We ended the year at 12–4 and were still gaining momentum as the play-offs got under way. In the last couple of games I felt as if I'd gotten back into a groove. Against the Giants, I made a couple of reverses, broke some tackles, and scored on a ten-yard run. Then, in the final game of the regular season, I got into the end zone twice against San Diego.

I wish I could tell you how it happens that a running back can suddenly step up his game; how you go from struggling for every yard one day to feeling like you can beat the world the next. Simplistic though it may sound, it just happens, and if I could come up with a formula for it, I could erase the national debt. Suddenly, with no real explanation, you find every sense heightened. You see things that you hadn't seen before; your reaction becomes automatic.

That's how I was beginning to feel as we entered the play-offs.

Against Pittsburgh in the divisional play-off, I ran for 121 yards on just thirteen carries and scored twice as we won 38–10. Then we faced Seattle, who had beaten us twice during the regular season, for the AFC championship.

At one point we were deep in the Seahawks' end of the field and preparing to run a play that called for me to serve as the lead blocker. Seattle safety Kenny Easley was up close to the line of scrimmage, staring directly at me. I looked across the line at him and gave him a little wink, as if to say, "Here I come." A few seconds later, he gave me a forearm to the face that brought the whole galaxy into view. I managed to get to my feet and stagger to the sidelines. Even before the game ended, I had the early makings of a black eye.

I gained 154 yards against them. And, with the Super Bowl two weeks away, I was finally feeling good about myself again.

In my opinion, the thing that sets the Super Bowl apart from all other professional sports championships is not the ring or the paycheck, or even the prestige that is attached to it; not the fact that millions are certain to be watching, or even the unprecedented media hype that routinely accompanies it. Unlike baseball's World Series, hockey's Stanley Cup play-offs, or the NBA's seven-game championship series, the National Football League champion is decided during a one-shot, sixty-minute sudden-death opportunity to prove yourself the best. From the off-season to training camp, through the pre-season, the regular season, and the play-offs, players work with a singular goal: getting to and winning the Super Bowl.

Believe me, it is an industrial-strength challenge. And team sports' ultimate mind game.

You hear the coaches endlessly lecture in the pre-game press conferences on the importance of focus and building intensity, using all the motivational buzzwords that players and sportswriters have heard for a lifetime. And, yes, they are important ingredients to getting into a winning frame of mind. What you rarely hear them mention, though, is something I believe is just as important: staying relaxed and composed, not allowing yourself to be so swept up in the emotion of the event that you fail to perform in the same workmanlike manner that got you there.

In that sense, the personality of the Raiders was ideally suited to deal with the pressures that accompany the game. For starters, the majority of our team had played in Super Bowl XV in 1981, soundly defeating the Philadelphia Eagles, and knew what to expect. Jim Plunkett had been the Most Valuable Player in the game. Rod Martin had intercepted three Eagles passes. Cliff Branch caught five passes. Their calm confidence quickly rubbed off onto the younger players.

And, more important, throughout the season we'd had a

unity and single-minded determination on the practice field
and on game days that most teams only dream of. No team
I'd ever played for displayed such a resolute calm on game
day, and I thrived in that atmosphere.

Away from the game, however, players had their fun.

After our first night in Tampa Bay, Flores dealt out something like $10,000 in fines to players who were out on the
town past curfew or late to the morning meetings. Believe
me, it wasn't a contrived thing; not a way of putting the time-
honored ''bad-boy Raiders'' image on display. It was just the
way the team was. And, rest assured, Flores was an equal-
opportunity disciplinarian. When Plunkett arrived at the first
quarterback meeting *one minute* late, he was fined $1,000.

Which only suggested to me that the coaches were more
uptight about the game than the players.

And, despite the fact the oddsmakers had made them a
three-point favorite, the Redskins seemed determined to push
every psychological button they could in the days leading up
to the game. And I seemed to be their favorite target.

On our first night in town, while having dinner at a place
called Confetti's, I looked across the room to see Dexter Manley, Washington's All-Pro defensive end, sitting at the bar
and staring at me. I nodded and looked away. Some time later,
I glanced over again to find him still looking at me, as if he
would love to rip off my head and stuff it into my plate of
linguini. So for several seconds we engaged in this schoolyard
stare-down. Finally, I just raised my arms in a gesture that
hopefully told him I didn't know what the hell kind of message he was trying to send. In fact, I began looking over my
shoulder as if to see if maybe it was someone else and not
me to whom he was directing his angry glare.

Then came the comments in the newspapers. When they
had beaten us during the regular season, I'd played just a
couple of downs because of the hip pointer I'd suffered the
week before. The strong suggestion by several members of
the Redskins defense, including my pal Dexter, was that I'd
been afraid to play against them then and that it would take
only one bone-rattling hit this time around to send me to the
sidelines where, according to some Redskins players, I would

prefer to be. Manley went so far as to say he thought I should play the game in a skirt.

Mind games.

On Press Day, a time set aside by the NFL powers-that-be for players and coaches to assemble on the field where the game is to be played so that thousands of members of the media can ask probing questions that always seem to begin with "How does it feel . . . ?" or—my personal favorite—"If you were a bird, what kind would you want to be?" I made a concerted effort to avoid responding to any observations by the Washington players that might fuel a verbal jousting match.

In the history of the Super Bowl, I wasn't aware of a single time when the winner had been declared on Press Day. I viewed it as nothing more than just another distraction to get past en route to kickoff. Still, just to be on the safe side, I wasn't about to add any motivational ammunition that might end up on the Redskins' locker-room bulletin board.

Actually, my only real objective that day was to avoid sportscaster Paul Maguire. I was still pissed off over the comments he'd made on ESPN, back on draft day when he'd expressed dismay that the Raiders had selected me; someone clearly too slow to make it as an NFL running back. Grudge-holding, I know, is hardly a virtue, but it would be years before he and I became friends. Even today when I see him, I make certain that he's reminded of his now fifteen-year-old comment. Actually, I owe Paul a debt of gratitude. His long-ago observation added fuel to my competitive fire.

Truth is, it would be easy to do interviews around the clock during Super Bowl Week if one were willing to make himself available. I had not the slightest interest in doing that. To avoid answering any more questions, I started hiding away in my room as much as possible when I wasn't on the practice field or in team meetings. Even the hotel lobby became an around-the-clock Mardi Gras celebration. I really couldn't understand what motivated so many people to hang out in a lobby from early in the morning until midnight, hoping to just get a glimpse of a player or an autograph.

I finally found a back entrance through which to come and

go. All I wanted to deal with was preparation for the job at hand.

For me, the most relaxed and enjoyable time spent in the week leading up to the game was on the practice field, away from all the hoopla. There, isolated with only my teammates and coaches, the world seemed to regain some sense of normalcy. I liked the routine, the planning, the physical exertion, the fine-tuning that was designed to move us closer to our goal.

Yet while our workouts at the Tampa Buccaneers' facility were crisp and upbeat, there was something missing.

It had long been a Raiders tradition to judge the quality of preparation by the number of fights that broke out during the course of our practices. Throughout the early part of the week there had not been a single temper tantrum, not a punch thrown.

Matt Millen, one of our All-Pro linebackers, became concerned and thus conspired with guard Mickey Marvin to set things right. Unknown to anyone else, they decided it would serve the best interest of the team to stage a fight in the middle of practice, convinced it was necessary to assure the rest of us that everything was normal. Frankly, it started out mildly, looking like exactly what it was—a staged fight that was pretty weakly choreographed—with Matt shoving and Mickey cursing and tossing his helmet to the ground. Matt delivered a punch that was light-years short of his best effort. Marvin then swung back with a little more authority. And in a matter of seconds things quickly escalated. The mock fight turned into an all-out brawl. Players trying to separate the two got into it themselves. Before the coaches managed to break it up there was an ample number of angry words, bloody noses, and scraped knuckles.

"Matt," I asked him later in the dressing room, "what the hell were you thinking? What if someone had been really injured?"

He shrugged it off and grinned. "Hell, I had to do it," he said, "to make sure everybody knew we were ready to play."

Certainly we needed to be. The Redskins were an even better team than they had been the previous season when they defeated Miami 27–17 in Super Bowl XVII. During the regular season they had become the first NFC team in history to win fourteen games—and their only two losses had been by less than a touchdown. Coming into the game, they had won eleven straight, including a 51–7 play-off win against the Rams and a 24–21 victory over an outstanding San Francisco team, when their kicker Mark Mosley hit on a field goal with just forty seconds to play.

During the Super Bowl buildup, the press had focused most of its attention on Washington's All-Pro fullback John Riggins. The MVP in the previous Super Bowl, he had rushed for over 1,000 yards during the regular season and scored twenty-four touchdowns. In the play-offs he'd added five more. And their quarterback, Joe Theismann, was having a brilliant year. They had a remarkable cast of receivers in Charlie Brown, Art Monk, and Joe Washington. What really made the offense go, however, was their great offensive line, a collectively talented group known as "the Hogs."

But what concerned me most was their defense, which had ranked number one in the NFL against the run. The more I thought about it, the more I found myself wondering if the one practice-session fight staged by Matt and Mickey had been enough.

As the game neared, I sensed a growing confidence within the Raiders' ranks. Despite losing to the Redskins earlier in the year, we had played well against them before losing, 37–35, after they managed to score seventeen points in the last six minutes of the game. Our coaching staff was convinced we could do some positive things with our passing game, and our defensive plan was devised to prevent Washington's hitting the deep passes this time around.

It was generally felt that if the Redskins had a weakness that could be exploited, it was their defensive secondary. Little was said about our mounting a ground attack of any substance against them. Nobody else had.

The night before the game I slept more soundly than I had in weeks. No dreams, no tossing and turning; just a quiet, peaceful rest that was not interrupted until a morning wake-up call came from the hotel operator.

There are times in an athlete's life, far too rare, when he finds himself in an almost surreal place that is called, for lack of a better description, "the zone." It is a state of mind every player aspires to but has no formula for. In over twenty years of game days, I've visited it no more than a couple of dozen times. It is difficult to even describe; part physical, part mental, with every sense heightened, every muscle feeling rested and almost bursting with strength.

The perfect night's sleep, I'm sure, was the birthplace of the frame of mind I would take into the game.

Suddenly, no distraction mattered. The maze of fans at the hotel became invisible. I ceased worrying about how my family was doing and if they would be able to get to the stadium okay. I felt a quiet, inner peace that allowed me to focus only on the game I would play in a matter of hours.

As I've mentioned, I've always made a habit of going to the stadium early, to enjoy the quiet of the locker room, to relax and read the newspaper or the articles in the game program, and, most important, to begin visualizing what I hope to do once the game gets under way.

For that reason I had no interest in waiting until the team bus pulled away from the hotel to deliver players and coaches to Tampa Stadium. The Raiders, in an effort to provide all the comforts possible, had made a number of rental cars available to the players throughout the week, and Odis McKinney and I decided to take one to the stadium.

Big mistake.

Odis was driving, and as we reached the stadium, he pulled into the first parking-lot entrance, only to be turned away and directed to another gate down the block. Trying it, we were again told we could not enter without a parking pass. Odis cursed as he made another U-turn back onto the street. After two more parking attendants refused us entry, Odis exploded. "We're the players, you fuckin' moron!" he yelled at the attendant. "How the hell are they going to play the game if you won't let the players in?"

Back on the street, we continued to circle the stadium as

pre-game traffic began building and Odis's temperature rose. "What the hell are we gonna do?" he finally asked.

I knew the entrance we'd used earlier on Press Day and directed McKinney toward it. When we reached it, I told him to pull over to the curb.

Parking the car, he turned to me. "Now what?"

"We're out of here," I said.

With that we abandoned the car, keys still in the ignition, motor still running, to God-knows-what fate, and walked quickly to the players' entrance. To this day I haven't the slightest idea what ever became of the car.

As the other players began filtering into the dressing room, the excitement that quickly permeated the place was incredible, almost electric. A few paced nervously, others huddled in small groups, talking. Some played the mindless card game Crazy Eights, others sat silently in front of their lockers, looking over the game plan one last time or idly thumbing through the game program.

I don't ever remember being more relaxed before a game.

When we finally went onto the field for the pre-game warm-ups, I was neither nervous nor apprehensive. The feeling was indescribable. Despite the bright lights and the roar of fans, I felt completely at peace, soaking everything in: the colors, the smell of the grass, the clean air. Everything seemed so perfect. The grass was cut short, making for the kind of fast track I like to run on.

On one hand, I was lost in my own comfortable little world, enjoying total focus. At the same time, I was keenly aware of everything going on around me: players and coaches offering words of encouragement to one another, the music that blared from somewhere high in the stadium. Irv Cross, the former Philadelphia Eagles defensive back, was standing on the sidelines to do a pre-game report for CBS, and waved in my direction just as Mike Ornstein, our public relations man, charged in his direction and yelled for him to get the hell off the field. Mike was obviously a little uptight. Irv, one of the nicest guys you'll ever meet, was stunned at Mike's reaction. "Hey, I'm on television," Irv said, ". . . we're live. I'm supposed to be here.'' Mike shrugged and stomped away, looking for someone else to vent his jitters on.

I saw all these things and they had absolutely no effect on me. I was riding the crest of the zone. You don't question it, you don't stop to wonder how you got there; you just go with it.

I couldn't wait for the game to get under way.

A half hour later, as we stood in the tunnel awaiting the player introductions, I took my customary place next to tight end Todd Christensen. We'd developed this bond during the time we played together, regularly reminding each other how neither of us had been given much chance of success at the professional level. Look, he'd told me when we'd first become acquainted, us underdogs gotta stick together.

And so before the Super Bowl, just as we'd done in every game we'd played together, we went through a routine that was simple but important to both of us. Just before running onto the field we shook hands and, in unison, said, ''Let's do it.''

As a guy gets older and has the advantage of hindsight and retrospection, he gains added appreciation for the enormity attached to the Super Bowl. For many who have played in the game, it is, I'm sure, the very highest point of their lives. Certainly, it is a memory I will forever cherish.

But for me on that late January day in 1984, the Super Bowl quickly turned into just another game. Once the action got under way, there was no more thought of Roman numerals or a worldwide television audience; just another challenge to be met, an opponent to conquer. A job to do.

And we did it damn well.

The early minutes of the game resembled a heavyweight fight during which the opponents spar, feeling each other out. And there was a lot of shit-talking going on. Cliff Branch, who isn't exactly a stunning physical specimen even for a wide receiver, was leading the chorus. It was comical listening to him, as he would go to the line of scrimmage and begin shouting across at whatever defensive back was assigned to him. ''No way you can cover me!'' he would yell. ''You better hurry up and get yourself some help over here.''

On defense, it was our linebacker Rod Martin who kept up a steady stream of profane chatter that would have made the National Truck Drivers' Association proud. I didn't say anything; probably couldn't have gotten a curse word in edgewise even if I'd wanted to.

We made a first down on our initial possession, then had to punt. Washington did the same.

As they lined up in punting position, Lester Hayes, who normally plays on the left corner, quickly shifted to the right, causing a brief moment of confusion on the Redskins' punting unit. That split second was all that our special teams captain Derrick Jensen needed as he bulled his way through the middle of the line to block the punt and chase the ball into the end zone, where he fell on it for a touchdown.

Derrick raced back to our bench, a mile-wide grin on his face, happy in the knowledge that he'd not only given us a lead with the game only five minutes old, but had been responsible for the first blocked punt the Redskins had suffered in three years.

Then it was the offense's turn. I made a couple of short gains despite the fact that it was clear the Redskins defense was keying on me. Early in the second quarter, Plunkett faked to me and threw deep to Branch. Even with Washington finally in double coverage, Cliff demonstrated his great speed and hands and made the catch for a 50-yard gain. Two plays later, he gave cornerback Anthony Washington a remarkable fake to the outside, cut back over the middle, and pulled in the pass for a 12-yard touchdown.

Theismann then began hitting his receivers, moving Washington into scoring range. But once the Redskins got into the red zone, our defense stopped them at the seven, forcing them to settle for a field goal that narrowed our lead to 14–3.

Then, with just twelve seconds remaining in the half, our defense came up with another big play.

Rather than run the clock out, Theismann attempted a screen pass to Joe Washington from inside the 10-yard line. It was the same play that the Redskins had completed for a 67-yard gain against us in the regular season, and our defensive coaches were determined not to let it happen again. Linebacker Jack Squirek had been assigned to forget about everything on the field except Joe Washington, to just stay with him on every play.

When Theismann turned to his left and lofted a soft pass over the outstretched arms of Lyle Alzado in the direction of Washington, Jack simply stepped in front of the ball, made the easy interception at the five, and took a couple of quick steps into the end zone.

Thanks to our defense, we were leading 21–3 at halftime. Not only did I like the advantage we had, I knew that in the second half Flores would likely put even greater emphasis on our running game. We'd been successful throwing the ball and our defense had been superlative. It stood to reason those were the areas that Redskins coach Joe Gibbs and his staff would concentrate on remedying at halftime.

While I'd managed to pick up good yardage on several plays, I hadn't broken a long one. Given the chance to carry the ball more, I felt it could happen. I was having success avoiding tacklers—as if I could feel them coming before I ever really saw them—and wanted the chance to show that we could run on the number-one rushing defense in the league.

The coaching staff, much to my delight, had the same idea. "What we want to do in the third quarter," Flores urged, "is dominate them."

The Redskins were hardly ready to concede. They took the second-half kickoff and drove 70 yards for a touchdown. John Riggins ran it in from the one to narrow the score to 21–9. Our special teams again came up with a big play as Don Hasslebeck broke through to block Mark Mosley's extra-point attempt.

It was important that we not allow them to let their first touchdown of the game serve as a springboard to the kind of momentum they'd enjoyed in the later stages of our first meeting. To assure that didn't happen, our offense needed to respond. If they could shut us down and get the ball back quickly, they could get back into it. Members of our defensive unit and specialty teams, quick to remind us that they'd already contributed two touchdowns to the cause, urged us to get our asses in gear and score some points.

The next few minutes were the most important of the game. The third quarter was one of the best fifteen minutes of football the Raiders ever played.

The Washington defense, also sensing the importance of the moment, became too aggressive, determined to close down our between-the-tackles running attack. With the battle going on in the middle of the line, I was able to pick up several sizable gains to the outside. Then Malcolm Barnwell went deep and Redskins defensive back Darrell Green, a world-class sprinter in his college days back in Texas, drew a thirty-eight-yard interference penalty. Five plays later I scored from the five and we were back in control.

Late in the third quarter, however, the Redskins got a lift when they recovered a Cliff Branch fumble at our 35-yard line. In three plays they advanced the ball nine yards, setting up a fourth-and-one situation as the quarter ticked away. Coach Gibbs obviously felt it was getting too late to settle for field goals, and left his offense on the field.

Attempting to pick up the first down, Theismann handed off to Riggins, who slid along the left side of his line, looking for enough daylight to get the necessary yard. What he found waiting was Rod Martin, who pulled him down for no gain.

With twelve seconds remaining in the third quarter, we took over at our own 26-yard line.

There are those moments in life that simply defy proper explanation, so magical that they beg a poet's talent for description. They pass all too soon, a blur in time so quickly gone that there is not ample opportunity to fully appreciate them as they occur. Such a moment for me began when Plunkett leaned into our huddle and called the play: 18 Bob Tray-O, an off-tackle power play.

As it is designed, I'm supposed to cut off a double-team block by our tackle and tight end, following the fullback, who is supposed to provide a kickout block on the cornerback.

For the first few steps the play went as designed and I broke past the line of scrimmage. From that point I was supposed to cut to the sidelines, but when I saw the safety racing to the outside to cut me off, I turned back toward the middle—and stepped on it. For an instant I was vaguely aware of arms reaching out at me, then slipping away as I ran toward the opposite sidelines, seeing nothing but open field in front of me.

Knowing that Darrell Green, Washington's fastest defender, had committed himself to the sideline and would therefore have a lot of turf to make up if he was to catch me, I knew long before I made it to the end zone that I was going to score. As I ran, I did something I'd never done before, sneaking a glance into the stands as I ran.

I felt as if I had wings while everyone and everything around me moved in super slow motion.

My 74-yard touchdown, announced as the longest run from scrimmage in Super Bowl history, took the air out of the Redskins. As my teammates ran from the bench to join me in the end zone, you could feel the Raiders' confidence soar. With a 35–9 lead and only fifteen minutes left to be played, we were not only in control of the game but carrying out Flores's halftime command. We were dominating.

The fourth quarter was little more than an exercise in frustration for the Washington offense. Forced into a passing game, Theismann was sacked three times, fumbled once, and then threw another interception.

Late in the game I broke free again, gaining 39 yards to move us deep in the Redskins' end of the field. It was my last play. With a few minutes still remaining, I jogged toward the sidelines, looking for Greg Pruitt. As a running back with the Cleveland Browns, he'd had a number of outstanding seasons during his career but had never made it to a Super Bowl. It seemed only fair to me that he get to play in this one. And so, for the first time in my life, I took myself out of a game and signaled my replacement onto the field.

Later Greg would come close to scoring on a sweep but was stopped short of the goal line by a shoestring tackle. By the time Chris Bahr went out to kick a 21-yard field goal that would increase our margin to 38–9, I was sitting on the bench beside Matt Millen, staring up at the message being flashed on the stadium scoreboard:

MARCUS ALLEN, 20 CARRIES, 191 YARDS. A NEW SUPER BOWL RECORD.

Then it dimmed before a second message appeared: SUPER BOWL XVIII MVP: MARCUS ALLEN.

It goes without saying that it had hardly been a one-man show. Our thirty-eight points were the most ever scored by a team in the game's history, and our margin of victory was also a new record. Plunkett had completed 16 of 25 for 172 yards, our defense had been incredible, and the specialty teams had blocked a punt and an extra point attempt. Just as Flores had urged, it was a dominating effort.

On that particular day, we could have beaten anyone in the world. Like announcer John Facenda said later on a NFL Films piece on the game, "Nothing that could run, block, or tackle could have stopped the Raiders on Black Sunday."

To be singled out as I had been didn't really soak in. Being part of a world championship aside, the greatest moment for me came in the final few seconds of the game when I looked over to see my parents being escorted to the sidelines where they were interviewed by CBS's Phyllis George. Not only had they been able to share the moment with me, they got the opportunity to actually participate, and that meant a great deal to me. I was also pleased to know that my grandmother was watching from the stands.

It might not have looked like it—I still had the shiner from the game and at some point during the Super Bowl I had chipped a tooth—but I'd never felt better in my life.

Naturally, the post-game locker room was bedlam. All the pain and pressure of the long season seemed to have melted away instantly, replaced by unbridled, childlike joy. We stood by to watch NFL Commissioner Pete Rozelle present the Lombardi Trophy to Al Davis, each of us silently wondering how these two longtime adversaries would deal with the moment. Rozelle was gracious with his congratulations. Davis, not missing the opportunity to point out that this was the organization's third Super Bowl championship, declared us "the greatest Raiders team ever."

It was one of the few times in our life together that I felt obligated to agree with him.

The celebrating went on long after all the cameras were turned off and the last member of the media had taken leave to begin writing his story. As I sat in front of my locker, sharing in the moment, wanting to lock it all into my memory, I looked across the room toward Lyle Alzado.

This hulk of a man, infamous for his rough style of play and roguish behavior, who had come to us after being discarded by the Denver Broncos, sat half-dressed, a portrait of exhaustion and sheer joy. Tears were streaming down his cheeks.

It occurred to me that being a part of a world championship meant more to him than any other person on our squad. In time, however, I would find myself wondering at the high price he'd opted to pay for that moment.

nine

Friends Too Soon Gone

Depending on the day or week—sometimes the hour—Lyle Alzado, the big defensive end who had come to the Raiders at age thirty-three, could be your best friend or your worst enemy. So drastic and lightning-quick were his mood swings that he was the only member of the squad afforded the privilege of a room to himself on road trips. Which, frankly, was fine with everyone.

The only player to even briefly share a room with Lyle was Howie Long, one of the most likable and easygoing people you'll ever meet. When not in the heat of game-day battle, Howie got along with everyone. But after only brief exposure to Lyle during his rookie year, Long quietly asked to be assigned another roommate. No one in management had to ask why.

Lyle fascinated me. His background, about which he openly talked in a self-deprecating manner, sounded like something out of *West Side Story*. He had grown up on the mean streets of New York and had the knife-fight scars to prove it. His mom was Jewish and his father of Spanish and Italian heritage, and he survived his boyhood days because he was big and mean enough to be the neighborhood bully. By age sixteen he was working as a bouncer at a bar he described as "one of those real-life bucket-of-blood joints."

His only goal in early life was to grow up to be a professional boxer. As long as you like beating hell out of people, he'd say, you might as well get paid something for it.

When Lyle talked about the good old days, there wasn't the slightest attempt to hide the sarcasm. He'd spent more than his share of nights in jail for fighting, drinking, and petty thefts. One night, he recalled, after waking in the Nassau County drunk tank, he removed all his clothes and began to jump up and down, screaming through the bars that he was going to kick every ass in the place if he wasn't released immediately.

Finally, an elderly prisoner looked up at him through weary, boozy eyes and quietly told him to shut the hell up. "You're just a bum like me, kid. Take it easy. You're going to be spending the rest of your life in and out of places like this."

For Lyle, the old drunk's observation was something of an epiphany. "At first," he recalled, "I didn't know whether to punch the old bastard or kiss him. No one had ever talked to me like that. But, hell, what he said was true. That's probably the biggest favor anybody ever did for me."

That's when Alzado decided to focus his strength and hostilities on football. By the time he graduated from high school, several small colleges expressed interest in offering him a scholarship—until they learned that his rap sheet made for more interesting reading than his academic transcript. Finally, a junior college in Kilgore, Texas, took a chance on him. Later he moved on to Yankton College in South Dakota, where his aggressive style of play caught the eye of NFL scouts.

His next stop was the Denver Broncos, where he became one of the game's most feared players, becoming an All-Pro defensive tackle and serving as point man on a unit that became known as the Orange Crush. The Broncos won the AFC title in 1977 and faced the Dallas Cowboys in Super Bowl XII. On that day in the New Orleans Superdome, however, Roger Staubach and the Cowboys proved to be the superior team, defeating the Broncos 27–10.

It was, Lyle would often say, the most disappointing loss of his athletic career. He'd never wanted anything so badly as he'd wanted to be a part of a world championship team. That, I have to think, was the reason for the emotion that overwhelmed him in the aftermath of our victory over the Redskins.

Like so many before him, Alzado had come to the Raiders after the rest of the league had dismissed him as over the hill. Denver had traded him to Cleveland, but the Browns quickly determined that his best days were behind him.

Convinced that Alzado could improve our pass rush, Al Davis had traded draft choices to the Browns for Lyle and thirty-one-year-old running back Greg Pruitt. Once again he'd resurrected careers.

In a manner of speaking, Lyle and I became rookie members of the team at the same time. And over the years we developed a strange sort of relationship.

It was tradition in those days for players to race from the morning team meetings into the parking lot adjacent to our practice facility and purchase lunch from a traveling catering service known to some as "Meals on Wheels," to others more cynical as "the Roach Coach." The driver offered a menu that was a nutritionist's nightmare—cold sandwiches, chili dogs, chips, soft drinks, and candy bars.

One day Lyle, in a particularly foul mood, literally threatened to kill me simply because I had been handed a sandwich he'd thought was his. Not that I'd taken the only remaining ham-and-cheese; just that I'd been given mine before he got his. He erupted into a rage, spewing profanity and threats, then stormed away, tossing his own sandwich aside.

If this scene strikes you as funny, think again.

There was the time in Miami's Orange Bowl when, as we returned to the locker room at the halftime of a game against the Dolphins, a drunken fan yelled obscenities at Lyle, then tossed a cup of beer into his face. Alzado went ballistic and began climbing the wall to get into the stands where the fan stood, beating his chest in a Tarzan-like manner. Lyle grabbed the man's shirt with one hand and began wildly swinging his helmet with the other. Realizing what was happening, several Raiders players quickly followed Lyle into the stands and began trying to pull him away with very little success. They managed to distract him just long enough for the foolhardy fan to pull away and run to safety.

One afternoon, during a dummy scrimmage—a practice session where the offense runs plays against the defense with blocking and tackling only simulated—I carried the ball past Lyle, then on upfield for another 10 or 15 yards. Turning to jog back to the huddle, I suddenly felt a forearm slam against the back of my head, causing me to momentarily see stars. When my equilibrium returned, I looked to see that it had been Alzado who had dealt the uncalled-for blow, and I was furious. I got right in his face, shoving him and cursing. He stood there for a moment, giving me this odd, bewildered look and asked, "Are you fuckin' crazy?"

That's when I really I lost it. *Me, crazy? Dammit, I wasn't the one who cheap-shotted a teammate from behind like a gutless coward.* And with that I did something no one on our team had ever done: I threw my absolutely best Sunday punch at Lyle's face.

I should say here that it was my good fortune that teammates and coaches rushed over to break things up before they went any further. Lyle had me by the face mask and was about to break my neck. And, bear in mind that he had, during his Denver days, actually gotten into the ring for an exhibition fight against heavyweight champion Muhammad Ali and fared reasonably well. He was the same guy who had caused the league to institute what came to be known as the Alzado Rule, forbidding a player to remove a helmet during the course of a game and use it as a weapon against an opponent.

It was in the locker room, after practice, that Lyle came up to me and made what for him was a profuse apology. Extending his hand, he said, "Look, I'm sorry."

"Forget it," I told him.

He began walking away but after a few steps turned and smiled at me. "I like you, Allen," he said. "You've got balls."

But every time I thought we'd become friends, something would happen to stir up old hostilities. One evening Lyle was a guest on sportscaster Roy Firestone's TV show. At one point during the interview Firestone asked Lyle what seemed to me a strange question. "What about Marcus Allen's heart?" he asked.

Lyle responded with an even stranger answer. "Marcus Allen doesn't *have* a heart," he said with a nonchalant shrug and a gravelly laugh.

I'm not sure who I was maddest at—Firestone for even asking such a strange question, or Lyle for his answer. The following day I summoned the most colorful language in my vocabulary to let him know how I felt about his unjustified remark. On this occasion, almost a week passed before I received yet another apology from Lyle. This time it came in a letter he'd written and left in my locker.

I dealt with Roy Firestone by ignoring invitations to be a guest on his show for the next five years.

In truth, the strange behavior of Lyle Alzado was a puzzle to no one. His unpredictable mood swings, the untamed behavior, and the barroom brawls that were a routine part of his troubled life were the result of the anabolic steroids he was taking. Like many in the league at the time, he denied it. But it didn't take a rocket scientist to tell.

I've always felt I could pick out the players using steroids just on the basis of one attempted block during a game. Under normal circumstances, a back my size can be pretty successful at moving linemen and linebackers, even if they do have a seventy-five- to hundred-pound weight advantage. It's all in getting the proper leverage. You get low enough and attack from the right angle, and you'll win the battle. Occasionally, however, no such science works. Over the years I've tried to block some defenders whose bodies felt like they were steel-plated.

They, I knew immediately, were using steroids.

Rob Huizenga, one of our team doctors, had spent countless hours counseling Lyle, urging him to stop.

For a long time, Lyle insisted that every rippling muscle on his 265-pound frame was the result of nothing more than long, dedicated hours in the gym. Up until the time a ruptured Achilles ended his playing career, he adamantly insisted that he was taking no form of performance-enhancing drugs.

His name never appeared on any report following the

league-demanded drug tests we were regularly subjected to. Officially, Lyle Alzado was clean.

In time he would admit the dangerous price he'd paid for his NFL success.

For several years after his retirement I saw Lyle only occasionally. He was busy doing movies and running a trendy sports bar in West Hollywood. Then, suddenly, at age forty, he visited Al Davis and told him he was thinking of making a comeback. Why? He wanted to do it for every forty-year-old man in the country, to prove that age is really nothing more than a state of mind.

Though skeptical, I thought his willingness to give it one more try was pretty courageous.

When he reported to training camp that summer, he didn't look as if he'd aged a day. He was a walking advertisement for Gold's Gym, his body even more sculptured than I'd remembered it. I was fairly convinced he was going to work his way back onto the Raiders roster for another season.

During the six weeks of camp, however, he suffered one nagging injury after another. Every day seemed to bring some new muscle strain or pull. Still, there was no move to cut him and he survived each roster reduction until we played the Chicago Bears on the final week of the pre-season schedule. In that game, played in historic old Soldier Field, Alzado started at his old defensive end position.

At one point, the Bears had moved deep into our end of the field and Lyle, seeing the opposing quarterback dropping back to pass, bull-rushed his way past a rookie tackle's block, arms held high. He batted the attempted pass skyward, then ran under it for an interception and lumbered 15 yards back upfield before he was tackled.

The fans loved it. So did Lyle. With arms outstretched in Rocky Balboa fashion, he jogged triumphantly to the sideline. The fact that the officials called the play back, ruling that Lyle had been offsides, did little to diminish his final moment as a professional athlete.

The next day, following a meeting with the coaching staff, Lyle Alzado "retired." Speaking with several reporters who regularly covered the team, he insisted that he'd accomplished what he'd set out to do. He made no mention of how difficult it had been trying to compete against players almost twenty years younger, nor was there any talk of that lost step of speed or the balking of forty-year-old muscles. No mention that even the steroids hadn't been enough for one more season in a game that worships youth.

I felt a certain degree of sadness as I watched a man who had been such a dominating force walk away from the game for the last time, aware finally that his time had passed.

It did not match the sorrow I felt when I learned soon thereafter that he had been diagnosed with inoperable lymphoma of the brain. Lyle Alzado, once the picture of health and endless stamina, was dying of cancer.

Convinced that his condition was the result of longtime growth hormones and steroid use, he finally went public. As chemotherapy treatments robbed him of that trademark wavy black hair, as one hundred pounds disappeared from his once magnificent body, as the tumor robbed him of equilibrium and eyesight, Lyle did something more courageous than anything he'd ever done on the playing field.

To anyone who would grant him an interview, he spoke out on the dangers of performance-enhancing drugs. For twenty-two years, he admitted, he'd been a nonstop user. When the steroids and growth hormones didn't get the job done, he'd added amphetamines to the mix. The price tag had been in the neighborhood of $30,000 a year.

All so he might continue to succeed in the athletic arena, to maintain his hold on the fame, the adulation, and the money to which we all, to one degree or another, become enslaved.

Toward the end, as his debts mounted, there was a $500-a-plate black-tie benefit staged in his honor. I was among those asked to speak, following the likes of actor Carl Weathers, Olympic gymnast Nadia Comaneci, and my teammate Howie Long.

It wasn't an easy thing to do. For all our differences, I had liked Lyle. He was basically a good person who had a very caring nature, but over time the drugs had turned him into someone else.

In May of 1992, Lyle Alzado died at age forty-three.

• • •

His was not the first senseless tragedy to visit the Raiders family. Before him there had been defensive end John Matuszak and strong safety Stacey Toran.

Matuszak, one of the standout performers in the Raiders' Super Bowl XV victory, had retired the year after attempting to stretch his career to one more season during my rookie training camp, but I'd gotten to know him on his frequent visits to practices and games. He'd been among the former Raiders players Davis had invited to accompany the team to Tampa Bay for the Super Bowl. One didn't have to be a member of the team long to hear the legendary 'Tooz stories. He was a six-eight, 280-pound combination of Grizzly Adams and Paul Bunyan, and stories of his off-the-field behavior made Alzado sound like a choirboy: arrested for possession of marijuana, hospitalized for overdosing on alcohol and sleeping pills, drunk driving, carrying a concealed weapon. In 1982 he'd posed seminude for *Playgirl* magazine. Legend had it that there was a member of the Raiders' front office whose only job was to look after Matuszak in an effort to keep him available for game days. In the week leading up to Super Bowl XV in New Orleans, pictures and stories chronicling his nocturnal behavior on Bourbon Street prompted Philadelphia coach Dick Vermeil to suggest to the press that if he had a player behaving in such a manner with the biggest game of his life on the horizon, he'd send him home on the next bus out of town.

John's football career finally ended when Howie Long moved him out of his job, but his wild ways apparently never slowed. They continued as he dabbled for a while in the movies and wrote a book.

In June of 1989, at age thirty-eight, he died of a heart attack, which medical authorities suggested was a by-product of too much booze and too many pills.

The untimely death of Stacey Toran was a different sort of story. A strong safety with the Raiders for six seasons, he had finally begun to gain the kind of recognition that results in an invitation to the Pro Bowl and inclusion on All-Pro selections. He was engaged to be married, had a nice townhouse in Marina del Ray, and was always looking ahead to business possibilities in life after his playing days were over.

We'd become friends one summer when we were part of a Raiders basketball team that traveled to Australia to play a series of exhibition games.

Stacey was neither a hard drinker nor a drug user. Rather, he was an example of what the vast majority who play the game are: a hardworking, God-fearing, decent guy trying to be the best he could be.

For years, one night a week had been designated as Camaraderie Night for members of the team. And, in theory, I always viewed it as one of the most positive traditions that we had. Players—black and white, offense and defense— would gather at some restaurant or bar for dinner and a few beers, shoot the bull, resolve differences, and generally become better acquainted. It was a tradition that added greatly to the sense of togetherness a team must have if it is to enjoy success.

When training camp opened before the 1989 season, I was a holdout, still trying to resolve a maze of problems I was having with Al Davis. As was always the practice, players would get one night off, free of the evening meetings and curfew that were a standard part of training camp. With the welcomed freedom, a number of players took leave of Oxnard late on a Saturday afternoon and headed southward toward Los Angeles for a relaxing evening on the town. Everyone, the coaches had announced, was free from the camp drudgery until Sunday evening.

Shortly after midnight, Stacey was driving toward his Marina del Ray home after having dinner and drinks with several teammates. Driving at a high speed, he failed to negotiate an exit and crashed into a concrete barrier. Not wearing a seat belt, he was thrown thirty feet from the site of the impact, his skull shattered. The coroner later said that in all likelihood he had died instantly.

And the autopsy revealed that his blood alcohol level was, in non-medical terms, well into the "disabling range."

When I received the news, I felt numb. It made no sense,

seemed so unfair. Still, it was hardly an unfamiliar story. I found myself making a mental list of players I'd known since joining the NFL who had died of alcohol-related deaths.

Stacey Toran, however, was different. He was a friend, a teammate; someone who I'd looked forward to seeing again just as soon as my contract problems were resolved and I rejoined the team.

As the news preyed on my mind, I did something for which I have no real explanation, aside from a frustrating search for some answer to the troubling questions that refused to go away. Late the following evening I drove to the site where the accident occurred and pulled over. For several minutes I sat there, staring silently at the marks on the embankment he'd driven into and the shards of glass that were still sprinkled along the roadside. Finally, looking up, I could see his townhouse, no more than a couple of hundred yards away, and I felt a wave of indescribable sadness sweep over me.

He'd been so close to home, to safety. To continuing on with his bright and promising future.

Three days later I took a seat in one of the pews at the Maranatha Community Church, where Stacey had been a faithful member, listening as his minister and several family members eulogized his all-too-short life. My coaches and teammates had arrived from Oxnard by team bus, practice canceled so they might pay their respects. Davis, who had discarded his traditional all-white outfit for an appropriate black suit, passed by me without a word.

And I really didn't give a damn. At that moment, contract negotiations, practice sessions, even the upcoming season, seemed of little consequence.

Historically, there has been a search for answers to why those who toil in a labor field where their bodies are their greatest tool, to whom peak physical well-being is so essential, would jeopardize their careers by using drugs and alcohol. The responses have routinely been simplistic and unsatisfactory: Generally immature young men blessed with great strength and speed, celestial contracts, and the adoration of millions, somehow deem themselves invincible against the dangers of the real world. There are pressures too demanding to be properly handled. In the highly competitive arena of professional sports, where there is always someone younger, stronger, and faster threatening to take your job, or an opponent who might make you look bad in front of millions on Sunday afternoon, there is an ever-desperate search for something—anything—that might give you even the slightest edge.

And in the search, the way is lost. I remember watching two players fall asleep during practice, their heads resting against their helmets, a white mucus coming from their noses. And though I didn't see it firsthand, one of the oft-told stories was about a player so blitzed on dope that he put his shoulder pads on over his street clothes and thought himself ready to practice.

They were the guys who were "on the pipe," doing the highly addictive crack cocaine. In the vernacular of the locker room, they were "smoking the Devil's dick."

All of which is a classic example of misplaced values and hard-core stupidity. I'm sure of this: In those days before he died, Lyle Alzado would have exchanged his prized Super Bowl ring for good health in a minute. Stacey Toran's fiancée would much rather have a husband, family, and future than a pro football player who brought home a big paycheck and felt that drinking with the boys was necessary to the team's success. Those who are forced to look back on drug-shortened careers would love the opportunity to go back and do it the right way. One of the cruel realities of sports is that it is stingy with second chances.

It is true that the pressures, both professional and social, attached to life in the NFL are real. There are millions of dollars at stake and little reward for those who don't succeed. Management protects its investment and collects its profit only when the team performs well. To do so it must field strong, well-coached teams made up of quality, productive players. So perilous is the public high-wire act that the weakest link in the chain can destroy the balance and set things on a downward spiral.

It is a fragile kind of existence, one filled with enormous pressures. Most can deal with it; some can't.

The public focus rarely strays from the high-dollar salaries being earned by today's professional athletes. It reads where So-and-So signs a multi-year, multimillion-dollar contract, complete with a huge signing bonus, and automatically assumes that he's set for life. And perhaps he should be.

But the reality is that there are far more financial horror stories than you could possibly imagine. You don't hear about the ex-players who have to do trading-card show signings to make a living; of once-financially-sound guys forced to sell their Super Bowl rings just to make a mortgage payment; or of the former players now literally on the streets with not the slightest idea where their next meal is coming from.

It seems unbelievable, but it happens. Why? Many of us are far better athletes than we are businessmen. At one time or another we have all been tempted by investments that proved to be too good to be true. A number of today's players were products of poverty-level social backgrounds and eagerly draped themselves in the luxuries of the rich when the money rolled in, giving little or no thought to the fact that one day the big paydays and the cheers would end. Too few stopped to realize the importance of preparing for a new career. In an era where bankruptcy has reached a rampant level, professional athletes have not been exempt.

For many, life after the game becomes an emotional horror. Having made no plans for the transition from the fantasy life of pro ball to the real world, they find it difficult to accept the fact that they're suddenly yesterday's news.

And they wonder where the money's gone, never stopping to realize that their salary, which was made known to the public, was a mirage to begin with.

For example, take a look at what happened to the signing bonus I received from the Raiders. Of the $400,000, half of it went straight to Uncle Sam. Then there was the percentage due my agent. By the time I made a down payment on a home and paid some bills, I was far less solvent than most believed. Then came the strike that reduced the season to nine games, cutting the salary I was to receive by half.

I give this example not as a "poor me" statement, but rather to demonstrate the fact that the numbers on a piece of paper and the dollars that actually find their way into your pocket are hardly the same. Nor am I holding myself up as some example of ideal financial housekeeping. I simply wish to make note of the fact that there is far more than meets the eye when the topic of pro sports salaries is discussed.

The smart player today is the one who not only asks that his boss "show him the money," but then seeks good advice on what to do with it.

It is not a lesson easily learned.

Mike Wise, a talented defensive lineman who was once among my teammates on the Raiders, was one to whom the pressures finally became more than he could handle.

Mike was a fourth-round pick in the 1986 draft, a six-eight 280-pound defensive lineman who wanted nothing more in the world than to play for the Raiders. Clearly, he'd worked on his "image" even before reporting, sporting a biker look and a Fu Manchu mustache. On one ankle he had a tattoo of the Grim Reaper. Despite the affectations, he was quiet and almost withdrawn, a loner who spent his every waking hour and every ounce of effort he could summon in an effort to win a place on the roster.

Though he would play sparingly as a rookie, he made the team as a backup defensive end and tackle. Then, in his second year, the break he'd hoped for came his way. Howie Long was injured early in the season and Mike got to start the last fourteen games. With each game his confidence grew.

By the time he'd gained veteran status, however, he began to consider the economics of his situation. No longer was just being a member of the Los Angeles Raiders enough. I have no idea what kind of contract he'd signed, but apparently he became convinced he was not being properly paid.

He'd apparently talked with some other defensive players who had been in the league for the same amount of time he was and who were seeing less playing time, only to learn they were making more. Loyal to the core, he agonized over his situation through most of the off-season before finally going to Davis and asking that his contract be renegotiated.

Davis finally agreed to do so, but for a figure still considerably below what Mike felt was fair. Thus came the dilemma few players anticipate back on that joyous day they are drafted. Bottom line: Mike could stay with the Raiders, accepting the fact that he was being underpaid, and remain out of Al Davis's doghouse, or . . . but for Mike Wise there was no "or."

By the time the season was to get under way, the boyish enthusiasm and loyalty to the Raiders organization had dissolved into bitterness. He sulked, fought with teammates over the most trivial matters, and then, just before the opening game, stormed out and went home to Sacramento.

The first couple of games of the season came and went and he stubbornly remained at home. Though I never spoke with him about it, I know exactly what was going through his mind. *They need me. I've busted my ass for them and they'll come around and realize they're going to have to give me a fair deal. I've just gotta be patient.*

But no one in the Raiders front office called.

Finally, at almost midseason, after months of no paychecks and mounting bills, Mike got word that Davis had released him.

He got a second chance when the Cleveland Browns picked him up on waivers, but soon found himself on injured reserve after tearing ligaments in a knee. Determined to make a comeback in '92, he severely injured his back lifting weights two weeks before training camp was to begin. The Browns cut him early that summer. And no other teams called. After four seasons, Mike's career in the NFL had come to an abrupt end.

Unable to accept his situation, he fell into a deep depression. Badly in debt, he was forced to put his home on the market. He rarely went out, unable to face the real world into which he'd unwillingly returned. To those few friends he did speak with, he tried to explain the overwhelming pressure he'd endured as a player and how now, with no sense of direction without the game, it was even worse.

On the first day of August in 1992, just a year after Lyle

Alzado had died, Mike Wise sat alone and fired a single shot from a 9mm Ruger into his temple.

The game had been his entire existence. Mike, like so many others I've come to know over the years, lacked the mature vision to see into the future and realize that there is a life after football, that there is beauty to be found in the world even if it is not accompanied by the cheers of seventy thousand voices.

Weary of attending funerals of friends far too young to die, I am angered and haunted by their stories. We all should be. And we have an obligation to seek solutions to the problem.

There aren't too many secrets in pro football. Everyone knows who is using drugs or drinking too much. And while I've seen the damage it can do, I've never completely understood the attraction.

Over the years, I've talked to a number of players who I knew had some degree of drug or drinking problems. It isn't an easy thing to do because you have to be very careful in your approach. I've had a few guys who thanked me for my concern and whatever advice I'd tried to pass along. To others, what I've said went in one ear and out the other. All I got was denial. They'll say they appreciate what you have to say and assure you they're either quitting or have their lives under control. They know it's bullshit; so do you.

It is very difficult to help someone who doesn't want your help. He's the guy who is going to do what he thinks is best for himself, regardless of how it might affect others.

That's where the all-important team concept comes into play. The good teams are those who have that core group of players who understand the importance of contributing to a collective effort. At another level you have that group that is on the fence; they want to be a part but haven't yet figured out how to accomplish it. Those are the guys who are more likely to listen to the advice of a teammate. Then, unfortunately, there is that small group that is completely apathetic about anything that doesn't directly concern them and their own gratification.

I've wondered why teams don't include conduct clauses in contracts, making it clear that if a player abuses drugs or alcohol, or runs afoul of the law, the consequences could be severe. On the surface that might sound harsh, but it is in virtually every endorsement contract I've ever seen. The quicker the latter element is weeded out, the better the chances of having a solid team are going to be.

I can honestly say that the great majority of professional athletes I know are attuned to the team concept. Unfortunately, there will always be those who just never quite get it.

As a player who doesn't drink or use drugs, I have a right to be angered by those who do, because ultimately the public paints us all with the same brush.

And while I certainly don't want to minimize drug abuse, I believe that the use of alcohol, though socially and legally acceptable, has done far greater damage. As I look back over the fifteen years I've been in the league, the list of players who have been seriously injured or lost their lives to drinking-related automobile accidents is staggering—and so damn senseless.

PART II

The only kind of dignity
which is genuine is that
which is not diminished by
the indifference of others.
          —Dag Hammarskjöld

ten

Fun, Friends . . . and One Fragile Relationship

Being young and single with money in your pocket isn't the worst thing that can happen to a guy. In a city that has made an industry of showering attention on its celebrities, being a member of the world-champion Los Angeles Raiders was a quick ticket to good tables at posh restaurants and invitations to more social functions than you could ever hope to attend.

But L.A. also loves its gossip. With little actual effort on my part, my reputation as a "man about town" really took flight. And while I did enjoy taking pretty women out to dinner and drove a new black Ferrari Testarossa, I hardly considered myself a creature of the Hollywood nightlife scene.

Which is to say I still wasn't living up to the image that some people seemed to have of me.

Actually, I found that it was becoming even easier to be credited for things I didn't do. For instance, one evening Mike Ornstein, who I had become friends with on that first day I attended the press conference where I was introduced as the Raiders' first draft pick, and I went out to the Forum to watch the Lakers in a play-off game. Afterward, we returned to his car in the parking lot and were preparing to leave when this guy who'd had a few too many walked by and banged his fist against the top of Orny's car. Mike made no secret of the fact he didn't appreciate it and yelled out at the guy. Big mistake. The guy staggered back to the car and slammed his fist against the roof a second time. Now Orny was really pissed, so he jumped out and they got into a shouting match.

There was some shoving, then Orny decked the guy with one swift punch to the nose, got back in the car, and we drove away.

But before we did, I heard someone in the crowd say, "Hey, did you see Marcus Allen pop that dude?" I hadn't even gotten out of the car.

I'm sure, though, that by the next day the story of how I beat the crap out of some innocent guy in the Forum parking lot was all over town.

Trouble is not something you have to go looking for in L.A.

One morning as I was driving along Melrose to a piano lesson, I saw the flashing lights of a police car in my rearview mirror and pulled over. I'd had my share of speeding tickets, but on this occasion I knew I was driving well below the limit. The street was under repair and I couldn't have been going more than ten miles per hour. I couldn't imagine why I was being stopped. Neither did I understand the patrolman's actions after I pulled over. Standing behind the door of his patrol car, pointing his gun toward me, he demanded that I get out of my car and lie face-down in the street.

The only deadly weapon I had in my possession was my piano lesson book.

As children in a nearby schoolyard looked on, he hand-cuffed me as other LAPD officers arrived and a police helicopter hovered overhead.

Actually, the explanation was pretty simple: A black guy driving a Ferrari had to be up to no good. No way he could afford a car like that, so it had to be stolen.

The officer explained that he'd pulled me over after running a check of my license plates and found they didn't match the car's registration number. As it turned out, he was right.

I had ordered plates for it months earlier, and when a set finally arrived, I immediately put them on. The problem was that the plates I'd received had not been for the Ferrari but, rather, the Trans Am, which I'd received for being the Super Bowl MVP and was planning to give to my brother Harold.

By the time a patrol sergeant arrived and finally listened to my explanation, the kids in the schoolyard were calling my name. Two women who lived in the neighborhood near my piano instructor had come out of their houses and tried to assure the police that I was who I said I was.

Finally, the sergeant apologized and sent me on my way with orders to get the right license plates on the right cars.

Suddenly, I wasn't just some black guy. I was Marcus Allen, football player, and in the eyes of the officer that somehow validated me. It wasn't the most blatant example of racism in Los Angeles history, but it pissed me off nonetheless.

Wanting to avoid finding my name somewhere in the papers other than the sports pages, I tried to adhere to the old rules my dad had set for us when we were kids. At the top of the list was to be certain to stay away from even the most remote association with drugs. I was so paranoid about it that on those rare occasions when I did join friends at some new "in" club, I would not even visit the rest room while we were there. It was generally known that a great deal of the drug activity that went on in such places took place in the privacy of the rest rooms. And the last thing I wanted to have happen was to be relieving myself when some narc busted into the place.

So, contrary to what you might think or have heard, I wasn't a hard-core night-on-the-town sort of guy. The truth is that a few of my friends labeled me a bit antisocial because of my lack of interest in hitting the hot spots.

I'm not suggesting I was a recluse by any means. During the off season A.C. Cowlings and I helped close Helena's, a nice dinner and dancing club, on more than one Friday night. We stopped in at the Improv on Monday nights as often as we could.

During the season, I rarely went out.

But because I was the only Raiders player living in Brentwood and therefore patronized some of the neighborhood restaurants also frequented by entertainment celebrities, I seemed to get far more credit for social activity than was due me. For example: I got involved in the Starlight Foundation, an organization that does wonderful things for disadvantaged children, and was asked by actress Emma Samms to be her escort to one of the Foundation's functions. The next day a local columnist wrote that we were dating. Emma was a nice, lovely lady, but we never dated.

Actually, my routine was far from a society-page columnist's dream.

On off-season weekends, I enjoyed just hanging out, sometimes at O.J. Simpson's, sometimes at the home of Allen Schwartz. A.C. and Orny could usually be counted on to stop by. We would meet on Saturday mornings and all go for some breakfast, then go back to someone's house in time to watch whatever sports event was on TV. Later, we'd shoot some hoops or play tennis, sit around talking, then maybe go out for dinner in the evening.

For the most part we gathered with no set plans except to spend time together. It was a good group of people to be around. And the membership seemed to constantly grow. More than anyone I've ever known, O.J. loved having people around. On some days it looked as if a major-league tennis tournament was going on as friends like Kareem Abdul-Jabbar, Ahmad Rashad, and Lynn Swann arrived with rackets in hand. On the Fourth of July, the action turned to an all-day softball tournament.

At times the tennis competition would move to Allen's. A great host, Allen once found out that my parents were coming to Los Angeles for a weekend visit and insisted on having them over for a Sunday brunch. When we arrived that morning, it was obvious that Allen had gone to great lengths, as a catered buffet awaited poolside. He had ordered every Jewish delicacy imaginable. I remember Mom and Dad looking over the food—lox, bagels, cream cheese, and the whole bit—and sharing wary glances. They nibbled politely while I did my best not to give away the fact that my dad's tastes rarely ran beyond T-bone steak and French fries.

Cowlings was one of the nicest and funniest guys I'd ever met. I'm convinced that he could have done well as a stand-up comic had he been inclined to pursue it as a career. And I've never met anyone who cared more about his friends. He was also the only one in the group who had been blessed with a mechanical gene. For example: For weeks, Orny had been troubled over the fact that the headlights would not go off when he returned home in the evenings. Convinced that there was some kind of electrical short involved, he nightly raised the hood and unhooked the battery. Finally tiring of the routine, he asked A.C. to see if he might solve the problem. Which A.C. quickly did, explaining to Orny that he had an automatic timing system built in that allowed the lights to remain on for a brief period of time after the car engine was turned off. Somehow, Orny had managed to set the timer for the maximum two minutes.

That's not to say A.C. knew everything. In the summer after the Super Bowl, he joined me on a trip to Italy, where I was to participate in a football clinic. Arriving in Milan, we checked into our hotel room, where our first order of business was to toss out what appeared to be spoiled fruit that filled a bowl on the table. Eager to test his limited Italian, A.C. then ordered up some orange juice. When two glasses of a thick red liquid arrived, we both assumed they were filled with tomato juice and placed another call to room service. A second time we were disappointed by what arrived. A frustrated waiter finally explained that he had brought us what we'd ordered. The juice was red because it came from a fruit called a blood orange.

We didn't bother mentioning that we'd tossed several of them into the garbage, thinking them spoiled.

Another who occasionally stopped by was Reggie McKenzie, one of O.J.'s Buffalo teammates. I remember him phoning late one afternoon to say he was stranded in Redondo Beach. Juice, A.C., and I went down to pick him up.

O.J. was driving his white Rolls, a magnificent-looking car, but one that had provided a very comfortable livelihood for several local mechanics for some time. Something, it seemed, was always malfunctioning.

But on this particular evening it purred smoothly along the freeway. We picked Reggie up and were headed back toward Long Beach when a violent thunderstorm suddenly erupted. O.J. tried to turn on the windshield wipers, only to find they weren't working. The rain was so heavy that it was all but impossible to see the road ahead, yet O.J. refused to pull over.

So there we were, four black guys, heads sticking out the windows of this fancy white Rolls, everyone simultaneously yelling instructions and directions. It had to look like a really bad vaudeville act.

Later, safely home, we laughed about it. We laughed a lot in those days.

It has been suggested that the two worst things that could have happened to me in my second year as a member of the Raiders were to be named the Most Valuable Player in the Super Bowl and have my picture appear on the cover of a popular national magazine.

The first was troublesome because it went against the Al Davis philosophy that the organization and team, not individuals, should be the focus of attention. Somehow, by being named the Super Bowl MVP, I had blatantly violated the credo. Thanks to a bunch of sportswriters who had cast votes, I was suddenly viewed by my boss as being self-centered and aloof. I hardly think that was the case, nor did I feel any of my teammates or coaches shared such concerns. Jim Plunkett certainly hadn't been looked on as a threat to team morale and a destroyer of the foundation of the Raiders organization when he'd received the same award a few years earlier.

Apparently though, Davis was not at all happy with the attention I was receiving. (I've never heard how he reacted to the fact that the San Diego Zoo named a baby hippo born immediately after the Super Bowl "Marcus," but odds are he wasn't pleased.)

To compound matters, someone published a commemorative picture book on our championship season and made the unfortunate decision to title it "Marcus Allen and the Los Angeles Raiders." To say the least, it did not sit well with the man who had long made it clear that the team was the sole creation and property of Al Davis and no one else.

Then came *GQ* magazine to toss its ration of gas onto the fire. Diane Shah, a sportswriter for the *Los Angeles Herald Examiner,* had done a lengthy article on the team, retelling all the old "rogue Raiders" stories that had become part of the team's lore. When a photographer for the magazine contacted me about posing for a cover photo, I agreed to do so.

What I didn't learn until recently was that Davis had been led to believe *he* would be featured on the cover. When the magazine arrived at the Raiders' offices, I'm told, secretaries hid it for days, knowing how eagerly Al had been looking forward to seeing it. His outraged reaction was predictable.

To that point, I'd had no real indication that our relationship was so fragile. He'd never been particularly friendly, but there were few of the players to whom he displayed a great deal of warmth. I dismissed it as an example of the time-honored big-business belief that it is never a good idea for management to be too chummy with the hired help.

If Davis had reservations about drafting me, I felt certain that I'd proven myself as a valuable member of the team. I saw no legitimate reason for his hostility.

I'd even tried from time to time to break the ice, but with little success. One afternoon, as I walked onto the practice field, most of the team was seated in front of Al as he delivered one of his impromptu pre-workout lectures. I walked up behind him as he spoke and acted as if I was going to place an arm over his shoulder. What the hell, it wouldn't hurt to demonstrate that not everyone on the team became a nervous wreck every time he came around.

Davis found absolutely no humor in the gesture. Turning to me with a frigid glare, he said, "Aw, fuck, you really think you're funny, don't ya?"

If nothing else, Al Davis has to be the most enigmatic, power-driven man I have encountered during my football career. And for all the faults the press and other owners around the league found in him, they had to admit one thing: He'd been successful.

And in the ledger of professional sports, that is the single most important measuring stick.

Described as a loner, a rebel, and an egomaniac, he went against the good ol' boy mentality of pro football ownership at every opportunity. In league meetings, the old joke went,

Al Davis was always the "1" in 27–1 votes on matters of rules and policies.

And the thing about it was he was fully convinced that he was right and twenty-seven other owners and general managers were dead wrong. In the world of Al Davis, there are but two kinds of people: those who agree with him, and the enemy.

This was a man who so strongly believed in himself that he'd repeatedly gone up against the NFL establishment and won. When no one blessed his plan to move the Raiders from Oakland to Los Angeles, he'd done so anyway, going to court to win a multimillion-dollar antitrust suit against the league. While most NFL teams belonged to a cooperative scouting combine to check out predraft talent, Davis refused to join. He felt he and his staff could better determine talent and pick players, and damn sure didn't want to share information with his competitors. It galled others that he constantly embraced players discarded by others and revived their careers. No fewer than twenty-two members of our Super Bowl team had been cut or traded away by some other NFL team.

In every way, big and small, he fought the establishment. It falls annually to NFL Films to produce highlight films for each of the league teams. Davis didn't trust them to do his team justice and therefore had his top administrator, Al LoCasale, produce the Raiders' highlight film. And in having control, Davis saw that it was done his way. When, for instance, the highlights of our Super Bowl season were shown, there was the traditional footage of locker-room celebration after the win over Washington, and shots of a beaming Davis holding the Super Bowl trophy. Nowhere to be seen was NFL Commissioner Pete Rozelle, a longtime Davis adversary, who had made the presentation. Ignoring the league rule that teams could spend only $2,000 for each Super Bowl ring and there was a limit of eighty that could be distributed, Al spent over $3,000 for each ring and ordered ninety, paying the difference himself.

He created a paranoia that was rampant throughout the league. Rival coaches were not only convinced that he spied on their practices, but that he even bugged visiting locker rooms so that he could listen in on pre-game and halftime strategy talks.

He was feared, and he loved it.

When drafted by the Raiders, I looked forward to becoming a part of the us-against-the-world mentality that Davis had fostered. The tunnel-vision focus on football and winning might not win him any social awards, but it was the kind of attitude I felt created the proper environment for success on Sundays.

And certainly his credentials were in order. Al Davis was not one of those billionaire philanthropists who viewed the team over which he presided as an expensive toy. He was a street-smart, Brooklyn-born football man, in and out, having climbed through the collegiate coaching ranks to become head coach of the Raiders in the early Sixties, turning a 1–13 team into a 10–4 contender in his first year. Later he'd served as commissioner of the upstart American Football League, battling the established NFL for players and prestige with such aggressive determination that he eventually forced the merger that expanded the league into what it is today.

And over the years he proved himself to be a shrewd if not always fair-handed businessman. He'd been allowed to buy into the Raiders during his coaching days for $18,500. Today, after a history of infighting and destroyed friendships, he is the majority owner of a team whose value has been estimated at roughly $100 million.

And, as overseer of the Raiders, he built the team into the most feared in the NFL, proudly pointing out that no other professional sport team—not baseball's Yankees, basketball's Celtics, or hockey's Canadiens—could boast the winning percentage of his beloved "Raid-uhs."

Al Davis—rogue, rebel, outlaw—had clearly made his mark.

I had not yet learned the price he demanded of those working alongside him, was unaware of the stark fear his domination of employees generated within the organization. What I would come to learn was that Davis presided over the Raiders with a monarch's zeal. No opinion was valid unless it was originally his, no employee was judged worthwhile without unquestioned loyalty, no effort, however mighty, measured up to his demands.

And if for some reason he harbored a grudge, it was for life. As I would ultimately learn.

But in the world of sports nothing deflects problems and criticism like winning. And that we were doing.

As the defending Super Bowl champions, we went into every game we played with a giant bull's-eye on our chest. Every team we faced, regardless of their talent or previous record, seemed to take their game to a new level against us.

Still, we opened the '84 season with a 7–1 record, losing only to Denver, before Plunkett was injured. Marc Wilson again stepped into the starting quarterback position, but the momentum was soon lost. Denver beat us a second time, opening the door for a three-game losing streak that eliminated our chances of repeating as division champions.

By the time we prepared to face the Pittsburgh Steelers in the final game of the regular season, we were headed to the play-offs, scheduled to face Seattle, our old nemesis, in a wild-card game.

To be assured of home-field advantage against the Seahawks, we had to beat Pittsburgh. And didn't.

Unlike virtually every other team in the league, the Raiders quarterbacks are required to hold on to the ball until they see a receiver break into the open. There are no timing routes, where the ball is thrown to a particular spot where the receiver is expected to be. It was a long-standing Al Davis rule that the quarterback not release the ball until he could see the numbers on the front of his receiver's jersey. That explains why we historically had more holding penalties charged to our offensive line and suffered more quarterback sacks than anyone in the league.

For all their greatness, quarterbacks like Joe Montana, John Elway, and Dan Marino would have been killed had they spent their careers in the Raiders offense. All succeeded because of their quick releases, because of their ability to throw timing routes. If required to hold the ball as long as our quarterbacks, they'd have spent most of their time in the training room or watching games from the sidelines in street clothes.

The Steelers took full advantage of our philosophy and blitzed Marc Wilson crazy, effectively shutting down our passing attack. Still, we persisted in trying to throw the ball.

For most of that frustrating afternoon, I played the role of pass blocker with marginal success. And carried the ball only thirteen times for a paltry 38 yards as the Steelers beat us, 13-7.

In the locker room afterward, Jack Disney, a reporter for the *Los Angeles Herald Examiner*, approached and asked my opinion of our offense—and I unloaded. Angered over the loss and the knowledge that we would have to travel to Seattle for the first round of the play-offs, I made no secret of the fact that I felt we should have tried to throw "hot" to the backs at least once. The constant blitzing by the Pittsburgh defense had been the ideal situation in which to break long gains, yet we'd rarely even tried. In a word, I'd felt our game plan stunk. We had allowed the Steelers to dictate what they wanted us to do.

In print, my comments looked like those of a prima donna. Reading between the lines, one got the impression I was more concerned with incentive bonuses and personal statistics than the overall good of the team. Actually, the only thing I was angry about was the fact that we'd lost. It had absolutely nothing to do with stats or incentives.

Al Davis was suggesting to the coaching staff that I had developed into a "selfish" player.

It was an unjust accusation that troubles me to this day. For all his talk, I never felt Al Davis had cornered the market on the desire to win. I was convinced that I wanted to win far more badly than he did.

My fears were realized a week later when we lost to the Seahawks, ending our hopes of repeating as world champions. Though I had ended the year as the league leader in touchdowns with eighteen, had rushed for 1,168 yards, and had been invited back to the Pro Bowl, I felt an emptiness as the season, which had held so much promise, abruptly ended.

And I felt a growing uneasiness about my relationship with

Al Davis. Clearly, there was a problem. Its cause, however, was a mystery to me.

Throughout the off-season I allowed the "selfish" remark to weigh on me. No criticism directed toward an athlete could be worse. I found myself replaying my entire football career, searching for overlooked signs that might justify such claims. And came up with none.

Angered, I wanted to challenge Davis to show me any Raiders player, past or present, more dedicated to the team and helping it win than I had been.

The concept of being a team player had been hammered into me since my days in peewee sports when my father was my coach. Vic Player had taught it at Lincoln High and John Robinson at USC. Not only had I abided by the philosophy but fully endorsed it. On one thing, Al Davis and I agreed: No individual is more important than the team.

And it was a message I had tried to pass on to youngsters. Aware that there were those who looked up to me, just as I had to a generation of professional athletes when I was younger, I felt a responsibility to project a positive image.

Being labeled a "selfish" player, even in the privacy of Al Davis's office or a coaches' meeting room, sent a message that was not only untrue but one that disturbed me a great deal.

Some may call it vanity, but I've always been image-conscious, concerned—perhaps to a fault—about how I am perceived by others.

For reasons I cannot understand, the question of whether or not high-profile athletes should consider themselves role models has become a topic of great debate. Does our stature and visibility in any way obligate us to a higher code of behavior? Are we responsible for giving direction to youngsters who wear our jerseys, collect our trading cards, and persuade mom and dad to buy the products we endorse?

A number of my peers and friends are quick to not only say no, but hell no. They argue that it is an unfair and unwanted responsibility society has cast upon them. It is, they point out, the job of the parent, not some stranger who can run and catch, to see that a youngster's moral compass is in proper working order.

And while I agree that a child should have to look no farther than the other side of the dinner table for the person he or she should aspire to be, the simple truth is—like it or not—there are millions who look to sports figures as models for what they hope their lives will one day become. In the minds of many, we have chased down the brass ring, and found the magic key that unlocks the American Dream. We're paid huge salaries and play to the applause of millions. Our faces are on magazine covers, billboards (and yes, book jackets). We interrupt your favorite sitcom to suggest that if you wear the athletic gear we favor and eat the fast-food products we eat, life will somehow be so much better.

How then can we expect to be invited into the homes and lives of millions and not feel that some degree of responsibility is attached?

The truth is we *are* perceived as role models. Is that fair? Perhaps not, but it is one of those facts of life from which there is no escape short of immediate retirement and life as a hermit.

I don't understand the fascination with celebrities today any better than I did back when I was a kid trying to emulate the sports stars who I saw as bigger than life. I never gave the faintest thought to growing up to become president or a famous doctor, but I spent a great deal of time daydreaming of how it must be to live the life of someone like Muhammad Ali or Dr. J. That was—and is—as much a part of growing up as skinned knees and the eventual discovery that girls are different.

Frankly, there are times when I find myself wondering why a total stranger would feel the need to have my autograph or seek my advice on some personal matter. I've found no cure for a life-taking disease, caused no great social change; I have not moved the world closer to peace. I view myself as nothing more or less than an ordinary person who happens also to be a football player.

Which is the message I feel most obligated to get across.

I have no visions of being viewed as a guru to the masses;

no profound wisdom to share. I am what I am, believe in what I believe, and can cause only a small effect on the course of human events. Yet I feel a responsibility to do what I can, always bearing in mind that my actions are not only being watched but constantly judged.

Still, there is no real formula by which we can judge our effectiveness.

A couple of years ago I received a letter from a man living in the Deep South who went to great lengths to explain the hatred his grandfather had expressed for blacks. Later, the man wrote, his father had taken up the racist banner. And from childhood, those attitudes had been passed along to him. "But," he wrote, "with the help of you and my own son, I'm now aware of the shortcomings of the teachings I received." His son, he explained, had a poster of me hanging on his bedroom wall. "He admires you more than you could ever imagine," the letter continued. "To my own child, the color of your skin makes absolutely no difference. He respects you for who you are. You have enriched both our lives and taught me a long-overdue lesson."

That letter made a great impact on me. Not only did it demonstrate the power we hold as athletes, it also told me how subtle our impact on the lives of others can be.

There is a fundamental truth to be considered: Kids do what they see. And a lot of what they're seeing today bothers me.

What kind of message is being delivered when an athlete dies his hair every color of the rainbow, spouts profanity on network television, or spits into the face of an official he disagrees with? I like to dance as much as the next guy, but I have no intention of doing it in the end zone. I like what someone once told me about how legendary Cleveland Browns running back Jim Brown always just handed the ball to the official after scoring a touchdown: "What Jim was telling everyone was that he'd been in the end zone before and damn sure wasn't surprised to be there again."

As you know by now, there have been times when I was not happy with the way my playing time was being rationed, but an angry shoving match with the coach in the middle of the game—in full view of fans watching in the stadium and on television—wasn't the place to resolve the issue.

Kids soak that stuff up like sponges. So do a lot of adults. And certainly the media loves it. But one outrageous incident should not be allowed to take precedence over the efforts of everyone else on the team.

When it does, the image of the game and those who play it loses some of its luster.

What has triggered such behavior in recent years?

It has always been my feeling that the game I play is nothing more than a reflection of our society. During the course of three hours on a Sunday afternoon, players are faced with many of the same decisions and roadblocks that cross the paths of people in everyday life.

What concerns me is that the emotional tool kit, which the Chiefs' running back coach Jimmy Raye often refers to, is no longer properly packed. And without it, we as a society are in big trouble. Sports figures are in no way exempted. There is nothing in an NFL contract promising that sudden wealth and stardom will bring about instant intelligence, diplomacy, and a heightened sense of right and wrong.

Today's streets are filled with young people who were never handed such tools.

It is not the NFL, NBA, or major-league baseball that is to blame any more than it is society in general. In recent years we've pushed the envelope further and further in every area of our lives. In the name of political correctness we've become tolerant of the intolerable.

The ballparks, stadiums, and arenas are now packed with fans who seem willing to shrug and dismiss all manner of social shortcomings if an athlete is still able to contribute to another win for the home team.

There seems to be a growing roar of approval on the part of the public for sports' "bad boys," sending the terribly flawed message that their no-rules attitude is to be embraced.

On the other hand, one of the game's great ironies is its rule against violence. As I view it, football is a fight from the opening play to the final gun. Yet the actual act of fighting is certain to earn you a penalty, possible ejection, and the good chance of a fine levied by the league. I know; I've been there.

In the '96 season, I was tackled out of bounds near the Seattle bench and came up fighting two Seahawks players while thirty-five of their teammates stood nearby. Almost immediately there were a number of my Kansas City teammates involved in the fray, there to protect me.

When all was said and done, I was fined $5,000 and three other Chiefs were fined $4,000 each for leaving the bench to help me out.

We appealed the league's decision and in the course of presenting our case to the NFL counselor, I asked him a question: What would he do if he were walking down the street and saw a couple of guys beating up on his brother while thirty-five others stood nearby?

He thought about it for a few seconds, then said, "Well, I don't know."

I found his answer totally unsatisfactory and let him know. "Don't insult me like that," I replied. But as I knew it would be, it was an exercise in futility. The fines stood. The guy hearing our appeal had no concept of the importance of supporting your teammates; could not empathize with the notion that a lack of response to such a situation could quickly fracture the morale of a team.

Understand that I do not believe that fighting should be a part of the game. But where do you draw the line in a sport that by its very nature is highly physical? There is violence on every play and emotions must run high if you are to be competitive. To ask that a player somehow ration his emotion in the heat of battle is pretty unrealistic.

Such are the gray areas that exist in the beauty-and-the-beast game of professional football.

Many of today's young players are coming into the league with little or no concept of the importance of teamwork; no real grasp of the idea that the worthwhile goals of sports can only be achieved through a collective effort.

When a player makes a tackle or a first down catch or scores a touchdown, it is now commonplace to see him immediately distance himself from all others on his team, rip off his helmet, and launch into a ridiculous solo celebration calculated to make certain that the television cameras focus on him.

And in that moment the concept of unity is tossed out the window.

Why? It is partially out-of-control ego, partially about exposure and money. Players are convinced that self-promotion is the fastest route to a few seconds on the ESPN highlights and the attention of promoters looking for their next pitchman. By calling attention to themselves, they're signaling the business world that they're ready to make a deal.

And impatient to get it done.

The idea of paying dues and establishing their place with excellent performances week after week, season after season, has become outdated. Raised in a society that wants its recognition and rewards immediately, they follow the outrageous self-promotional path laid out by the so-called rebels and bad boys of sports.

And the media and product marketers encourage it.

Even Nike's "Just Do It" campaign seems to have sent a mixed message to some. While most see it for what it is—a positive challenge that simply urges athletes to reach for their dreams—there are those who have chosen to interpret it to mean that all rules and consequences should be ignored and the job done at any cost. Critics have wondered why it is necessary to build a commercial story line around the fact that a tennis player or basketball star is too nice, too polite, and therefore in need of instruction on the fine points of being a more aggressive, in-your-face, to-hell-with-sportsmanship kind of competitor. They ask what demographic study determined that an angry glare sells more shoes than a smile. How did we reach a point where bad is considered good? What makes an outlandish act more newsworthy than the constant, reliable play of someone who has never been disciplined by the league? It seems to me that people are reading far too much into a slogan whose intent is to offer positive encouragement.

Why is it that the moment an athlete wants to speak out

about his religious convictions, sportswriters and broadcasters quickly switch to another subject? My only guess is that market research has shown that the good guy just doesn't sell.

I absolutely refuse to believe that.

Somewhere along the way the principles of determination and hard work have been replaced by the ongoing search for the shortcut to fame and fortune. Youngsters see Michael Jordan and dozens of other sports celebrities and have no idea of the years of practice that enabled them to reach the status and financial bracket they now enjoy. There's the indication that all you have to do is "Be Like Mike" and fame and fortune will instantly come running. The message offers no indication of how that is to be accomplished.

For many, young and old, money has become the panacea, the cure to all problems. The ultimate equalizer. If you have a pro athlete's money and can live in a house like his and drive a car like he does, the world will suddenly become a perfect place.

There is no warning that people of wealth and fame also deal with problems. You see no commercials featuring the guy who was suspended for repeated cocaine abuse, no celebrity treatment afforded the player arrested on a DWI charge.

The world of sports depicted in commercials and on the highlight films is more the product of fantasy than reality.

It is important that the public be made aware that athletes are really no different from any cross section of society. Pick any NFL roster and you will find the same mix that exists down at the local mall on any given Saturday afternoon. There are blacks and whites, mature and immature, varied personalities and intellects, people from different social and economic backgrounds with various degrees of self-importance and feelings toward their fellow man.

The problem works both sides of the street. There is an arrogance in the stands today that didn't exist when I first came into the league. The number of fans who display little or no respect for the players has grown dramatically. Their curses and taunts have grown louder and louder. The guy who

misses a block or drops a pass is not afforded the same for-
giveness routinely granted an accountant whose addition is
faulty or the secretary who might be having a bad day. What
does it say about society that major-league baseball teams
have discontinued the practice of giving away free balls to
ticket buyers for fear they will throw them at the players on
the field?

Because of the I-bought-a-ticket-so-by-God-you-perform
attitude, the mutual respect that once existed between player
and fan has been eroded. And there is a growing distrust on
the part of the athlete. Why not, when tennis players' lives
are being threatened by knife-wielding nut cases? When a
police officer admits hiring a hitman to kill a player he's upset
with? When a so-called fan extends a congratulating hand to
a quarterback who realizes only at the last second that the
man has a razor blade clutched between his fingers?

On a rainy Monday night in the Oakland Coliseum during
the '96 season, I remember looking up at the stadium scoreboard during a television timeout and seeing Raiders defensive tackle Chester McGlockton doing a public service
announcement about an innovative crime-prevention program
in which the Raiders were involved. In an attempt to help get
firearms off the streets, the team was offering free tickets to
anyone who turned over a gun to the local police.

Before the game ended, several of us would wonder if perhaps they should have included ammunition in the deal since
we were being peppered with bullets that were thrown from
the stands in the direction of the Chiefs' bench.

They are isolated incidents, of course, but just cause for an
athlete to consider keeping his distance.

Such are the by-products of today's society, not simply
sports.

When I visit schools, the majority of the youngsters I speak
with are respectful and receptive to what I have to say. At
the same time, I can always expect a handful of thirteen- and
fourteen-year-olds to take a challenging, almost hostile stance.
It is as if by getting the better of me in an argument, they are
somehow elevated among their peer group.

They are the sons of those who pour beer on the coach as

he leaves the field and yell vindictive curses when a block is missed or a pass dropped. The kids are only emulating their role models.

Which is to say it is a problem that must be dealt with by society as a whole, not just the few hundred people who play games on Sunday.

Still, I firmly believe it is an obligation of the professional athlete to do whatever he can to set the pace. The nature of our job has provided us a platform from which to do so.

And it can be done simply. Not everyone is good at standing in front of a group, speaking out against drugs or pointing out the importance of education. Not everyone has a cause or the inclination to step into the spotlight. We can all, however, do our best to conduct ourselves as good, decent people.

And when we fall short of perfection, the message is still worthwhile: We, too, are human.

My friend Charles Barkley has been one of those who has loudly disclaimed the idea that he should be viewed as a role model. Yet I know for a fact that Charles does a great deal of charity work, quietly reaching out to people in need of a hand. As the old saying goes, his actions speak far louder than his words. I think that the message Charles is really trying to get across when he publicly refuses the label of role model is that he labors with the same human imperfections as everyone else. Because the game of basketball comes easy to him, it should not be assumed that he has found all of life's answers.

Nor have I. But for a society to flourish, we must all be accountable and acknowledge respect and responsibility for our fellow man.

It is said that sports do not really *build* character, they only *reveal* it. And the vast majority of those I have played with and against stand as positive examples. Too often, however, their efforts and contributions are forced into the background by the thoughtless behavior of a few.

In all honesty, I am not completely comfortable with the fact that I am viewed as a role model. Certainly there are those better qualified to fill the position. I don't wish to give the impression that I have reached some rare level of self-awareness that allows me the right to pat my own back and urge others to do as I do. My imperfections are many.

The day will come when I have children of my own, and, like all kids, they, too, will grow to that stage in life where they feel the urge to look beyond the dinner table for examples of what they hope to be.

It is my sincere hope that their social and emotional tool kits will be well-stocked. And that they will be able to find role models who have recognized—and accepted—the importance that accompanies such admiration.

DAVE HOUGHTON, FORMER RAIDERS EXECUTIVE: *I've never been around a player who interacted better with kids than Marcus. I was the business manager for the Raiders during his years there and remember a time in the late Eighties when we were in Seattle to play the Seahawks.*

After the game, I was standing in the parking lot adjacent to the dressing room, watching our players walk through the ever-present crowd of fans to get onto the bus that would drive us to the airport.

As Marcus made his way through the crowd, this little kid, maybe seven or eight years old, locks himself around one of Marcus's legs and begins to cry. Marcus thought maybe he'd stepped on him. As he knelt down to check on the kid, the parents came up and quickly explained that their boy was only crying because he was so excited over the opportunity to finally meet his hero.

They said his name was Jason Mix, but that he insisted on telling everyone he was "Marcus." Even in school, he signed the name "Marcus" to his papers.

Marcus lifted the little boy up and carried him onto the team bus and sat, talking with him—about how he was doing in school, what sports he was interested in, things like that. And it was as if the youngster had died and gone to heaven. Finally, before we had to leave, Marcus gave the boy an autograph and got his home address so he could send him a photograph.

The whole scene played out in ten or fifteen minutes and

would have been enough to last the little guy a lifetime. But Marcus didn't stop there.

By the time we returned to play the Seahawks the following season, he and little ''Marcus'' had become pen pals. And Marcus had left tickets for the boy and his parents at the will-call window. And of course ''Marcus'' was again waiting for his hero near the bus after the game.

That whole thing just blew me away. And it told me a great deal about the kind of person Marcus Allen was. Watching him give of his time and himself to a stranger who clearly thought he was the greatest person in the world, I gained a better understanding of a comment that Dan Reeves, then the Denver Broncos coach, once made to the press. ''I'd love for my son to grow up to be like Marcus Allen,'' he'd said.

eleven

Uneasy Lies the Head That Wears the Crown

I wish someone would erase the word *dynasty* from the dictionary, at least as it applies to the NFL. It seems that every time a team puts together a series of good seasons and manages to win a Super Bowl, you can count on it being labeled a dynasty in the making. And, frankly, if it's your team they're talking about, it is hard not to buy into the idea. After all, it is what everyone's working for.

In truth it isn't likely to happen. Unfortunately, there is nowhere to go but down after winning it all. And that's the direction most go. The Redskins found that out when we replaced them as champions. It was a lesson previously learned by some of the most impressive teams in modern pro football history. The Steelers had an outstanding run, but eventually their star dimmed. Same with the Dallas Cowboys, who experienced a lengthy dry run between outstanding teams. And the Miami Dolphins and Chicago Bears and . . . you get the idea.

We had only added to the familiar trend when we stumbled out of the play-off picture in the first round just a year after winning it all.

Actually, there are few teams in the game today that are that much better than the others. No longer are there sure wins on anyone's schedule. There is a simple formula that I've long felt produces winning teams: You have to (1) win at home, (2) win at least three-fourths of your road games, and (3) make damn sure you win those rare games you're clearly supposed to win. But in today's climate, even that's not really enough. The team that now finishes on top not only has to be good and well-coached. It also has to remain reasonably free of injury and enjoy a little luck along the way.

While we won in 1985, it was neither easy nor the result of good fortune. We just went out every Sunday and found a way to get the job done.

Marc Wilson had taken over as quarterback, and as the new season got under way, there seemed a change in the atmosphere that surrounded the Raiders organization. I sensed an unspoken urgency to get a grip on something that all of a sudden seemed in danger of slipping away. Confidence still prevailed, but it was tempered by an unfamilar degree of concern.

Figuring that out was easy. Reading Al Davis wasn't. I continued to get mixed signals despite the fact that he and my agent had agreed on a four-year renewal of my contract during the off-season. If he didn't like me, why make me the first back in the league to receive a million-dollar annual salary?

I determined that the best thing for me to do was to quit worrying about the front office and tend to my job.

And as the season progressed I got ample opportunity. Without Plunkett's near mind-reading sense that had allowed him to seem always in sync with receivers, our passing game became erratic. And as it did, the game plans relied more and more on the run.

Which was fine with me. I've never felt the need to apologize for wanting the ball. Any running back will tell you that the more often he carries, the more apt he is to get into that groove that pays off in big yardage. History is filled with games in which a Jim Brown or Walter Payton or O.J. Simpson was held to little gain the first dozen or so times he carried, but then suddenly began to pick up yardage in large chunks. Repetition is the key to a running back's production. It allows him to become familiar with the track, get a feel for the flow of the game, and gain an awareness of the strengths and weaknesses of the defense he's facing.

For me, 1985 was a dream come true. Physically and mentally, I felt at the zenith of my game. And as it became increasingly obvious that I was going to be the focal point of our offense, I had no reservations.

Already it had begun as one of those seasons when I felt I could do no wrong. In the opener against the Jets, I even completed a pass to Todd Christensen—not one of those loopy bombs that just fell into his hands, but a tight spiral that hit him in the numbers as he ran a well-covered hook pattern. That was even more exciting than the two touchdowns I scored.

And while our offense was putting thirty-one points on the board, our defense was even better, shutting out New York. It was exactly the kind of beginning we needed. In the next two weeks, however, some of the optimism faded as we lost back-to-back to the Chiefs and 49ers.

It was at that point that we began to depend even more heavily on the running game and won five in a row. Feeling more confidence with each passing week, I barely missed the 100-yard mark against New England, getting 98, then had a 126-yard day against the Chiefs. Against the Saints, I gained 107 and scored twice.

We beat the Cleveland Browns in a real war, 21–20, to improve our record to 6–2 at the midway point of the season. I gained only 81 yards that day, but knew I had found that sweet groove—that zone—that was going to make the remainder of the season a lot of fun. Not since college days had I felt such a level of enthusiasm for what I was doing.

Beginning in Week 8 against the Chargers, I had a nine-game stretch in which I gained over 100 yards, setting a new NFL record. In a 16–13 overtime win against Denver, I had my best day of the season, gaining 173 yards in twenty-four carries.

By season's end I had carried the ball 380 times for 1,759 yards and became the first Raiders running back in the franchise's history to win the league rushing title. Additionally, I caught sixty-seven passes for an additional 555 yards, so my combined total of 2,314 was an NFL single season record. I was named the league's Player of the Year and voted to the Pro Bowl for the third time. Modesty aside, I was feeling pretty good about myself—and about the Raiders.

We were taking a 12–4 record and revitalized confidence into the first round of the play-offs against the New England Patriots. Not only was our offense on a productive roll, but our defense had led the league with sixty-five quarterback sacks. Things couldn't have been better.

One of the harsh truisms of sports is that things can change with eye-blink quickness. Euphoria and heartbreak are separated by the thinnest of lines; yesterday's hero becomes today's scapegoat. In the first week of the new year, everything came crashing down.

Marc Wilson had a terrible day against New England, completing only eleven of twenty-seven passes and was intercepted three times. I rushed for 121 yards, but our inability to mix in a real passing threat proved fatal. The Patriots beat us, 27–20.

Afterward, Al Davis made no attempt to hide his displeasure to the press. "We're never again going to be so dependent on one guy," he said. "This team has become too one-dimensional."

I can only guess that the "one guy" to whom he referred was me. And while I agreed that we needed to regain a balance to our offense, I could not help but feel I was somehow being singled out as the reason we'd again fallen short.

On that one afternoon all the joy of the season drained away. Yet even in my depression I had no hint of the dark days that lay ahead. There was no way to know that our loss to the Patriots would mark the Raiders' last appearance in the play-offs in the Eighties.

Nor did I know that I would soon take up permanent residence in Al Davis's doghouse.

ODIS McKINNEY: *To this day, I don't know what the deal was between Al Davis and Marcus. Everyone I know has speculated, but I think the only person who really knows is Al himself. The only thing I've ever been able to figure out was that because of Marcus's USC background—the Heisman and all that—and the great early years he had with the*

Raiders, Marcus got more attention from the people of Los Angeles than Al did. And Al Davis didn't like anyone to be out in front of him.

I remember when I first came to the Raiders as a player, he told me that there was no individual who was above the team. I think he felt Marcus had somehow violated that rule.

One time, after I'd become a coach and we were losing, Al asked me what I thought the problem was. I told him we didn't have enough leadership on the team. He wanted to know who I felt the leader was on offense. I told him it was Marcus Allen. How about defense? They all looked to Marcus. Special teams? Marcus, again. It obviously wasn't what he wanted to hear. But the fact was, Marcus was the only guy we had who could really pull the team together.

I think Al resented the fact that all the players looked up to Marcus.

Stealing advice from military history, I decided that if my boss was my enemy, it would be in my best interest to know as much about him as I could.

In the years that I'd been with the Raiders, the conversations we'd had were all similar. Davis would approach me in the dressing room or on the practice field and, careful to remain out of earshot of anyone else, would ask my opinion, usually of one of my teammates or coaches. I sensed he was looking for some form of criticism or negative reaction that I had no reason to provide. And he clearly didn't like certain observations I made in response to his questions. For instance, I remember telling him that I had become concerned that the attitude of the team seemed to be changing. We no longer had that nasty edge that had always been so important to our success. If he did not share whatever opinion I offered, it was made eminently clear, usually with a response preceded by his standard "Aw, fuck . . ."

What was even more interesting was watching as he eventually found his way to the person he'd just asked about to get his opinion of me. It was a game I found to be not only silly, but potentially divisive. And he played it constantly.

As he did others. He had this hypothetical test he loved to

administer. If, he would ask, you could have a choice of money, fame, or power, which would you choose?

Anyone who did not immediately pick power was lectured on its value over all other commodities.

Al Davis is obsessed with power. It is what defines him and he clearly loves using it, whether on a major battleground like a courtroom, taking on NFL rules and tradition, or in the course of his daily routine. Upon his arrival at the office a tension gripped all in his path. It was standard procedure for the first person to see him pull into the parking lot to quickly begin a telephone version of the jungle drum-warning system. The message was always the same: "Al's heading toward the building." A similar system was utilized in the adjacent building where the coaches had their offices.

It was not unusual for him to make a stop in the equipment room, take a fresh towel from one of the stacks, and then, without so much as a word, ceremoniously drop it at his feet. It was a signal for one of the ball boys to shine his shoes. When he worked late in his office, sometimes past midnight, reviewing tapes of games or workouts, he would not give a second thought to phoning some administrative assistant at home, waking him, and order him to deliver a burger.

Then and now it puzzled me that so many people would subject themselves to such daily abuse. Obviously for some it was as simple as the need to feed families and pay bills. For others, though, it was a price they seemed willing to pay just to be able to say they were a part, however small, of the grand tradition of Raiders football. It was those who earned Al Davis's infrequent smiles. In his mind they were the loyal ones; they were the people who recognized and acknowledged the power he so cherished.

I empathized with them all. I had bills to pay, responsibilities to meet. And even as I hated it at times, I also wanted to be a part of something successful.

I think what bothered me most was Davis's picking such inappropriate times to make his dislike for someone known. Particularly me. For instance, I remember attending the funeral of legendary Heisman winner and sports broadcaster Tom Harmon. I was seated in one of the back rows of the church with Sean Jones. Before the service got under way, Al turned from his seat up front to see who was in attendance. When he saw me, he mouthed those two favorite little words of his. Later, as he was called to deliver the eulogy, he mentioned a number of people in attendance, ending the roll call by saying, "And we have the great Marcus Allen here." For reasons I had no way of understanding, his words dripped with sarcasm.

Just as the team and coaches hoped for a season that would return the Raiders to glory, so did the secretaries, switchboard operators, mail-room employees, and errand boys. Only winning would ease the oppressive atmosphere in which they worked.

And we opened the '86 season with three straight losses.

In the third game, our home opener against the Giants, I had broken up the middle, cut to my left, and was clobbered by three New York defenders. I felt a stabbing pain just above the ankle and for a moment was certain that I'd broken my leg.

Getting to my feet, I signaled for Vance Mueller to replace me and began hopping one-legged toward the sidelines. My string of 100-yard days, which I'd stretched to eleven in our first two games, had come to an end.

I accompanied the team's doctors, Robert Rosenfeld and Rob Huizenga, to the dressing room, where the leg was X-rayed. To my relief nothing was broken. "See if you can walk on it," Dr. Rosenfeld urged.

I could, but the pain was unlike any I'd experienced in my entire career.

The game hadn't been over five minutes when Davis entered the dressing room and went directly to the training room for his customary injury report. That done, he headed in my direction.

"I'm sorry you were hurt," he said. "How ya feeling?"

"I think it's going to be okay."

He was always sending mixed messages. He was sorry, but it was clear he wanted me back in action immediately.

I assured him I'd be ready to play against San Diego the

following Sunday. But no amount of treatment or rehabilitation seemed to work. The swelling was gone and additional X rays had failed to detect even so much as a hairline fracture, but putting any weight at all on the leg brought a quick return of the pain. There was no way I would be able to make any quick cuts since I seemed to have no power there.

And so Mueller started while I watched from the sidelines for the next two weeks. And he played well as we narrowly beat the Chargers, then San Diego.

In four years of pro ball, I had dealt with elbow surgery, a numbness in my right arm, sprains, strains, cuts, and bruises, but had never missed a game. Suddenly, an ailment even the doctors could not diagnose had me hobbling around like an old man.

As preparation began for our game against Seattle, I made up my mind to play through the pain. Ineffective, I carried the ball only six times for 11 yards before Vance came in to finish out the game.

A week later against Miami, the leg felt much better as I gained 96 yards and we won our fourth game in a row. The good news was that we were fast taking on the look of a play-off contender again. The downside was that late in the Dolphins game the pain had returned, worse than before.

I missed the Houston game and our winning streak came to an end.

Though limping, I returned to the lineup the following week. I didn't threaten any land-speed records. In fact, I found myself wondering if I should even be on the field. I had difficulty making sharp cuts and couldn't hold onto the ball for the life of me. As badly as I wanted to play, there was part of me that questioned just how much good I was doing the team.

It was before a crucial Monday night game against San Diego that Steve Ortmayer, one of our assistant coaches, approached me. "Mr. Davis says you're still favoring the ankle," he said. "He wants you to take a shot."

For weeks the doctors and trainers alike had been suggesting they could give me an injection that would mask the pain at least for the duration of a game, but I'd ignored them. It was a time in league history when injured players routinely did it. There was some measure of courage assigned to taking a shot to play. When we'd won the Super Bowl, I'll bet there were a dozen guys on the team who were injected before the kickoff.

It was one of the realities of big-time athletics. Certainly I'd taken them before. If the only way I could get through a game was with the help of a heavy dose of medication, I would agree to a shot of novocaine or Xylocaine, but only after being assured that it would do no further damage to my injury. Still, I avoided injections whenever possible. While they mask the pain as you're playing, it is sure to return—more severe than before—just as soon as the drug wears off. You play, then you pay.

I took the shot. And, thanks to medical science, had my best game of the season. It was one of those seesaw battles that found us trailing by three late in the game. Finally, Chris Bahr kicked a field goal that brought us into a 31–31 tie as regulation time ended.

In overtime I was able to make one of those zigzag runs that finally got me into the corner of the end zone with a couple of Chargers defenders dragging along behind—and was almost instantly aware of my mom and dad celebrating wildly in the stands. A few hours later, after the effect of the shot had worn off, the pain was worse than ever.

The disastrous start to the season now old history, we were 8–4 and looking ahead to hosting a Philadelphia Eagles team that was struggling badly at 3–9. We were getting so close to a play-off berth we could taste it.

And I put the torch to the whole thing.

It was one of those days of big plays that resulted in a 27-all tie at the end of the fourth quarter. For the second straight week, we found ourselves working overtime.

In short order, however, we were in a position to win the game. Howie Long had fallen on a Randall Cunningham fumble, then I caught a well-thrown pass over the middle for a 27-yard gain that got us down to the Eagles' 20. By the time we had driven to the 12-yard line, Flores sent in word for us to just run the ball into position so that Bahr would have a point-blank field goal to end it.

Taking a handoff just inside the hash mark, I was headed toward the middle of the field when an Eagles lineman got his arms around my waist. Jerking in an attempt to free myself, I felt the ball slip from my grasp. Defender Seth Joyner somehow managed to bat the ball in the direction of his teammate, Andre Waters, who ran all the way to our four-yard line before he was dragged down from behind by Dokie Williams.

Cunningham scored two plays later.

The loss devastated me. Never before had I felt so singularly responsible for a defeat. Despite the efforts of several teammates who tried to assure me that there was blame enough for everyone, I sat in front of my locker replaying the horrifying moment of the fumble over and over in my head.

Finally, I looked up to see Al Davis standing over me, his face burning crimson, lips pursed. He just stared angrily at me for what seemed like an eternity before finally spitting out what was on his mind. "Aw, fuck," he said. "I shoulda traded ya." And with that he turned and stormed away, never to speak kindly of me again.

In a post-game report, network sports announcer Jim Gray made an observation that I might well have played my final game in the Coliseum as a member of the Los Angeles Raiders.

To this day, there are those who point to that loss to Philadelphia as the last hurrah of the once-proud Raiders tradition. In a position to win our division before that day, we became a struggling, lifeless team thereafter. We finished with four straight losses as the mood grew increasingly dark and hopes of a play-off berth vanished.

In the Raiders' front office, I had taken on the new role of a pariah. And for the first time, I began to seriously think of moving my career elsewhere.

Though I had gained 759 yards despite missing three games, I judged my year a disaster and was surprised when

My role models sat across the dinner table from me every evening as I grew up—my mom and dad. (*Photo courtesy of Gwen Allen*)

Even when I was very young, I was fascinated by the world that television brought into our home. One of my earliest memories is of watching the funeral of President John F. Kennedy when I was just three years old. (*Photo courtesy of Gwen Allen*)

It was flattering to receive scholarship offers from other schools, but the idea of wearing the cardinal-and-gold uniform of the University of Southern California Trojans was always foremost in my mind. (*Photo by Doug Gray, courtesy of USC Sports Information*)

With the kind of blocking I had in my senior year at USC, I knew a 2,000-yard season was a realistic goal. (*Photo by Bob Hagedohm, courtesy of USC Sports Information*)

Winning the Heisman Trophy at the end of my senior season at
USC was a dream come true.
(*Photo courtesy of USC Sports Information*)

Lyle Alzado's emotions ran from one end of the scale to the other. Despite his unpredictability, I liked him. He was more than a teammate; he was a friend. *(Photo by Jerry Wochter,* Sports Illustrated)

Though the Denver Broncos held me to just 45 yards in this game in the 1983 season, I stongly felt we had every tool necessary to make it to the Super Bowl. And we did. (*Photo by Peter Read Miller,* Sports Illustrated)

The puzzled look on my face is there for good reason. Throughout my career with the Raiders I never completely understood what made Al Davis tick.
(*Photo by Craig Malenhause,* Sports Illustrated)

It might not have been Wimbledon, but we had some pretty interesting off-season tennis matches when I was with the Raiders. Here, Ahmad Rashad (center) and I offer our critique of O.J.'s game. (*Photo by Peter Read Miller,* Sports Illustrated)

For years I congratulated the Los Angeles Rams' Eric Dickerson (left) on outstanding games he had against us. Then one day he joined the parade of running backs Al Davis brought in to try and take my place in the Raiders backfield. (*Photo by Paul Spinelli, NFL Properties*)

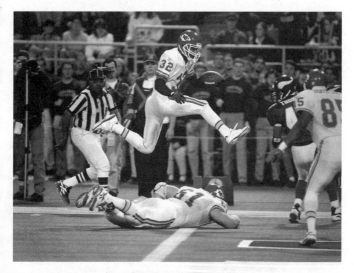

With my career resurrected by the Kansas City Chiefs, I proved I could still find my way into the end zone. Here I had to hurdle over my buddy Tim Grunhard after he cleared the way against the Minnesota Vikings. (*Photo by David Liam Kyle,* Sports Illustrated)

That quarterback Joe Montana (left) joined the Chiefs the same time I did was a real bonus. It was a lot more fun playing with him than against him. (*Photo by Al Messerschmidt,* NFL Photos)

The form isn't likely to make Tiger Woods envious, but I can assure you my golf game is going to improve dramatically once my football-playing days are over. *(Photo by Colin Braley, EGI)*

I was notified that I'd been named to the Pro Bowl as a replacement for the injured Sammy Winder.

Upon my arrival, I was not the least disappointed when the Pro Bowl medical staff ruled against my playing after examining my ankle.

twelve

Strike Two

One of the most interesting side issues of this country's passionate affection for sports is that it has never fully come to grips with the idea that once an athlete reaches the professional level, he becomes a card-carrying member of big business. The fan, weaned on evening visits to the Little League parks, Friday-night high school football, and nostalgic memories of the pageantry of collegiate athletics, finds it difficult getting past the idea that there comes a time when the fundamental reason one plays a game is to earn a paycheck.

Sure, we've all professed our love for the game, even going so far as to suggest we'd do it for free if we had to. Yeah, right.

The hard truth is that NFL players, just like the guys in the NBA and major-league baseball, hockey players, and professional boxers, want to be fairly compensated for their bruises and broken bones. We want our cut of the multimillions the owners and promoters are earning.

And, most important, we want a fair shake.

As the 1987 season neared, the collective bargaining agreement between the owners and the National Football League Players Association (NFLPA) was coming to an end and yet another strike was being called. Once again the rallying cry would be a demand for unrestricted free agency that would allow players to test their value on the open market. Simply put, we wanted the same right everyone else in the American workplace enjoyed. In the real world, if the corporation across town wants you badly enough to offer you an increase in salary and perks to make the move to his firm, you rush home, tell the wife the good news, and give the boss two weeks' notice.

Under the unique rules of professional sports, however, you are held in bondage. So unrealistic is the price Team A would have to pay Team B for the right to hire a player away that it makes the whole idea of free agency a sham.

As teams gathered in pre-season camps that summer, a strike vote was taken. The Players Association assured us that this time things would be different. Demands were outlined and a plan set. We would play the first two games of the season, then walk out, leaving management backed into a tight corner. Rather than lose millions of dollars from lucrative television contracts and ticket sales, the owners would finally be forced to bargain fairly.

Gene Upshaw, the former Raiders All-Pro who had become executive director of the NFLPA, sent out the word that solidarity would serve as our greatest weapon. There would be no repeat of the failed efforts of my rookie season when the eight-game walkout had accomplished nothing.

After winning our first two games, the Raiders joined NFL players across the country in a strike that was supposedly driven by great resolve.

We walked out on feet of clay.

In anticipation of the strike, the owners had made plans of their own. The last thing they wanted was another cancellation of games and empty stadiums. Too many ticket buyers and television viewers had discovered in 1982 that there were other things to do on a fall Sunday afternoon besides watch football.

Thus, after only one gameless Sunday, NFL football—or at least a minor league version of it—was back. Franchises fielded "replacement teams" made up of free agents rejected from earlier training camps, ex-collegians who scouts had at one time judged too lacking in talent for serious consideration, and an occasional former NFL player who welcomed the opportunity to come out of retirement and earn a quick $6,000 per game.

Vince Evans, the Raiders' "replacement" quarterback, had been selling cars for three years when he was called to sign a contract.

It quickly got ugly.

Curses flew from the picket lines as the "scab" players daily reported for meetings and practice. Fans predictably lashed out at what they perceived to be a money-driven work stoppage. All the while, owners and general managers locked arms, vowing to break the strike at all cost. Tex Schramm, president and general manager of the Cowboys and a member of the NFL's powerful management council, made no friends among players in the league when he referred to them as "cattle" during one of his attempts to explain how the importance of the game far outweighed that of the individuals who played it.

Occasionally, we would have team meetings where players would address the pros and cons of our actions, but they seemed to get us nowhere. Meanwhile, the league's propaganda machine was working full tilt. Players were regularly receiving pro-NFL literature that painted a dramatically different picture than that offered us by the union.

Meanwhile, coaches were up in arms over a league decision that the replacement games would not simply be frivolous exhibitions, but instead count in the standings. In theory, a scab team could win its way into the Super Bowl. In the event the real players did decide to return to complete the season, we would do so with the help or hindrance of the won-lost record of a bunch of guys we didn't even know.

Solidarity didn't last long.

As the season reopened, our scab team beat Kansas City's scab team. There weren't enough fans in the Coliseum to create a decent wave.

I had mixed emotions about the players who were taking our place. Part of me resented them greatly; part of me was sympathetic to what they were doing. I disliked the fact that they were helping the owners in their efforts to break the strike. At the same time, it was difficult not to place myself in their shoes and realize that, through no fault of their own, they had been given an opportunity to live out the dream of a lifetime. Years later they would be able to tell their kids and grandkids of the time they had played pro ball with the Raiders. They could put their own spin on their recollections, carefully avoiding mention of the brevity of their stay, or the fact that they had been called "scabs" more often than "Raiders."

If there were to be any winners in the whole misguided mess, they were the ones.

Veteran players, having already lost one game check, soon began crossing picket lines and returning to work. Before our replacement team was to travel to Denver, Howie Long and Bill Pickel gave up the cause and returned to the team. Howie, disgusted with what he considered futile and untrustworthy efforts by Upshaw and the NFLPA, said his first loyalty was to his wife and kids.

Throughout the league, players were waving white flags and crossing picket lines in increasing numbers. For all practical purposes, it was over.

With Howie and Bill back in the fold, Al Davis turned up the pressure. Calling on the tradition of camaraderie that had so long been a Raiders trademark, he urged players to return before the season was destroyed.

When Davis and I finally had a discussion, I listened as he talked of the sympathy he felt for our cause. Still, he believed, by remaining on the wrong side of the picket line, his players were betraying him. Hell, he'd been fighting unfair rules handed down by the NFL all his life, he explained. But there was no way we were going to win this fight. Everybody— players, owners, fans—was going to lose.

Among the strongest arguments he made was the fact that I was losing $80,000 every time some guy named Joe lined up in my position on Sunday.

"Do the smart thing," he said, "and come on in."

I told him I would, but soon had second thoughts. I knew that if I didn't cross the line, he would forever view it as a blatant act of betrayal. I'd been told that he was so sure of convincing me to give up the battle that I had already been written into the game plan for the following Sunday. I knew that Davis saw me as something of a bell cow, a leader others were likely to follow. Yet even as I resented his subtle threat and his efforts to have me influence the decisions of others, I knew he was right about at least one thing: We weren't going to win.

Still, I strongly believed that free agency had to occur if ever players were to expect fair treatment. I wanted to see better medical benefits for everyone, and the establishment of programs that would help players as they left the game and established themselves in other walks of life. I wanted us to unite and demand the abolition of the synthetic turf that had been responsible for so many unnecessary injuries in recent years. I wanted the players of today to do something for the players of the next generation.

And I knew we would get nothing. It was going to be 1982 all over again.

Ask any player in the league today and he will tell you that the system remains a smoke-and-mirrors illusion. The salary cap that all teams are now forced to work under has only added to the problem.

There is example after example of veteran players signing new long-term contracts with escalating salaries they'll never receive. By the time the money is supposed to dramatically increase, owners hit them with the news that if they hope to continue playing, they will have to renegotiate their salary—down—so the team can remain under the salary cap. The alternative is to be cut from the roster.

So the player, often driven by ego to agree to the escalating salary contract that promises him millions, will never see the big numbers he was promised. More likely, he is going to be told that the $1 or $2 million he's making will have to be dramatically reduced if he wishes to continue playing.

By the time I phoned Davis to tell him I had decided not to cross the picket line, twenty-six of my teammates had already done so. When they played San Diego, the Raiders had more veteran players on their roster than any in the NFL. And the $6,000-a-game Chargers kicked their ass.

Begun with such resolve and high ideals, the strike ended with a whimper.

The replacement players returned to the lives from which

they'd come, except for Vince Evans and a safety named Eddie Anderson, who had impressed the coaches enough to be asked to remain with the team.

Sean Jones, the Raiders' player representative to the NFLPA who had fought gallantly to keep the striking players united, began counting his days. Accused by Davis of "ruining his team," Sean would soon be traded.

As the team returned to work, one more "replacement" player arrived. Recruited from major league baseball, he was coming to replace me.

For years Al Davis and Dallas's Tex Schramm had engaged in a not-always-friendly competition for recognition as the most innovative, forward-thinking CEO in football. Different in so many ways—Schramm had immersed himself deeply into the inner circle of NFL leadership while Al stood apart as the ultimate rebel—they shared a common sense of their own place in history, both racing to see who would gain induction into the NFL Hall of Fame first.

While Al could pridefully point to his countless successes at turning discarded veterans into Raiders stars, Schramm countered with the fact that his team had set the pace in drafting obscure players from little-known schools and watching them become great players. Both had Super Bowl trophies to back their boasts.

Davis and Schramm cursed each other, admired one another, and each claimed credit for having built the most successful franchise in professional sports.

Al had gone one-up on Schramm during the 1986 draft when, in the seventh round, he'd selected former Auburn Heisman Trophy winner Bo Jackson. At the time, it seemed about as frivolous a pick as the one Schramm had made two years earlier, when he drafted Olympic sprint champion Carl Lewis—who had never played a down of football in his life—in the last round.

The only difference was that Bo Jackson was clearly an outstanding football player. The problem was that he'd decided to pursue a career in professional baseball after college. Even before Tampa Bay had picked him in the first round in

'85, Bo had warned them that he had no interest in continuing his football career. A year later, when Tampa Bay's rights to Jackson ended, the Raiders selected him. By then Bo was firmly established in the starting lineup of the Kansas City Royals, and there was no indication that he had changed his mind.

Which is to say Al Davis knew something no one else did. He had devised a plan that he was sure would not only turn the rest of the league green with envy, but would make headlines coast to coast.

Bo had agreed to Davis's suggestion that he become a two-sport professional. The arrangement that had been worked out was that Bo would complete the baseball season with the Royals, take a ten-day vacation, then join the Raiders for the last half of the season. As we gathered to try and rebuild the momentum of the two pre-strike wins, we were joined by Bo Jackson.

And, yes, I felt resentment, though I kept it to myself. At best, I would be sharing my job with him. More than likely the grand plan was for him to ultimately have it to himself if only Davis could figure some way to lure him into football full-time.

While I recognized that Bo had an incredible amount of athletic ability, I was in no way ready to concede that he was the better football player. And as a highly competitive person himself, he understood that.

In fact, Bo and I got along well from the beginning. My resentment was not focused toward him. Like many of my teammates, I had been taken aback when I learned the terms of his contract: a five-year, $7.5 million deal—to play what amounted to half a season annually. "Bo's hobby," the newspapers were calling it. Truthfully, I regarded Bo's presence as just another way Davis had discovered to slap me in the face. That aside, I was sure that the special accommodations being made for Jackson—the huge salary for playing only half a season—were destructive to the chemistry of the team. But, again, any jealousy or anger toward Jackson was misdirected. He hadn't come to Al Davis; Davis had gone to him.

If you're going to be pissed off, I told more than one teammate, be pissed at the guy standing over there on the sidelines, wearing the white jogging suit and dark shades.

There would be no storybook ending written to the strike-marred 1987 season. We would finish the year with only five wins—and one of those had to be credited to the replacement team.

Initially, I continued to start at running back, splitting time with Bo. And neither of us felt comfortable with the arrangement. After three straight losses, I went to Coach Flores with a suggestion that seemed to surprise him.

"Maybe if we're both on the field," I said, "we can get something going. Put Bo at running back and I'll play fullback."

The following Sunday, Jackson very nearly got his first 100-yard game, carrying thirteen times for 98. I had 42 yards in eleven carries. A running game that netted 140 yards was an improvement—but not enough to end our losing streak.

That would finally come a week later when we visited Seattle for a Monday-night game. On one evening, our offense provided most of the footage for the team's annual highlights film.

Bo brought the Silverdome crowd to its feet with a 91-yard touchdown run—the longest in Raiders history—and ended the night with a club record 221 yards rushing on eighteen carries. Paltry by comparison was the 76 yards I gained from the fullback position as we beat the Seahawks, 37–14.

The following week we defeated Buffalo, but things went downhill from there as we finished with three straight losses. Jackson suffered a badly sprained ankle against Kansas City and sat out the final two games of the year.

If you're keeping score, the comparison looked like this at season's end: Jackson, in seven games, gained 554 yards rushing and caught sixteen passes for 136 yards. In the twelve games I played, I gained 754 rushing and led the team in receptions with fifty-one for 410 yards.

Never before had I gone through a season in such a poor frame of mind. Jackson's joining the team had very little to do with it. Davis's remark the previous year after the fumble against Philadelphia had continued to haunt me. The more I thought about it, the more I wanted out. And the ineffectiveness of the strike had disappointed me greatly.

Most disconcerting of all was the realization that we were a team on the decline. Recent drafts had failed to fill holes left by retirements, and trades had offered little improvement. I found myself wondering if we could turn things around any time soon.

Obviously, I wasn't the only one concerned. Before planning could get under way for the next season, Tom Flores announced that he was retiring as head coach of the Raiders.

thirteen

"Red Alert"

No one was more disappointed to see Tom Flores leave than me. Not only did I consider him an outstanding coach, but I had grown very fond of him personally during our years together. Though he'd never mentioned it, I knew he had played a big part in my being drafted by the Raiders. If for no other reason, I had wanted to do all I could to justify his belief in me. And once joining the team, I learned that he had worked hard to convince Davis that our offense would function best with me running out of an "I" formation instead of the full-house backfield the Raiders had traditionally used.

Though generally quiet and soft-spoken, he had a firmness about him that I admired greatly. He was a gentleman's gentleman. While he made it clear that he cared for his players, he also demanded their best effort in practices and on game day, and was quick to give his "shape up or ship out" speech to anyone he felt wasn't carrying his part of the load. He was not one to make idle threats or screaming speeches.

Perhaps most important, he had come up through the ranks, advancing from Raiders player to assistant to head coach. Tom was familiar firsthand with the unique Raiders' operation and knew how to deal with Davis constantly looming over his shoulder.

While he had obviously been frustrated with the turn the team had taken since winning two Super Bowls, his resignation still came as a shock. There was a great deal of speculation among the players that it had not been an altogether voluntary decision. Publicly, Tom said that he just wanted to spend more time with his family, that the long hours and endless work schedule had taken their toll on his energies and enthusiasm.

The general feeling of the players was that Al Davis, despite his "Once a Raider, always a Raider" preachings, despite having at one time hailed Flores as "one of the greatest coaches in NFL history," had decided his usefulness to the organization was at an end and was ready for him to step aside.

The most popular rumor that circulated among the Raiders' employees was that Flores had received a very attractive cash settlement to put a positive spin on his decision to "retire."

Frustrated by the downward spiral of the team, Al deemed it time to seek new leadership.

More surprising than Flores's departure was the announcement that he would be replaced by Denver offensive coordinator Mike Shanahan. For the first time in the franchise's history, Davis had gone outside the Raiders family to select a head coach.

His reasons were promptly questioned by the Los Angeles media. Some went so far as to suggest that Davis had finally awakened to the fact that the philosophies he'd jealously held to for almost three decades had become outdated. A team could no longer expect to win with an offense that relied on the deep pass; that the bump-and-run defense he'd helped design and perfect had been abandoned by others in favor of an increasingly complicated mixture of zone coverages.

Perhaps by bringing in an "outsider," Davis might be able to catch up with modern football techniques.

Clearly, Shanahan had put an impressive offense together for the Broncos. Directed by John Elway, it mixed the idea of ball control with a fast-paced passing game. The philosophy was basic but exciting: You can pick up first downs with short, quick passes just as easily as you can by sending a back into the middle of a bunch of three-hundred-pound linemen. At the same time, the running game would be able to take advantage of the defense's constant concern that you were going to throw the ball on any down. To me, it sounded like the best of both worlds.

The idea of a more equal distribution of the ball fascinated me. While I was convinced we would never desert our running game, the idea of getting into more pass patterns, catching the ball in the open field, was exciting.

Those looking for more devious intent behind Davis's decision to hire Shanahan pointed to the fact that the Broncos had, in their previous two Super Bowl seasons, kicked our butts the last four times we'd played. By stealing away a key member of their staff, Al could kill two birds with one stone. He could build new fire under his Raiders—and hopefully do damage to the chances of a division rival's continued success.

It was the kind of master gamesmanship Al Davis lived for.

Adding to the new look was Steve Beuerlein, a former Notre Dame All-American, who would take over the starting quarterback role.

Despite all the excitement and high expectations, we spent most of the season running everywhere and getting nowhere.

The departure from Raiders tradition seemed doomed from the get-go. Almost immediately, there was a line drawn in the sand between former Flores assistants and those Shanahan had brought with him from Denver. Before all was said and done, Shanahan tried to fire Joe Spinella and Tom Walsh, two of the holdovers from Flores's tenure, but Davis stepped in at the last minute and and blocked the move. Later Al fired Nick Nicoli, one of the assistants whom Shanahan had hired.

Todd Christensen, never the most laid-back guy anyway, was far from happy after a meeting during which Nicoli had him watch film of Clarence Kay, the Denver tight end, running routes. An All-Pro, Todd had considered the suggestion an insult.

It wasn't difficult to see that the marriage was not going well.

Among many things that contributed to the new disharmony among the players was a lengthy list of disciplinary rules that the new coach put into effect. The thing that brought the greatest ire from the veteran players was the rule that stated that players must wear their helmets at all times while on the field. No longer would we be allowed to sit on our helmets while on the sidelines. Several reacted as if they'd been fined a game check. Didn't this new guy understand that there were certain rituals and customs that had long been part of the personality and persona of the Raiders?

The answer was no. To understand the mentality of the Raiders, you had to have been a part of the organization, the family; you had to be familiar with all its quirks and habits and understand that they are all—good, bad, and trivial—judged important.

I wondered if Shanahan understood how little real authority his new title provided him. Did he really think Davis would allow him to come in and revamp the Raiders' image and style of play without front-office interference?

If anything, Al would be watching even more closely, making sure the ''outsider'' did things his way. That was also a big part of the Raiders tradition.

While other front-office executives in professional sports busy themselves with the business side of their operations, Al Davis had long ago determined that his confusing title of president of the general partners included the right to help coach the team.

Appearing at practices in his all-white jogging outfit, dark glasses, and Super Bowl jewelry, he looked like a character from a Mario Puzo novel, standing with arms folded as if ready to make any and all an offer they couldn't refuse. It was not unusual for him to bring a workout to a halt while he dressed-down a receiver for not making the proper cut on a pass route or critiqued a lineman's blocking technique.

He was never hesitant to order a player onto the practice field to replace one he felt was not performing at a proper level. And it always amazed me. I tried to think how John Robinson might have reacted if the USC athletic director had suddenly appeared at one of his practices and taken over.

Davis would routinely sit in on the coaches' weekly meetings, lording over them. No game plan or depth chart was finalized without his approval.

Even during pre-season, Al had the final say on the amount of playing time dealt out to rookies and free agents attempting to make the team.

A self-proclaimed ''genius'' during his own coaching days, Al Davis continued to jealously guard the title.

Game days were an exercise in insanity. Though high atop the stadium, seated in the owners' suite or a corner of the press box, Al ran the show, maintaining contact with the sidelines. No criticism, however small, was allowed to wait until game's end. And if he decided a particular realignment of the defense was in order or a certain play should be called, the message went quickly to the sidelines.

In most stadiums around the league, he had easy access to the box where Raiders assistants were located, communicating with the sideline coaches through headphones. Knowing that Al or one of his messengers would be regularly popping in with caustic notes or plays hastily diagrammed on napkins, they had devised a signal to prepare those on the sidelines. The second Al or one of his aides appeared in the doorway, one of the assistants would lean forward and whisper into his headphone: ''Red alert.''

Aware that the television cameras would often be pointed in his direction during critical moments of games, no doubt hoping for visual proof of the oft-told stories of his visits to the coaching booth, Al had a secondary plan of communication.

To this day, Mike Ornstein, then the Raiders' public relations man, insists he initiated the now common fashion of wearing running shoes with a suit and tie. He did so because of the repeated trips from press box to sidelines, delivering Davis's messages.

Previous Raiders coaches like John Madden and Flores, who had grown up in such a controlling environment, had learned to deal with it. They could anticipate Davis's whims and outrages, and often made calls and decisions before the orders were issued.

But for Shanahan it would be a strange new world.

• • •

Actually, the only thing about Davis's new system that fell into place was that we did beat the Broncos twice. Otherwise, little went as planned.

Beuerlein immediately fell from favor and after the second game of the season Davis hurriedly traded for Washington's backup quarterback, Jay Schroeder, in an attempt to get a quarterback who Shanahan could hopefully mold into the Raiders' version of John Elway.

And Jay had the perfect history to be a Johnny-come-lately Raider. He'd been an All-Pro in 1986, but had never been able to accept the criticism that he threw the long bomb far too often to suit the Redskins' offensive scheme. He had ultimately been benched, replaced by Doug Williams. Sitting on the sidelines with very little hope of ever regaining the stature he'd briefly enjoyed in the nation's capital, Jay soon earned the label of malcontent when he began a public campaign to be traded.

It must have seemed Los Angeles was the perfect place for him to attempt the resurrection of his career. For at least one Monday night, it looked as if he was going to do just that. We were 1–2 and the underdog when we traveled to Mile High Stadium for Shanahan's first encounter with his old team.

For the first thirty minutes we were terrible. Elway was slicing up our secondary, the Denver defense was intercepting Jay and generally making his life miserable, and our running game looked as if it had been left behind in Los Angeles.

By halftime we were trailing, 24–0. In the locker room we heard such adjectives as "pitiful," "horrible," and a wide assortment of expletives that all underlined the fact that we were stinking up the place.

It was our defense that first came to life. Early in the third quarter, safety Eddie Anderson stepped in front of one of the few passes Elway had underthrown all evening and made the interception at the Denver 40. On first down, Schroeder faked to me up the middle, then flipped a quick screen pass to fullback Steve Smith. Even as I was trying to work myself from beneath the pileup I'd run into at the line of scrimmage, Steve was racing down the right sidelines for our first touchdown of the night.

Suddenly, there was a spark. Our defense again held, forcing a Bronco punt that gave us the ball on our own nine. I got nine up the middle, then Schroeder hit Willie Gault for gains of 11 and 15. At last we were moving the ball and you could almost hear the adrenaline flowing in the huddle.

At Denver's 42, Jay called the same quick pass to Smith that had resulted in our first score. And again, he was all alone, racing down the sidelines as the stadium suddenly grew quiet. Wide receiver Mervyn Fernandez threw a final clearing block, and Steve went into the end zone for his second touchdown. Down by only 10, we were back in the game.

And as the fourth quarter opened, we narrowed the margin to seven when Chris Bahr connected on a 28-yard field goal.

Then we got the break that had eluded us all night. On the kickoff following Bahr's field goal, special teams player Reggie McKenzie raced downfield and collided with Denver return man Ken Bell. The ball popped free and Steve Strachan fell on it at the Broncos' 17-yard line.

Four plays later, I got in from the four-yard line and Bahr's conversion pulled us into a tie.

If you're even a casual student of NFL football, however, you know of the legendary last-minute heroics that John Elway has routinely performed throughout his career. This night was to be no exception. It suddenly looked like the first quarter all over again as he launched a lengthy drive that didn't stall until Denver had reached our eight-yard line. With 3:01 remaining in the game, a field goal put the Broncos back into the lead.

But Schroeder retaliated with some magic of his own. Starting from our 20, he connected with Smith for 16, then threw to me for 11. On a fourth-and-four at the Denver 43, he got the ball to me in the flat and we picked up the first down with a yard to spare.

Finally, with the clock showing only eight seconds left in regulation play, Bahr came on to again tie the game with a 44-yard field goal—his longest of the still-young season.

In overtime, it looked as if we'd won it early when rookie

Tim Brown displayed his remarkable speed, breaking for an apparent 74-yard touchdown on a punt return, but the run was wiped out by a penalty. Twice our defense held Denver in its own end of the field before our safety Zeph Lee intercepted Elway and ran the ball down to the Broncos' 31-yard line. Smith and I alternated on short runs to move the ball to the 17, from which Bahr kicked the field goal that finally ended it.

Technically, it would not be remembered as one of the great games in Raiders history. But for pure drama, it had to be right up there. And it was, at least, a long-overdue positive moment in a troubled season. The post-game celebration that erupted as soon as we made our way into the locker room signaled a renewed belief that we just might be on the road to putting things in order.

Still, Davis very nearly ruined the moment. He burst into the locker room and stood glaring. Had Mike Ornstein not distracted him, what most certainly would have occurred next would have been a standard Al Davis tantrum. As he'd done so many times before, he would have berated coaches—he seemed to delight in accusing them of being "just a bunch of high school coaches"—and every player within the reach of his voice. Among his favorite admonitions was that we did a "fuckin' horseshit job . . . just fuckin' horseshit," but Ornstein had whispered a plea before he could begin. "Al," he said, "don't spoil this. Let 'em enjoy it for a little while. We won the damn game—on national television—and it just might be what we need to get something started."

Al's only response was a frown, yet he did nothing more than pace among the players, keeping his feelings about our performance to himself. It was obvious that he had derived little pleasure from our victory.

I was convinced there was absolutely nothing that would satisfy the man and found myself wondering what demons must haunt a person so displeased with the world around him.

Unfortunately, he would have ample opportunity to vent his anger as we lost three of our next four games.

• • •

The Raiders' attempt to join pro football's modern age never materialized. By the time Bo had ended his season with the Royals and reported to football, few held any real hope that the idea of a hurry-up, short-pass offense would become a reality.

We were once again a running team that occasionally threw short to the tight end or tried to get the ball deep to one of our Olympic-speed wide receivers.

What had apparently been overlooked in this sudden urge to transform the Raiders offense was the fact that the personnel that had been assembled over the years were simply not suited for that kind of game. Everything, from drafts to free-agent signing, had been done with the old brand of Raiders football in mind.

And so Shanahan had retreated to something he thought might work. And occasionally it did.

Just weeks after Jackson had left the Kansas City baseball team, he was back there to play against the Chiefs. With fresh legs, he got the bulk of the carries, gaining 70 yards. I had only eleven carries for 20 yards but did score a touchdown as we won the game, 27–20.

A week later Bo suffered a hamstring injury early in the game and I had my only 100-yard day of the season, with 102 yards on twenty carries. Afterward, some suggested that my performance had been inspired at least in part by Bo's return to the roster. If so, it was unconscious. I'd long since passed the point in my career where I felt the need to prove my abilities.

Though we would manage a three-game winning streak late in the season, beating Kansas City, San Diego, and the 49ers, the year had disaster written all over it. With two games remaining we were playing .500 ball but were beaten by Buffalo and Seattle to wind up 7–9.

And the statistics spoke loudly of the failure of our grand experiment. For the seventh season, I led the team in rushing with 831 yards. Jackson had added 580 to the total. On the other hand, in a year when we'd anticipated catching a great number of passes, I had thirty-four and Bo only nine.

Not only did we have a very unhappy owner, but it was

clear—at least to me—that our new coach had decided he had made a very bad career move.

While the turmoil would not end with the completion of the season, 1988 did have its bright side.

Since college days I had been so fixated on football that I viewed time away from the game as little more than a brief and necessary respite. I knew full well that the all-work-and-no-play philosophy was valid, so it was nice to attend an occasional party or take someone to dinner. On the other hand, I wasn't looking for anything like a serious relationship. The right woman was out there somewhere, but I'd not felt any urgency to find her.

Suddenly that changed.

Early in the fall I had met a beautiful woman who fascinated me more than any person I'd ever met. Her name was Kathryn Eickstaedt and she had come to Los Angeles from Wisconsin to pursue a career in modeling and advertising. She had a wonderful sense of humor and a smile that lit up the room, yet seemed to have no idea how really stunning she was.

And she didn't know me from Adam. She had grown up a basketball fan and had absolutely no interest in football.

While I had seen her on a number of occasions, it was not until we were seated together at a dinner party hosted by one of her friends that we really got acquainted. Still, months would pass before we had our first date. She finally agreed to have dinner with me shortly after phoning to ask how the broken wrist I'd been playing with was mending.

Which is to say of all the injuries I've dealt with over the course of my career, that one was the best to ever happen to me.

Soon we were seeing each other regularly and by the time the new season approached she had moved into my condo and immediately set about redecorating.

Not only did her presence take my mind off my problems with the Raiders, but the more I was around her, the more convinced I became that I'd met the person with whom I wanted to spend the rest of my life.

fourteen

History in the Making

Since my contract had again expired, I waited through the off-season for word from the Raiders. Ed Hookstratten had phoned Davis several times but got no response. The word we were hearing was that Davis had made it clear he would decide whether to offer me a new contract in his own good time.

I hated the gamesmanship. We'd been through it enough to be convinced that Al was simply flexing his management muscles. It was a strange little dance that had to be performed annually before the deal could be done. And certainly I wasn't the only one backed into a hurry-up-and-wait corner. With no collective bargaining agreement, players throughout the league had no leverage in negotiations whatsoever. Ed urged me to be patient; he said things would work out like always.

I was still hearing that when training camp opened. I was in excellent shape and, like everyone else on the team, was looking forward to helping prove we were a better football team than the previous year's record indicated.

But with no contract, I stayed away from camp. Not by choice, as people might have assumed, but because of the league rule that clearly stated that if one was not under contract, he could not participate in any team activities.

And while I certainly would have entertained the chance to continue my career with some other team, I knew there was little chance of me playing anywhere other than Los Angeles. Under the restrictive NFL rules that would force another team to give the Raiders two first-round draft picks before they could even begin negotiations with me, my chances of going elsewhere were slim to none.

Briefly, there was a rumor afloat that the Cleveland Browns might be interested in trading for me, but that was soon followed by a call from a friend in the front office who related Davis's response to the offer. "I'll never trade him," he reportedly said. Then, when someone in management asked why he was so determined to keep a player he obviously didn't like, he explained, "As long as the son of a bitch keeps scoring touchdowns, I don't have to like him."

Only when the pre-season games got under way did the negotiations finally begin in earnest. And even then they were tedious. Finally, with the first regular season game just days away, George Karras, the Raiders' director of scouting, contacted me. He was not one of my favorite people.

It was after nine in the evening when he called to say that the final draft of the one-year contract had been drawn up. Could I drive down to training camp and sign it so that I would be allowed to begin practicing with the team?

As I read over the one-year agreement, there were several things that I was sure had been discussed but weren't included. Karras argued that everything Davis and my agent had agreed to was written into the contract.

"What about the medical benefits that I had last year?" I asked.

"We can't do that," he insisted. Understand, this was not the Raiders' chief counsel talking. Not the owner. This was a guy who heads up the scouting department telling me what the organization could and couldn't do.

They were still fucking with me. I took the contract, folded it, and told George that I was going to take it with me and think about it for a while.

His expression was a combination of panic and anger. "When can I expect you back?" he asked.

"Later," I said. It was my turn to play games.

It was sometime after eleven before I returned. We argued for another half hour or so, my medical benefits were added, and I signed to become a Raider for another year.

As I was leaving I could hear George dialing the phone. "It's done," I heard him say. I knew he was speaking to Al Davis.

I was already in the parking lot when I saw Karras running after me. "Marcus," he yelled, "you can't do this to me. This contract is a mess. We've got to draw up a clean one."

His reference was to the marginal notes I'd made and the unsatisfactory wording of certain paragraphs that I'd circled or revised. At that point it seemed to me that neatness counted for nothing, so I refused and drove away.

I reported to the team the week before the opening of the regular season. In what had become a commonplace occurrence in recent years, I immediately found my attention drawn to the tenuous nature of life in the NFL. Players, I'd come to realize in my seven years, were the game's most disposable commodities. I'd lost count of teammates who I'd seen released or traded, quickly replaced by those younger, stronger, and faster.

Missing this time was Todd Christensen, his career ended when his name had appeared on one of training camp's final roster cuts.

His story had been one of the most inspirational I'd encountered during my association with professional athletes. An outstanding running back at Brigham Young, he had originally been a high-round draft choice of the Dallas Cowboys. But Dallas scouts and coaches had agreed that Todd's professional future was as a tight end. And Christensen had balked, stubbornly insisting to head coach Tom Landry that he wanted to make his mark as a running back or not at all. Landry had wearied of arguing the point and agreed to give Todd his chance to succeed or fail at the position of his choice. And the Cowboys, in no real need of another back, let him go late in the pre-season.

He'd been picked up off the waiver wire by the New York Giants and was active for one game before they, too, released him. After that had come a series of unsuccessful tryouts with four or five other teams. Only when the Raiders found themselves in need of someone who could snap the ball for punts and place kicks did Todd get one last opportunity to make it as a professional.

After spending his rookie year on special teams, he had gone to the coaches and volunteered to do that very thing he'd so stubbornly argued against in Dallas. He wanted a shot at playing tight end.

In time he became one of the best at the position, leading the Raiders in receiving five straight years and earning All-Pro status.

But, like everyone, he had known that his days with the Raiders were winding down as the '88 season had ended. During the off-season, Todd had visited Davis to ask an honest evaluation of his chances of playing another season. If he did not figure into the team's plans, he wanted to know. If he had no realistic chance, Todd simply didn't want to go through the demanding regime of conditioning and training camp. Al urged Todd to begin getting into shape and assured him he'd be given every opportunity to extend his career for one more year.

Davis had only proven once more that he was not a man to be trusted.

Immediately upon joining the team for the season opener against San Diego, I did the one thing that Davis expected of me. I ran the ball well and scored a touchdown.

And we won the game.

The following weekend was not nearly so much fun. While making a block against Denver's Steve Atwater in the second quarter, he gave me a forearm shot that forced my helmet down against my forehead, opening a three-inch gash over my left eye. I knew it must look pretty bad by the way people on the sidelines were clearing a way for me as I trotted off the field. It was like the parting of the Red Sea. Whatever had happened to me was cause for a full-scale gross-out and everyone gave me plenty of room. The doctors only glanced at me before waving me toward the locker room. Once inside, I removed the helmet and looked into a mirror to check the extent of the damage. The skin above the eyebrow had slid down over the eye. Part of my skull was exposed and blood was flowing freely.

But in a matter of minutes Dr. Rosenfeld, a gruff, white-haired man who had served as the Raiders' team doctor since 1968, had cleansed the wound with saltwater solution and was suturing the skin back into place. Dr. Rob Huizenga watched silently from a distance.

I was back on the field as the second half began.

It was only after the game, when I'd showered and dressed and was preparing to leave, that Dr. Huizenga came up to me and slipped a piece of paper into my hand. "Go to this address immediately," he whispered. "It's the office of a very good plastic surgeon. I've called him and he'll be waiting for you. The suture job you've got is okay—it'll hold things together—but there's no reason for you to have the kind of scar that it is going to leave."

Meanwhile, our season continued to be a frustrating roller-coaster ride. And one of new upheaval.

Four games into the season, Al Davis called Mike Shanahan into his office and fired him.

Few on the team were surprised. There had been widespread speculation throughout the summer that the differences in philosophy between Davis and Shanahan had become an unresolvable problem and that a coaching change might come at any time. As I've said, I respected Mike's knowledge of the game, as did just about everyone on the team. And he had initiated some good things, including replacing the infamous roach coach with a noon buffet catered daily in the locker room. But his relationship with the front office had been rocky from the day he accepted the job.

I learned that Shanahan had not actually been Davis's top choice when he made the decision to venture outside the Raiders "family" to replace Flores. Joe Bugel, the Washington Redskins' line coach, had been the first to be interviewed and the widely circulated story was that he'd angrily stormed out of Davis's office after a two-hour conversation that had quickly dissolved into a heated argument over who would actually be in control of the team.

Shanahan, then, had been the second choice. And ultimately an Al Davis experiment that failed.

In retrospect, I'm convinced that Shanahan had reached the point where he was hoping to be fired and set free from the discomfort he'd endured from his first day on the job.

And while I was genuinely sorry to see Mike go, I was elated when I heard the announcement of his replacement. No longer interested in another league-wide search, Davis stayed within the organization.

Art Shell was to become the first black head coach in the fifty-year history of the NFL.

I would be playing for someone I'd long viewed as a bona fide legend; coached by a man who was being given the opportunity to usher in a new era of professional sports. The contributions he now had the chance to make were endless. He could be the catapult for a number of other qualified black coaches waiting their turns. He could do so much to disprove the tired old racial adage that blacks lacked the intelligence needed to effectively take on the role of head coach. Art Shell had been placed in a position that transcended the game.

No player in the team's history better exemplified the championship tradition of the Raiders. From 1968 to 1982—my rookie year—he had played the left offensive tackle position like none before him. At six-five and 305 pounds, he was a man among boys, knocking defenders away, clearing holes. *Domination* is a term loosely tossed about in sports today, but it served as an honest description of the way Art played his position. When I joined the Raiders, one of the first of many legendary stories I would hear was of the game Art had played in Super Bowl XI at the end of the 1977 season. Minnesota Vikings defensive end Jim Marshall, himself an All-Pro, had been assigned the unfortunate task of going against Art. And by game's end Marshall had been shut out. No tackles, no assists, no sacks.

No one ever played the game more fiercely, while at the same time being such a likable, easygoing person. Away from football, Art Shell is one of the most gentle men you'll ever meet.

Raised in North Charleston, South Carolina, his mother had

died when he was fifteen and his father worked in the paper mills. Art rarely spoke of his roots, but I had the distinct impression that his childhood had been far from easy.

Though an outstanding football and basketball player in high school, no major colleges offered him a scholarship. The only recruiters to come calling were from the small black colleges. Eddie Robinson, the legendary Grambling coach, had badly wanted Art to come to Louisiana but at the last minute Shell decided to attend Maryland State. There he started in both the offensive and defensive line and soon gained the attention of NFL scouts who had learned not to overlook the potential of players at lesser-known schools. In 1968 the Raiders made him a third-round draft choice despite not knowing whether he would play offense or defense.

In the years to come, a number of Raiders running backs, myself included, would be thankful that Art landed on the left side of the offensive line, shoulder-to-shoulder with guard Gene Upshaw. Fifteen years later, I still haven't seen a tandem that comes even close to equaling their talent.

Immediately following his retirement, Art became a member of the coaching staff, passing his knowledge on to new members of the offensive line. When Flores had abruptly resigned, there was talk that Art was among a shortlist of candidates for the job.

It had been clear that Shanahan felt little need for Art's expertise, resigned to keeping him a member of his staff only because Al Davis had decreed it.

It finally reached a point where several of the veteran players and some of the old-guard assistants had urged Art to look elsewhere for a coaching job. As Shanahan's assistant, he would forever be in limbo.

It was an idea Art would not even consider. "As long as Mr. Davis is the owner of this team and wants me here," he said, "this is where I'll be. When he tells me to leave, then I'll leave. But not until then."

Such was Art Shell's loyalty, and you could not help but admire it.

Finally, his patient dedication paid off. Suddenly, Art was on quite a roll. The previous summer he had been inducted into the Pro Football Hall of Fame, selecting Al Davis to introduce him at the ceremony in Canton.

With the summer mind games and the frustration of holding out behind me, I was determined to focus all my efforts on making a solid contribution to the team. Art's elevation to the head coaching position only strengthened my resolve.

And things had been going well until we went into New York for a Monday night game against the Jets.

That evening, as we were getting off the bus, I heard a rumor that Davis was again talking to the Cleveland Browns and I might soon be traded. If that was the case, I was more than ready to pack my bags. First, though, there was a game to play for Art Shell. Nothing seemed more important than seeing that he won his first game as a head coach.

Early in the game I felt good, getting to the holes quickly and picking up yardage. Before halftime I had carried nine times for over 40 yards and had caught four passes. On my tenth carry, I had planted on my right leg to make a cut just as a Jets defender collided with my knee. I immediately felt a hot, knifing pain.

It is a football player's worst nightmare. Nothing can so abruptly end a season, a career, as a serious knee injury. Even with the pain, it is the first thought that races through your mind after such an injury occurs. My question as I lay on the turf was hardly original: Was my career over?

Once the pain subsided and the doctors assured me the damage was not irreparable, I got up slowly and walked from the field. On the sidelines, I waited for a few minutes, then tested it. I tried to jog, only to have the knee buckle.

I was through for the night and as the game progressed without me, I felt cheated. We played well and won, making Art's head coaching debut before a Monday-night audience a roaring success. I had badly wanted to be more a part of the historic event.

My disappointment would soon be compounded when I was placed on the injured reserve list. It would be eight weeks before the rehabilitation process was complete and I could return to the active roster.

I watched from the sidelines in street clothes as we defeated Kansas City, then lost to Philadelphia. With Bo Jackson getting into stride after his late arrival from the Royals, things took an upswing as we won two in a row. Then, just as quickly, we lost back-to-back games to San Diego and Houston.

It had developed into a season no one was happy with.

By the time I was reactivated for the Denver game, we were 6–6 and I was told that I would be allowed to suit up for the game but wouldn't play unless Bo got hurt.

We managed to win 16–13 in overtime to avoid dropping below .500.

As we prepared to play Phoenix in the Coliseum early in December, I was feeling good about my knee. To be safe, I wore a brace for the first time in my career and had become reasonably comfortable with it. After a half season of inactivity, I was eager to play, but the coaching staff had been instructed to keep me on the bench.

I knew where the edict had come from. The only question was the motivation that had prompted it. Was I being kept out because of concern that I might re-injure the knee? Or was it payback for staying out of camp? For getting hurt? Was I being held up to blame as the number-one cause of our disappointing record?

Though the season had been a personal disappointment, it was still a very interesting one. It had been fascinating to watch Art Shell as he functioned in his new role. Despite the fact that we ended the year with an 8–8 record, Art had won seven of twelve games after taking over the job. And, modesty aside, I think it might have been better had I not spent two months on the sidelines. Still, everyone believed he had the team headed in the right direction.

If he felt any pressures beyond those that all other NFL head coaches deal with, they were well hidden. He knew that he was shouldering the hopes of an entire generation of African-American coaches who aspired to one day be in charge of an NFL team. He had to know that his every move was being closely watched and that there were whispers throughout the league suggesting he'd been elevated to the head coaching job not so much because of his qualifications, but rather because of Al Davis's egomaniacal eagerness to again be viewed as a pacesetter.

But he seemed to have a remarkable ability to put such things aside and concentrate only on that over which he had some degree of control.

He had made the transition with style and grace, maintaining a good relationship with the players while at the same time keeping the distance that is necessary for a head coach to maintain. He had rekindled a unity within the coaching staff.

I watched him and cheered for him. Yet all the while I found myself asking the same question about Art Shell that I had about every coach I've ever known: Why the hell would he want such a job?

Over the years there have been a number of coaches who I've greatly admired. But I can honestly say I've never envied one of them. For every brief reward they realize, there are twice as many setbacks. So demanding is the job that it requires a person be selfishly willing to sacrifice time with family and friends just to be as ready as possible for next Sunday's game.

And for coaches there is never a finish line, only brief pauses along the way to take a quick breath, then continue on with the race. Win or lose, there is always another game just a week away, a player draft to prepare for, playbooks to revise, minicamps, quarterback camps, training camps, and then the beginning of yet another season.

In my career as a professional, I've gone to the practice facility at all hours for one reason or another. And no matter how early I might arrive or how late I stay, there is one certainty. There will always be coaches there.

And there is what I've long viewed as the greatest frustration the coaching profession offers. For all the hard work and long hours of planning, there always comes the time when those best-laid plans are placed in the hands of the players. On Sunday afternoon, the coach turns things over to a group of young men, some whose level of desire and ambition are not as great, and he must rely on them to win the game.

It is no wonder to me that so many of them suffer burnout. And at the same time, I have a great admiration for the dedication they bring to their craft.

As Art Shell's first season as head coach progressed, his confidence grew. His assistant coaches rallied around him, as did the players. Though our record was far shy of Raiders expectations, a new energy, a new sense of purpose was developing.

A year later our won-lost record would be the proof.

fifteen

Pioneers

The announcement that Art Shell would be the Raiders' new head coach made headlines throughout the country. For the first time in the fifty-year history of the National Football League, a black man was handed the mantle of authority, and the significance of the moment was not lost on members of the team. No member of the Raiders organization had ever received more respect than Art, and everyone, black and white, was eager to do whatever he could to help the new coach become a success.

I'm sure that black coaches everywhere were praying that Art would prove himself quickly. In a sense, he would carry the torch for an entire generation of new, young black coaches.

To not only have a front-row seat from which to witness the historic event, but to be able to participate in it as well was exhilarating.

I'm not sure at what point I became interested in the history of black athletes who paved the way in their respective sports, but for years I had found their stories—many of which my father had related to me—fascinating. And the older I became, the more I realized the debt owed them by modern-day players.

Blacks in professional sports have their grievances, both valid and trivial, but when compared to the players of past generations, the truth of the matter is we have precious little cause for complaint.

For instance, I can't imagine how Jackie Robinson dealt with the hatred and pressure of being the first man across major league baseball's color line. When, back in 1947, Brooklyn Dodgers owner Branch Rickey picked Robinson from the remarkable talent pool of the Negro Leagues to forever change the face of baseball, it had to have been incredibly difficult. How could someone lend the proper concentration to his craft with such a storm swirling around him? Today we cringe at occasional boos from the stands and critical fan mail; Robinson worked daily amidst a chorus of racial slurs and death threats. Today's athlete is upset over the fact that room service is delayed fifteen minutes; Robinson was not even granted the privilege of staying in the same hotels as his white teammates.

I've marveled at the degree of courage and determination that Robinson must have had. And wondered what might have happened had he lacked the strength to focus on his goal of becoming a big league baseball star. How easy and understandable it would have been for him to simply pack his bags and walk away from the enormous pressures forced on him, to leave the work of social groundbreaking to some player more courageous. No doubt there would have been someone to follow him and break down the barrier. But how much longer would it have been delayed? Another decade?

In my opinion, no athlete has left a greater legacy than did Jackie Robinson.

He was, however, not the only one to look racial prejudice squarely in the eye and triumph over it. Jesse Owens captured the hearts and imagination of the entire world with his four gold medals at the 1936 Olympics in Berlin, the cradle of Adolph Hitler's Aryan supremacy philosophy. Heavyweight champion Joe Louis shouldered the hopes of a nation as he went into the ring against Germany's Max Schmelling and won the heavyweight title. In both cases, it was a black athlete who was given the responsibility of representing a country against Nazi ideology and white racist propaganda, and who emerged successful. I remember reading an interview with legendary Grambling coach Eddie Robinson, who recalled listening to the Louis-Schmelling fight on the radio. "When

Louis won," Robinson remembered, "it was the first time I ever heard a black man referred to as an American."

The importance of such moments is immeasurable.

Every time I go out to play a round of golf, I'm reminded of the uphill battle fought by Charlie Sifford. A big, cigar-smoking man who had taught himself to become an outstanding player, he was long prevented from competing against the best by a clause in the PGA bylaws that restricted membership to whites only. There were courses throughout the country on which he was not allowed to tee up a ball simply because of the color of his skin. But, fortunately for every black player, from Tiger Woods to wanna-bes like me, Sifford kept banging on the door, demanding his rights.

It was a letter to the PGA from Jackie Robinson, pleading for Sifford to be given his rightfully earned chance, that finally set in motion the effort that resulted in the removal of the Caucasian clause in 1961.

The dynasty that the NBA Boston Celtics would become is traceable to their 1956 signing of Bill Russell, the first black player to wear their uniform. A year later, when they'd won the league title, franchises throughout the league were in a frantic search for more talented black players. While Russell's remarkable abilities were in themselves enough to assure him a legendary spot in the sport's history, it was his concern for human rights that elevated him another notch. Once, when preparing for an exhibition game in Lexington, Kentucky, the team, which by then included several black players, entered a local restaurant for their pre-game meal and was told that the establishment's policy dictated that blacks would not be served. It was Russell who convinced the team that it should make a statement on the matter by not playing the game.

Naturally, the decision was unpopular with fans and promoters and, as instigator, Russell was the target of most of the resentment. But the principle, the quest for respect and equality, was more important to Russell than the cheers. He refused to willingly accept the decades-old social standards that he knew to be wrong. Years later Russell was still fighting the cause when he became the NBA's first black head coach.

No athlete in modern history has had a more powerful effect on me than Muhammad Ali. As a youngster, I remember listening to his fights on the radio, bouncing around my bedroom, arms flailing, doing my thirteen-year-old best to emulate his famous rope-a-dope, sharing every tense moment, every jab, with him.

He captured the sports world's imagination like no athlete before him, and the public—young and old, black and white—was taken by his incredible talent, his looks; even charmed by his outrageous behavior. If ever there was an athlete with feet planted squarely on top of the world, it was Muhammad Ali. Then it all came crashing down when he broke with tradition, refusing induction into the service because to do so would violate his strong Muslim beliefs. Overnight he became a traitor, a coward to many, and was stripped of his title. Yet Ali stood his ground, so strong in his beliefs that he was willing to risk the loss of status and millions of dollars.

Could I have done it? Risk everything I'd worked so hard for? I only wish I could say I had such rare inner strength and conviction.

Muhammad Ali was and remains one of a kind.

But he is not the only great black athlete who has been willing to risk a white nation's ire in favor of his strong beliefs. I remember watching the 1968 Olympic games on television, mesmerized by the grace and style of those competing, at the time youthfully ignorant of the degree of growing racial unrest in America; not knowing that many of the black Olympians had gone to Mexico City with a mission that went beyond winning a gold medal. I did not fully understand the gesture at the time, when U.S. sprinters Tommie Smith and John Carlos raised gloved fists from the victory stand as the national anthem played. I wasn't sure why they were summarily dismissed from the team and sent home.

Only in time would I understand that they had been willing to set aside the glory of their finest moments to demonstrate their concerns about racial injustice. Had they simply stood

at attention, basking in their accomplishment, they would today be remembered only as warm footnotes in Olympic history. Instead, by making their shared statement, they did their
part to advance the cause of an entire race. That is a greater
legacy than even a treasured Olympic medal.

Years later I met John Carlos and asked him about that
long-ago event in Mexico City. I was interested in knowing
how he dealt with the public outcry from those who suggested
he'd tarnished the spirit of the games with his demonstration.
It had not been easy, he admitted. "But," he said, smiling,
"I caused people to stop and think about the things we were
fighting for at the time. It got people talking. And until people
talk about problems, they don't get solved. See, that's one of
the great advantages sports figures have. They have a platform
that the guy working down at the post office or selling alu-
minum siding will never enjoy. I felt we had a responsibility,
an obligation, to take advantage of that position, that moment.
If I had it to do over, would I do it again? I damn sure
would."

It is not black athletes alone who owe a debt of gratitude
to Carlos and Smith and Lee Evans, the 400-meter champion
of those same games who later joined in their statement. It is
African-Americans from every walk of life who live in a
world they helped improve, one that is a little more fair, more
socially conscious, because of their efforts.

If there is one thing that all those I've mentioned have in
common, it is their courageous willingness to risk their own
futures for their beliefs and the betterment of others.

Curt Flood, the great centerfielder for the St. Louis
Cardinals in the Sixties, was such a figure. In 1969, after years
of batting over .300 and routinely winning Golden Gloves for
his gifted fielding, Flood was suddenly traded to the Philadelphia Phillies. And refused to go. Instead, he decided to
take a stand against the reserve clause that bound players to
a particular team, then allowed owners sole right to trade
players if and when the mood struck.

Despite the concerned advice of friends, family, and fellow
players, all warning that a legal battle with management was
not only likely to end his playing career but would surely

block any chances of one day coaching, managing, or taking his rightful place in baseball's Hall of Fame, Flood chose to fight the unfair system that perpetuated a virtual enslavement of players.

It would take six agonizing years for him to finally win the battle and demolish the century-old system. A thirty-two-year-old black outfielder, with little support from even his fellow players, stood up against the commissioner of baseball, presidents of the American and National League, and executives of all twenty-four major-league teams, to make a simple statement that ultimately revolutionized professional sports: "I wish to be traded not to the team you want me to go to but, rather, the team that makes me the best offer."

Taking a stand at the risk of great sacrifice and personal attack, Curt Flood succeeded in making things better for us all.

And we are all in his debt. Just as we are to those who pioneered the entry of the black athlete into the game I play.

I look back on my experiences of playing in the Rose Bowl while at USC as a fun, exciting, and energizing time. There was no concern over how many blacks and how many whites were listed on the team rosters, no threats of violence, no racial epithets being tossed around. The sports world had long since become color-blind.

I think of what Woody Strode had to endure when the Los Angeles Rams signed him to a contract in the early Forties, making him professional football's equivalent of Jackie Robinson. Or Marion Motley, the great Cleveland fullback, who signed with the Browns that same season.

As late as the Sixties, long after blacks had become commonplace on NFL rosters, they were still not allowed to stay in the same hotels as their white teammates or eat their meals at the same restaurants. When teams traveled to Dallas, the white players were routinely housed in a local hotel the night before the game while the blacks were bused over to Fort Worth to stay in the home of a dentist.

By comparison, the difficulties of the black athlete today are small. While we don't function in a perfect world, there are no death threats, no segregated housing arrangements, no blatant displays of racism to endure. In the fifteen years I've been in the league, I can think of only one time an opponent has called me a "nigger." That's once too often, but insignificant when measured against what the Woody Strodes and Marion Motleys were forced to deal with.

Which is to say that in the grand scheme, today's athletes have it far better than at any time in the history of sports. We're better paid and have more economic opportunities than even the most visionary of our athletic forefathers likely ever dreamed possible. And it is a state of affairs for which we owe a great deal to those who preceded us—enduring, fighting long odds, changing attitudes, demanding that injustices be dealt with. We are obligated to do our part to see that the improvement continues for the benefit of the next generation.

It troubles me that today so many of the young players, black and white alike, seem to lack any real sense of their game's history. More often than not, when I mention the names of the heroes of my youth, I am met with a blank, disinterested response. The "me generation" mentality that is now so much a part of our nation's culture has found its way into the sports arenas, leaving little time to consider the importance of history or heritage.

That major-league baseball dedicated its 1997 season to recognition of Robinson's historic accomplishment is a step in the right direction. When Muhammad Ali lit the torch to open the 1996 Olympic games in Atlanta, there was a revival of interest in his remarkable history. The sad thing to me is that there were so many young athletes who previously had no real idea of who these men were or what they had done.

I owe them. And I salute them and so many others whose efforts have made my life so much easier.

While the elevation of Art Shell was cheered as a move long overdue, I could not help but wonder if the real significance of the moment was as fully appreciated as it deserved to be. Regardless of what Al Davis's motives may have been— some suggested it was a move Al felt necessary to ensure his own induction into the game's Hall of Fame—naming Art as head coach went light-years beyond Raiders football.

Art Shell had become a pioneer whose name would forever be attached to one of the major milestones in the game's history.

It was our job as players to do our damndest to see that it would treat him kindly.

sixteen

Held Hostage

Steve Beuerlein fell into a carefully laid Al Davis trap in the summer preceding the 1990 season. Though the starting quarterback the previous year, he was reportedly earning considerably less than Schroeder and therefore felt a significant raise was in order. Al, who had made no secret of his belief that the team's future was with Jay, steadfastly refused to negotiate with Beuerlein and his agent. By keeping Steve at arm's length, all the while placing blame for his absence on the nonexistent contract negotiations, Al could be assured that Jay would establish himself as the team's offensive leader.

When it came time for training camp to begin, Steve joined me as one of the expatriate Raiders. We worked out on our own while the remainder of the team gathered for pre-season preparations. However, there was a difference.

Though we were both referred to by the media as holdouts, that was only half true. Steve was holding out until such time as his contract was renegotiated. I was simply waiting for a contract, just as I'd done the year before.

The only reason I wasn't in camp was because league rules prohibited me from being there. Earlier in the summer I'd gone to the Raiders facility and while there had decided to do my daily workout. I'd been told that I couldn't, and was invited to leave and not return until I became an official member of the team.

By the time Beuerlein finally signed—for an increase in pay considerably shy of his asking price—he had missed the

entire training camp and pre-season schedule, allowing
Schroeder to establish himself as the number-one quarterback.
Thus, Beuerlein joined the team, anticipating a fight to regain
his job—only to find out he really didn't have one. Davis
immediately placed Steve on the inactive roster, where he
would remain for the entire season. His punishment would be
to serve as nothing more than a practice player, never to see
action on Sunday.

My situation didn't look a lot better. I arrived in camp a
week before Steve and found that I was listed fourth among
the running backs on the depth chart. Vance Mueller, who
has been a reserve since 1986, was listed first; Greg Bell, who
had been picked up from the Rams, was number two; and
some rookie I'd never heard of was third.

Apparently, I had some work to do.

For our final pre-season game, we were to fly to London
and play against the New Orleans Saints in famed Wembley
Stadium. It was part of the NFL's campaign to draw added
international attention to professional football.

Earlier in the off-season, a league publicist had contacted
the Raiders about sending a player to London for a few days
of interviews to generate interest in the game. They had asked
that I go as a Raiders representative, but, as I was told later,
the idea was quickly nixed by Al.

Our early August trip to London was not to be confused
with a leisurely vacation abroad.

We arrived suffering major jet lag and went immediately
to a park near our hotel for a practice. To the curious Brits
who gathered to watch, we must all have looked like giant
zombies as we stumbled and staggered through drills.

On the day of the game, Joe Scannella, one of the Raiders
assistants, began going over the amount of playing time those
on the roster would be assigned. Though you want to win
pre-season games, their purpose is also to give coaching staffs
a chance to determine the quality of their players. They are
the showcases for rookies hoping to earn a job and, in some
cases, older veterans trying to prove they deserve to play another year. Routinely, the first units open the game but play
sparingly, soon giving way to backups. By game's end there

are so many rookies on the field that you can't tell the players without a program.

"You'll be playing some in the fourth quarter," Scannella told me.

My response was one I'd never thought I'd make as a football player: I told Joe that I wouldn't play.

I knew who had final okay of the depth charts and rationing of playing time. "Tell Davis that I'm not going to go out there with a bunch of rookies and get my ass kicked."

Thus, if you look back on the statistics of the 1990 American Bowl, you will see that I was invisible. No carries, no yards, no nothing.

Afterward, Davis had stormed into the locker room to demand an explanation of Scannella. Joe could only shrug and shake his head. "He said he wasn't playing," he explained.

Al's reply was predictable. "Aw, fuck . . ."

Next came rumors of a trade. San Francisco running back Roger Craig was injured and the 49ers were reportedly in a desperate search for a replacement. Davis indicated that he might be persuaded to let me go. It soon became obvious that he was not remotely serious when he demanded Charles Haley, the All-Pro end who was the anchor of the 49ers defense, in exchange.

It was also becoming increasingly obvious that my reasons for still being in a Raiders uniform had little to do with playing football. I was being held hostage. The coaches, I soon learned, were being told not to play me. Schroeder confided that he'd been given instructions not to throw to me.

I was fast becoming little more than a third-down back, called on when short yardage was needed for a first down. And even that was a tenuous situation.

Terry Robiskie, our offensive play-caller, had actually ignored instructions from the owner's box on several occasions in '89, inserting me into games when the staff had been instructed not to play me.

Against the Cardinals, when we'd still had a chance at the play-offs, we were behind but driving toward what we hoped would be the winning touchdown. Faced with a fourth-and-two situation late in the game, Shell had called time-out to discuss our options with Robiskie. Finally, it had been Terry who made the call. "If I'm going to get my ass fired," he told Art, "it's going to be because I played him, not because I was stupid enough not to." With that he'd called to me and sent me into the game and I got the first down.

Later, with only six seconds and the ball on the Phoenix 2, Terry sent me onto the field a second time. I got the ball in the end zone and we won the game, 16–14.

Afterward Davis was waiting for Robiskie at the entrance to our locker room. Grabbing him by the arm, he pulled Terry aside. "Goddammit, you defied me," he said.

Terry, assuming his days with the Raiders were over, admitted that he had knowingly done so, and braced for the consequences.

To Robiskie's surprise, Al smiled. "What the hell? We won the game," he said.

The message seemed to be that it would be okay to allow me to play occasionally—but only if the situation demanded it.

In the locker room, my teammates seemed to assume that I had been freed from the doghouse and was again in the fold. Several approached me to say, "Welcome back." Davis was not one of them.

Whatever charity he had expressed to Terry did not carry over to me. As he made his rounds in the locker room, head down, hands buried in his pockets, he finally approached the area where I was dressing. Lifting his head, he looked me in the eye, muttered his tired "Aw, fuck," then turned away without further comment.

During practice the next week, it was clear that nothing had changed. As Davis stood on the sidelines, he said something to George Karras. George, in turn, sought out Shell and delivered a message: Al wanted Vance Mueller to get more practice time at running back.

I saw what appeared to be a look of disappointment, maybe even frustration, on Art's face. As George walked away, I yelled across the field, "Don't worry, Art. They can't beat me.'' I was sure to speak loud enough for Davis and his messenger to hear.

The following Sunday against Seattle, we were in one of those short yardage situations where I was routinely called on to deliver. Terry looked at Art and said, ''Hell, I'm not putting him in.'' Shell's response was, ''Me neither.'' The word had obviously come down that I was not to play.

For me, the only positive of the 1990 season was that we began to win again. Our defense suddenly blossomed and through the first four games of the season had given up an average of only nine points per game. And I was getting a lot of time to admire their work as I sat on the sidelines.

The busiest afternoon I had in the first month of the season came in a 24–10 victory over Chicago. Subbing in on short yardage situations, I carried twelve times for 57 yards and scored a couple of touchdowns.

In years past, I'd always been one of those players who stood near the sidelines, into the ebb and flow of the game, ready to get back on the field at a moment's notice. I had always wanted to know everything that was going on in a game. I wanted to be totally involved. But, knowing that my playing time would be limited, I found it increasingly difficult to maintain any real enthusiasm.

I found it impossible to leave my frustrations at the office. Thus Kathryn found herself caught up in my woes. One evening I opened the freezer compartment of the refrigerator and was surprised to find, of all things, a photograph of Al Davis that she had clipped from a book. A friend of hers who was fascinated by everything from unexplained phenomena to Tarot cards and voodoo rituals had offered the suggestion. The friend had read somewhere of a hex one could place on an enemy simply by exposing his image to subfreezing temperatures. It was an amusing variation on the old pins-in-the-voodoo-doll form of retaliation.

''Hey, I thought it was worth a try,'' Kathryn explained.

What made things even more difficult was the fact that I was allowing my personal conflicts to cloud the enjoyment I knew I should be feeling over the season we were having.

There is nothing in football more gratifying than feeling a part of a winning team. The tension had disappeared from the locker room, Shell had worked hard at creating a fun atmosphere in practices and meetings, and confidence seemed to grow with each passing week.

Meanwhile, I could not pull myself from my funk. I tried to put on a happy face around my teammates, but in private I was absolutely miserable. I hated going to work.

Ironically, when Bo Jackson reported to the team after baseball season, my workload actually increased. Art, confident in our defense's ability to hold down the opposition's scoring, felt our best chance of finishing the season strong was the attack with a strong running game. The vertical passing game that Davis had hoped Schroeder could bring to our offense had not developed.

Bo proved quickly that he was ready to oblige, immediately stringing together 100-yard games. Though I was still primarily a short-yardage specialist, I did get nineteen carries and 79 yards in a 13–10 win over Miami.

We were 8–4 by the time we visited the Silverdome to play the Detroit Lions on a Monday night. And it was one of those games that seemed to have become our *Monday Night Football* trademark.

Before the first quarter ended, we trailed 21–14. The Lions extended their lead to ten with a field goal early in the second period, but we got a big lift just before halftime when Bo broke on a 55-yard scoring run that narrowed Detroit's margin to 24–21 at the half.

In the third quarter Schroeder put us ahead with a 10-yard touchdown to Mervyn Fernandez, then connected with Tim Brown for another, and we went up by eleven with just fifteen minutes left to play.

But when the Lions pulled to within four points with only six minutes left, the crowd turned into a roaring chorus in anticipation of one more scoring drive. But our defense held. And, when Jeff Jaeger added a late field goal, we were able to leave town with a 38–31 victory.

It would help us to close out the regular season with five straight victories.

There were those who, while quick to admit that Bo Jackson—230 pounds, great speed and strength, less than 3 percent body fat—was a remarkably talented athlete, expressed doubt that he could excel as an NFL back as long as he gave the game only part-time attention.

Those doubters needed only to have been in the Coliseum and watched his performance against Cincinnati. We were on our own 11-yard line when Jay pitched the ball to Bo, running toward a defense that was stacked to that side of the field. Seeing the wall of defenders, Jackson pivoted, gave ground, and shook off the attempted tackle of a Bengals linebacker before running toward the opposite side of the field. Schroeder, seeing that Bo had reversed his field, attempted to throw a block and fell directly in Jackson's path. Bo hurdled Jay and turned upfield.

Finally, Bengals defender Rod Jones dragged him down at the Cincinnati two-yard line after one of the most incredible runs I'd ever seen.

Knowing the drill—that I was routinely called on when we needed to score from a few yards out—Jackson began trotting toward the sidelines.

I met him at the hash marks and grabbed him by the shoulder pads to spin him around. "Get back in there," I said. "This one's yours. Go get it." Bo looked at me for a second, grinning.

"Man, I'm shot," he said.

"Go get your touchdown," I said, pushing him in the direction of the huddle.

As it turned out, Bo *was* out of gas. The 88-yard run, which probably had covered more like 120 yards, had totally drained him. He attempted a run up the middle that gained nothing before Jay decided to fake it to him and flip the ball to the tight end for the score.

By season's end, Jackson had rushed for 698 yards in ten games and was picked to play in the Pro Bowl.

Unfortunately, it would have to serve as the closing statement of his football career.

Once more champions of the AFC West, we faced the same Bengals in the first round of the play-offs and Bo and I were having the best combined effort we'd ever enjoyed. Then, early in the third quarter, he was hit hard along the sidelines following a long gain. Slow getting up, he told trainers of hearing something pop in his left hip as he'd tried to break free of the tackler. It was first assumed that he'd suffered a painful hip pointer that would only sideline him for the rest of the day.

With Bo out, the running game fell to me, and by day's end I'd had my most productive day since midway through the 1988 season: I carried twenty-one times for 140 yards, proving to myself and anyone else interested that I could get the job done if given the opportunity.

More important, we won, 20–10, earning a trip to Buffalo to play the Bills for the right to represent the AFC in the Super Bowl.

All the news, however, was not good. We would make the trip without Jackson. Doctors had discovered that he had a degenerative condition that would likely require hip-replacement surgery. It was very likely that his athletic career had been abruptly ended.

So did any thoughts we had of revisiting the Super Bowl. On a bone-chilling day when absolutely everything that could go wrong did, the Bills defeated us, 51–3. It was over almost before it began as Jay threw interceptions, our running game went nowhere, and Buffalo gained almost 400 yards against our defense in the first half alone.

In one arctic afternoon, everything we'd accomplished during the season seemed instantly swept away. Our twelve victories, the fact that Shell had been recognized as Coach of the Year, the revitalized crowd support we'd begun to enjoy in Los Angeles, suddenly meant little.

In professional football, I'd long ago learned, you were judged only by your last game.

And I knew the unfortunate departure of Bo Jackson would have no real effect on my ongoing situation.

When the 49ers' Roger Craig had regained his health, Davis made a deal that brought him to L.A. He was still determined to find a running back to his liking.

seventeen

Race

Despite all the theories and secondhand rumors that I heard, I could neither understand nor determine for certain why Al Davis had declared war against me. It made no sense.

For all the motives suggested, however, none involved the possibility that the issue might be racial.

Al Davis was many things I didn't admire, but he was no bigot. And the truth of the matter is, the organization he watched over was as color-blind as any you're likely to find in sports today.

The topic of racism was a battle for another front.

In the summer of 1991, *Sports Illustrated* conducted an extensive survey of athletes in pro football, basketball, and major league baseball in an attempt to judge the state of race relations in sports. Two decades earlier, a writer named Jack Olsen had done a series of articles on the black athlete for the magazine and it had been viewed as a groundbreaking event in sports journalism. Now, *SI* wanted to take measure of the progress.

If its editors had anticipated their survey would detail some happy quantum leap, they were misled—and likely disappointed by the responses they received.

Among the things the magazine learned was that 61 percent of the black players who responded felt their salaries were less fair than those earned by whites; 73 percent saw their opportunities for endorsements worse than white teammates; and 77 percent of the blacks felt their chance of moving into a position of team management once their playing days ended was virtually nonexistent.

None of those figures surprised me in the least. What I found most interesting was the fact that of the 2,290 players on the rosters of NFL, NBA, and major-league baseball teams polled, only 301—just 13 percent—responded despite the promise that their answers would remain confidential.

In New Orleans, the Saints strongly discouraged their players from participating in the survey. Mike Kenn, an Atlanta Falcons tackle who was president of the NFL Players Association, made teammates aware that he did not feel it was in anyone's best interest to fill out the questionnaire.

In the Nineties, the subject of race relations has gone underground. The angry street-corner speeches about inequality and injustice have turned into whispered grumbling in secluded corners. For purposes of marketing and maximum goodwill toward the ticket-buyer and corporate sponsors, the sports world has put on a happy face that suggests it has found the magic answer to racial peace and harmony.

Such is no more the case in sports than it is in society in general.

On my questionnaire, I wrote: "I think racism is at its highest point since the civil rights movement in the 1960s and 1970s. I would call it our cancer. There is definitely a lack of awareness and a lack of education. We're not only talking in sports, but in every segment of our society."

I've had little reason to change my opinion since. The cancer remains and continues to grow. It troubles me to see our government so concerned with matters beyond our borders when our greatest problem—racism—is in the streets of our own country.

Yet the majority of today's athletes seem increasingly hesitant to stand up and speak out. They've fallen victim to the social mind-set that causes each of us to think first of ourselves and our own welfare before taking a hard look at the needs of those around us.

The black athlete of today has gone silent. Unlike Muhammad Ali in his day and Jim Brown in his, we, too, seldom take the risks that accompany speaking out on unpopular sub-

jects. We have allowed our opinions to be bought off with
multimillion-dollar contracts and big-buck endorsement deals.

It only emphasizes the incredible courage of those athletes
who pioneered the black cause. Ali spoke out at the height
of his career, with millions of dollars at stake—because he
so strongly believed that the status of his fellow man was
more important. Jim Brown could so easily have been quietly
satisfied with the adulation heaped on him when he was setting all those rushing records for the Cleveland Browns. But
he not only chose to speak his mind but to become an active
participant in the movement for equality. He concerned himself with the plight of the black businessman just as emotionally as he did getting the Browns to another championship.
The quest for popularity never ruled his decisions; fear of
retribution never slowed him. And for that I admire him
greatly.

Today's athlete has become too conditioned to traveling
the safe route, anxious on one hand to show pride in being
black, while at the same time careful to offend no one. The
fear of retribution in the workplace or socially has become a
powerful deterrent.

It is an attitude being encouraged by all around us. Team
management stresses the market value of racial harmony;
product manufacturers make it clear they are not in the business of sponsoring causes.

We would all do well to stop and look at the unselfish
efforts of people like Reggie White of the Green Bay Packers,
who works tirelessly to find new ways to empower the
African-American community.

A football team is made up of a bunch of guys who are
part of the society and culture they've grown up in. Some are
better educated than others, and they come from different economic backgrounds. Some are outgoing, comfortable in
crowds; others more private and relate to only a close circle
of friends. Some like vanilla ice cream, some favor chocolate.
I was taught to be color-blind by my parents. Some weren't.

But is it a signal that racial tension, however subtle, exists
when white members of the team seek seats together on a
charter flight or during a team meal and blacks seem more

comfortable segregating themselves into their own group? I don't think so. Do some players resent it when management and the coaching staff decide it is in the best interest of interracial harmony to mix blacks and whites when making up training-camp rooming lists or hotel assignments on away games? Actually, it is generally a decision made by the athletes themselves. Are there white players who look with disdain on the flashy clothes and jewelry worn by some of the brothers? Again, the answer is yes, just as it would be if you asked some blacks about the cowboy boots, jeans, and western hats favored by some of the white players. But, to take it a step further, it should be pointed out that all white guys don't appreciate the fashion of their white teammates, just as all blacks don't approve of the style favored by some of the brothers. We're talking about personal tastes and personality differences more than black and white.

But, while there may not be full-fledged acceptance of each other's lifestyles, there is generally a tolerance that allows everyone to coexist and work together toward a common goal. And that in itself is a step in the right direction.

There are other issues that concern me more. While the players are generally color-blind, management still has a long way to go.

Some years ago the league initiated a program that had teams invite the coaching staffs from small, predominately black colleges to spend an all-expense-paid week at their training camps, observing, asking questions, getting acquainted. On the surface, it sounded like a wonderful idea, a step toward moving more black coaches onto NFL staffs.

It was a grand public relations gesture and nothing more.

With only the rarest of exceptions, those black coaches, many of them intelligent, enthusiastic, and certainly qualified to move up the professional ladder, remain where they are.

One who I remember speaking with readily admitted that his dream was to work in the NFL. "But," he said, "I'm too good at what I do to be somebody's 'get-back' coach." I wasn't sure what he was talking about and asked him to explain. "Aw, hell, you see them on game day, down there on the sidelines, not really doing much of anything but making sure players don't move too close to the field and draw a penalty. The guy's job is to keep telling the players to 'get back.' That's not what I'm looking for. I'm a coach, a teacher.''

There was a look of resignation in his eyes that troubled me for some time after our conversation. I sensed that he knew the day wasn't likely to ever come when he'd get the opportunity to prove himself at a higher level.

He shares that same unfulfilled dream with black coaches throughout the United States.

With an exception here and there, even those who have managed to get a job on the staff of a pro team face long odds of one day ever becoming the man in charge. When Art Shell was named head coach of the Raiders, there was a great wave of excitement and refueled optimism that finally the doors were swinging open. And, yes, he was eventually followed by Dennis Green at Minnesota, Ray Rhodes with the Eagles, and Tony Dungy at Tampa Bay. But from where I'm sitting, that hardly represents any wholesale change in the timeworn structure of the game. Four head coaches in a half century is not exactly a stampede.

If there is a legitimate effort to catch up with professional basketball and even major-league baseball, and place black men in positions of authority, it is being done in baby-step fashion.

Last year is a prime example. No fewer than eleven head coaching jobs came open in the NFL. And there were precious few black assistants' names on the interview lists. Instead, we saw coaches who had been out of the game for years—Mike Ditka and Dick Vermeil—being called back to duty. I mention their names not because I lack admiration for their coaching abilities. I respect their experience and their accomplishments. But surely there were black coaches, groomed and eager, who deserved some consideration from some owner. Somewhere.

During the course of my career, the two people who have taught me more football than anyone else are Terry Robiskie when we were together with the Raiders (he's now an assistant with the Redskins) and Jimmy Raye, my backfield coach in Kansas City. But you never hear their names mentioned when a head coaching job comes open, despite the fact that each has been in the NFL for twenty years.

To at least some small degree, the fault is their own. Both have so devoted themselves to developing their craft, learning the game inside and out, that they've never concerned themselves with the political skills that today's business world demands. They are not self-promoters, nor have they played to the cronyism that so often seems to determine who moves up the ladder, gets the recognition, and earns the big salary.

They are football coaches and feel a single-minded obligation to concentrate their efforts and energies on making their teams and players the best they can be. That leaves little time for cocktail parties, glad-handing, and backslapping on the banquet circuit.

Yet if I were looking for a coach, their dedication and talent is exactly what I'd want. And the color of their skin would have absolutely nothing to do with it.

Robiskie and Raye are hardly unique. Sherman Lewis, the brilliant offensive coordinator for the Green Bay Packers, is obviously ready to take over a team. I think it's time Elijah Pitts of the Buffalo staff and Emmitt Thomas in Philadelphia got their chances, but I've yet to hear their names come up.

Is there some magic number of blacks allowed into the NFL coaching fraternity? In a time when 67 percent of those playing the game are black, is there still some unspoken but adhered to quota for the number of black head coaches? Does management still hold to some archaic notion that black coaches lack the intelligence and leadership qualities necessary for success?

In a time when major cities throughout the country have black mayors and police chiefs, when the military and the political arena have black men and women making an impact on national policies, when the arts and entertainment world is bursting with black talent—why is it so damn hard to find a few more black men who can coach football at the professional level?

I'm afraid the answer is a complicated one that creates

something of a Catch-22 for many of the established black assistants. To find it you have to understand the paranoia and jealousies that populate the game.

A young coach who suddenly finds himself in the position of authority is often wary of anyone—white or black—around him who might demonstrate a greater knowledge of the game. The safe and easy thing for him to do is man his staff with people he's not only comfortable with but in no danger of feeling inferior to.

Most NFL owners seem comfortable with the low risk that maintaining the status quo offers. While every year or so a successful college coach makes the jump to a head coaching position in the NFL, there has long been a trend that suggests that there are only a select few who have the proper level of expertise to function at the professional level. And they are shuffled around the league in a never-ending game of musical chairs. If a coach is fired in one NFL city, more often than not he quickly moves to another. Then the people in search of his replacement immediately pick someone from the staff of another pro team. It is a recycling process that is bound to run dry of new ideas and fresh innovations at some point.

There is an old two-part adage that suggests that, first, the most difficult task an aspiring coach will ever face is gaining entry into the NFL. But second, once he does, he's got a job on someone's staff forever. I can give you a laundry list of assistant coaches who have been dismissed by a half dozen pro teams during pretty unremarkable careers. Yet their next job is only a phone call away, to an old coaching buddy somewhere in the league who has a favor to repay.

The circle is a very tight one and so select that new membership is a rarity.

The new St. Louis Rams staff that the sixty-year-old Vermeil has put together sounds like the NFL version of the Supreme Court. Among the assistants he initially hired were Bud Carson, sixty-five; Jim Hanifan, sixty-three; Dick Coury, sixty-seven; Mike White, sixty-one; and Jerry Rhome, fifty-five. They're all white and, granted, have had exceptional careers. I can honestly say I have a great deal of admiration for every one of them.

But I was also pleased to later hear that Vermeil had added Carl Hairston, a fine black coach who had worked for Kansas City, to his staff. I'm sure Carl will be a big help to Vermeil as he makes the transition back into the game after his fourteen-year absence.

When will the time come that NFL front offices realize the coaching talent pool is so much deeper; that there are new faces and new ideas out there that will not only benefit their teams but the game as a whole?

It is all part of the invisible blockade that the black coach, hoping to get a foothold, constantly runs up against.

And things aren't getting better. In fact, I'm afraid they're going in the opposite direction. Today the names you hear most often mentioned as bright stars with the potential to become pro head coaches are not NFL assistants, but, rather, successful college coaches like Steve Spurrier at Florida and Rick Neuheisel of Colorado.

The most troubling social problem in pro football today is not in the locker room but in the front offices where hiring and firing decisions are being made.

Is there some concern that white players not give maximum effort for a black head coach? They need only to look to those who played for Shell and the Raiders for the answer to that one. Or talk to Ray Rhodes's Eagles.

In the minds of players, a wonderfully simple logic prevails: A coach is judged by his ability, by his won-lost record, and how he treats his players; not the color of his skin.

The problem becomes something of a Gordian knot that can only be sliced by those who control the game. The all-white ownership in the NFL has to address the fact that it has but a token number of blacks in front-office, decision-making positions. Where is the black general manager who could step up to champion the cause of a qualified assistant who has dutifully prepared himself for a head coaching job?

He doesn't exist, and likely won't until the day comes when there is black ownership.

It is a problem with many layers and too complicated for any person to solve. But as players we have to quit hiding behind the our-job-is-just-to-play-well-on-Sunday attitude and involve ourselves in the issues that affect so many others. It is not a pleasant admission, but we've become too caught up in our individual dramas to look at the big picture.

And I have been one of the guilty parties. But as I've grown older, taking more time to view the world around me, I've realized that a person can't live his life in the comfort of a vacuum. There are people who deserve our help; there are changes we are obligated to make happen.

If our stand is judged unpopular yet shines light on an important truth, then the effort has to be judged worthy.

As the saying goes, a person is rich by what he gives, not what he keeps.

Personally, I have no coaching ambitions. Neither do a number of the black athletes I've played with and against. But that is no reason to ignore those who do and are being denied the opportunity to realize their dreams.

And it my responsibility to speak out for them.

Despite great improvement—particularly on the part of the players—there are still racial problems in the NFL. Just as there are in every corner of American society. We are nothing more or less than a reflection of the world in which we live. And we still have a great deal of work to do.

The most immediate thing I had to deal with as the '91 season got under way was a bad knee. In our opener against the Houston Oilers, I attempted a cut to avoid an onrushing defensive back and felt a posterior ligament pop. It was an injury for which I could give full credit to artificial turf—which I despise—since no Houston player even touched me.

The best way I can describe artificial turf is to liken it to a giant slab of concrete covered by a thin rug. It does not give at all to the force of your body as you run or are pounded into it by a tackler. And since something has to give—all that force has to go somewhere—it is absorbed by the body, rattling your eye teeth. Natural turf, on the other hand, not only has give to it, but offers a far more comforting cushion for a fall.

· · ·

Craig and Mueller would have my job by default, as I spent two months on injured reserve, missing eight games while attempting to rehab myself back into playing condition.

The separation I felt from the team was even worse than it had been in '89. By the time I returned in early November, I held little hope that I would play much, despite the fact that our running attack had been almost nonexistent.

I was surprised when I was told I would start against Kansas City in the final game of the regular season. It wasn't one of those spectacular comebacks that all athletes fantasize about, but I did get 55 yards on just nine carries and caught five passes for 45. The Chiefs beat us by a touchdown, and at 9–7 we headed into the play-offs as a wild-card entry.

Ironically, our opponent was again to be Kansas City. Playing in Arrowhead Stadium this time, they proved the previous week's win had been no fluke. This time we didn't even score a touchdown as they eliminated us, 10–6.

The Raiders were once again headed in the wrong direction. And my future didn't even really seem to exist.

One off-season evening, I recently learned, Al Davis had emerged from his office to make conversation with an administrative assistant who was working late. "Let me ask you something," Davis reportedly said. "Who do you think is the best player we have on our team right now?"

The assistant pondered the question, knowing that the answer would not be the one his boss wanted to hear. "Very honestly, Mr. Davis," he said, "I'd have to say it is Marcus Allen."

"Aw, fuck," Al said before retreating back into his office.

I did everything I could think of to put football out of my mind during the off-season. I played golf. I tried white-water rafting. I did some salmon fishing in Alaska. Kathryn and I traveled a good deal.

Yet rarely was my mind off the seemingly unresolvable problems I was having with the man I worked for.

eighteen

Monday Night in Miami

The mind games escalated as the 1992 season began.

It had been a long-standing practice of the Raiders to make room assignments for training camp early in the summer when everyone reported for the first off-season minicamp. Ronnie Lott, my old USC teammate and All-Pro defensive back with the San Francisco 49ers, had become a free agent and, to my delight, was signed by the Raiders. It seemed natural to ask if he would like to be my roommate during training camp.

I felt he'd be more comfortable with someone he knew, and at the same time I wanted to help him get to know the other members of the team as quickly as possible. It would also simply be nice to spend some time getting reacquainted.

Thus we both asked to be assigned to one of the suites at the Radisson when camp got under way and considered the matter closed.

But on the day I reported to Oxnard, offensive coordinator Terry Robiskie called me aside and told me that Al Davis had sent word that he didn't want Ronnie and me rooming together. More specifically, Davis didn't want Lott rooming with me. Terry didn't have to explain further. No doubt Davis feared that I would set about poisoning the mind of our new defensive back the minute we were behind closed doors.

So I enjoyed the luxury of having an entire suite to myself throughout the drudgery of camp. And I don't think any of my teammates minded, since rooming with me had become something of a jinx. My three previous roommates—Rod Martin, Frank Hawkins, and Matt Millen—had seen their careers as Raiders end shortly after sharing living space with me.

I lived alone, feeling as if I was being quarantined, in the spacious living accommodations the Raiders provided. Each suite had two bedrooms, a loft, a kitchen, color television, fireplace, private phone—and thanks to Al, Lott and I wound up being the only players to enjoy such luxury in private.

I also learned upon my arrival that I was again listed fourth among the running backs on the depth chart. No longer even considered the team's third-down specialist, I would be used in short yardage situations—if at all. The latest back Davis had imported to replace me was Eric Dickerson, the former Rams All-Pro.

By the time the regular season got under way, I was being told even before games that I wouldn't be playing.

So I decided on a silent protest. On Sundays I took a spot at the far end of the bench and remained there until I heard my name called. What that would immediately tell me was that it was third or fourth down, short yardage was needed, and the play I would be called to run would be I-Right-14.

Immediately after the play was run and the pile would untangle, I would jog directly back to my spot on the bench to await my next call.

Emotionally drained, I had made up my mind that if all they wanted was a third-down back, that was all they would get. I'd made up my mind to give no more, no less than what was being asked of me.

Following one game, my mother asked about my new routine. "Why are you sitting way over there, away from the rest of the team?" she wanted to know. I told her it was my way of calling attention to my situation.

She seemed surprised, even disappointed. "Son," she said, "I've never known you to call attention to yourself."

As I look back on it all, I was probably hurting myself far more than those with whom I was so angry. But I must admit that I got a kick out of the T-shirts that some people began wearing to the Coliseum on game days. Across their front was printed the message FREE MARCUS ALLEN.

One Friday afternoon we were in the meeting room, going over the game plan with Joe Scannella. As the meeting broke up and we were leaving, Joe called me back inside and told me that I wouldn't be playing at all the following Sunday.

The more I thought about it, the angrier I got. By the time we went out onto the field for our regular Friday run-through, I couldn't even talk. When the offensive players began trotting to one end of the field and the defense to the other, I just pulled off my helmet and sat on it at the 50-yard line. I sat there for some time, staring into space, saying nothing to anyone while practice went on around me. In retrospect, I must have looked pretty ridiculous. After a while I got up and walked into the locker room.

I was in no mood to practice. Why should I when I knew that hell would freeze solidly before I got the opportunity to get into Sunday's game?

I showered, dressed, and was preparing to leave when Terry Robiskie came in. "What the fuck are you doing?" I think he was concerned that I was walking away from the team for good.

Even before I could answer, he began offering advice. "Go ahead, take the day off. Do what you've got to do to cool down. But you're going to be back tomorrow, right?"

"Why should I? I've already been told I'm not playing Sunday."

"Marcus, listen to me. You can't let them get to you. Tomorrow's payday. You get your ass here and pick up your check just like everybody else. Don't do something stupid like giving them their money back."

Leaving, I took a long drive, trying to sort things out and decide what I might be able to do to get myself out of the hopeless trap I was in. And I found myself thinking about what Terry had said about the money.

And that was the greatest paradox of the whole mess. There I was, seething with anger and indignation, wanting so badly to be treated fairly and to stand by principles that I honestly believed were important. But like everyone else, I was also a slave to the money.

Finally, I drove home and telephoned Art Shell to apologize and try once again to explain to him the frustration I was feeling. "Art, I'm tired of being treated like shit. I've had all of it I can stand. I don't want to play here any more."

There was a long silence before he replied. He and the coaching staff had been resigned to the idea of trading me for some time. He knew how unhappy I was. "Marcus," he said, "you know I don't have anything to do with this. But Mr. Davis won't let you go."

If there had ever been any question in my mind about what was going on, that answered it. Al Davis would rather torture me, teach me some sadistic lesson, than let me go somewhere and play. And get on with my life.

It wasn't long afterward that I learned that the Green Bay Packers had called and asked about making some sort of deal for me. Davis, I was told, had unleashed a barrage of expletives directed at me, then said, "I'm never trading the son of a bitch."

After we'd lost our first two games of the season, I tried going directly to the source of my problem. It was rare when a player ventured into the waiting area of Al Davis's office, but there I stood, telling his secretary that it was urgent that I speak to him.

Once inside, I unloaded. "I've tried every way I know to do things the right way!" I shouted. "I've worked my butt off and it doesn't seem to matter. So now I just don't care. You can trade me. Hell, even cut me if you want to. But I want the fuck out of here."

The entire purpose of my tirade was to upset him, push him to that infamous anger point I'd heard so much about. With a snap of a finger, he'd fired people over seemingly trivial matters. Maybe I'd get lucky and be one of them.

Instead, he leaned back in his chair and simply nodded. "Of course, the final decision is that of the coaches," he said. "But, okay, I'll see what I can do."

Several days later he sent word to me that he'd done some

checking around the league and found that nobody was interested in me.

Thus I made a decision that had not come easy. I filed a free agency lawsuit against the Raiders and the NFL, fully aware that I was literally risking my career. I carefully weighed the consequences and knew that there was a chance that I would be branded a troublemaker, maybe even blackballed by the other owners in the league. It was a tricky situation in which I knew I would be damned if I did, damned if I didn't. I had nothing to lose and everything to lose. But the bottom line was that I had become convinced that it was the only chance I had to free myself from Davis's hold.

Needless to say, Al wasn't pleased.

RONNIE LOTT: *To me, the mark that Marcus has made on the game goes well beyond the remarkable things he's accomplished during his career, beyond the fact that he continues to play at such a high performance level after fifteen years in the league. Marcus has always wanted to make a difference, to offer encouragement to others. By his own actions, on and off the field, he's made a lot of people better.*

When I was thinking about joining the Raiders toward the end of my career, I talked with him about it and never once did he mention anything about the personal difficulties he was having. Instead, he praised Art Shell, said he was going to be a great head coach, and urged me to come on board and help him out.

The first indication I had that Marcus was having problems with the front office came during my first meeting with Al Davis. I'd made up my mind to sign with him and we were discussing what my general role would be. I'd made it clear that I wanted the opportunity to compete for a starting position and he assured me that would be the case. "And, don't worry," he said, "this thing with 'your guy' won't have any effect on your chances here."

I didn't even know who he was referring to, who "my guy" was supposed to be. Only later did I realize that he was talking about Marcus.

Watching what was done to Marcus Allen during the time

I was with the Raiders is, without a doubt, one of the low points in my football career. I hope I never have to watch another person go through what he endured.

And what was it all about? To this day I'm not sure anyone really knows. There was a lot of speculation: Some suggested that Marcus had not been Mr. Davis's draft choice and he resented the fact that someone he hadn't hand-chosen had done so well. Others said it was because Marcus enjoyed greater popularity in Los Angeles than Mr. Davis. There was even the suggestion that Mr. Davis felt Marcus's performance in the Super Bowl took the spotlight away from him and the Raiders organization that he was so proud of building. Some wondered if it could be as simple as the fact that Marcus lacked the kind of speed Mr. Davis felt essential for a running back.

None of which made much sense to me. I'd always been a great admirer of the Raiders and their "commitment to excellence" policy. Mr. Davis, obviously, was a winner. But so was Marcus Allen. They were pursuing the same goal. They both wanted to win as badly as any people I've ever been around.

Despite what some might have you believe, football isn't that complicated. The cardinal rule is that you put your best people on the field if you want to win. Period. No rocket science involved. I could never understand—and don't to this day—why the Raiders wouldn't give one of the greatest players in the game's history the opportunity to help us accomplish that objective.

If it was personal, as so many have suggested, why should everyone be made to suffer? Why couldn't whatever differences existed be set aside for the good of the team? The whole thing sent a conflicting message about what the club's "commitment to excellence" slogan really meant.

As I said, I've always admired the Silver-and-Black and the things they have accomplished: the Super Bowl championships, the incredible winning percentages, the manner in which they could bring in such a divergent collection of personalities and mold them into great teams, all the Hall of

Famers they have produced. The Raiders organization has built a remarkable legacy.

Unfortunately, there will always be an asterisk attached that need not have been. The Raiders will forever be remembered as the team that wouldn't let Marcus Allen, a certain Hall of Fame selection, play.

As I watched this weird situation play out, I was amazed at how Marcus managed to deal with it. Everyone knew he was dying inside, but outwardly he remained upbeat, as if to prove to everyone that he had no intention of letting Mr. Davis beat him down.

He put on a damn good face, but everyone on the team recognized his suffering. It was like seeing a man in bondage.

Then, when they came out with the statement about Marcus Allen being a "cancer" on our team, I couldn't believe it. They weren't talking about the man I had known since USC days. Or the one I'd faced as a defensive back while playing for the San Francisco 49ers.

I remember all too well the first time we went against each other as pros. He was in his rookie year and I was determined that I was going to give him a sample of what the NFL was all about. We'd both learned the same lesson at Southern Cal: On every play you hit the other guy as hard as you can. If he doesn't get up, that's his tough luck.

Early in the game Marcus took a handoff, slid off-tackle, and turned up the sideline. I had a clear shot at him and was thrilled at the opportunity to rattle his teeth. I was already envisioning the kind of blow that was sure to make the highlights film. But just as I prepared to deliver it, he did this quick 360-degree turn and went on his way while I lay there with my mouth full of grass.

I know where Marcus's heart is. I've always believed that one of the greatest things about sports is that it puts a person's true character on display. And Marcus is a winner. Even when he was forced to sit on the bench, not allowed to contribute, there was not a player on the team who wanted us to succeed more than Marcus.

I remember a stretch of games early in the '92 season when nothing was going right. We'd lost four in a row and were *getting ready to travel to New York and play the Giants. After a rather lackluster practice, it was decided that we needed to have a players-only meeting to try and get things headed in a positive direction.*

It was Marcus who did most of the talking. Though he had been in on just a handful of plays during the season and wasn't even mentioned in the game plan for the Giants, he took the floor and spoke his mind, offering criticism and suggestions, urging everyone to focus on the task at hand.

You could have heard a pin drop in the locker room as he spoke of Raiders football, of the responsibility we had to the coaches, and the proud team tradition we weren't living up to.

For all his inspirational efforts, however, we played terribly in the first two quarters against the Giants and trailed at halftime. Marcus hadn't played a down.

But in the locker room he again went on a tirade, getting into the faces of his teammates. "This isn't Raiders football!" he yelled. "I saw quitters out there and I'm embarrassed. Damn it, that's not the Raiders' way. We're better than this."

In the second half we got it together, made a pretty remarkable comeback, and won the game. Yet Marcus wasn't allowed in for a single play, wasn't given the courtesy of being even a small part of what at the time was a very important victory for us. This despite the fact that it had, in my opinion, been his words at halftime that provided the spark we so desperately needed.

I knew that afternoon as I walked off the field that there would never again be any fairness for Marcus so long as he wore a Raiders uniform.

Inside the locker room I made my way through the celebration that had broken out and walked in the direction of his locker. I found him sitting there alone, tears streaming down his face.

I wasn't feeling sorry for myself. They were tears bred of a degree of anger I'd never before experienced. The last straw had been broken. I'd gone up to Terry Robiskie after the game and asked him why I hadn't played. He'd just raised his palm, shrugged, and said, "Marcus, I don't know."

I did. And as I sat in the locker room, bawling, my hands shaking with rage, I began looking around for Al Davis. "Where is the motherfucker?" I asked Vince Evans.

"Marcus, calm down."

"I'm going to kick his ass," I replied. "I'm going to . . ." Even before I could complete my threat, I felt Vince's grip on one arm and Robiskie's on the other. Steve Smith and Ronnie Lott had me by the waist. They hurriedly steered me into an adjacent room and shut the door, standing guard while waiting for me to calm down.

On Monday, as we gathered to review game films, Art passed out game balls and congratulations on the much-needed win, then paused and cleared his throat before dismissing us. "One more thing," he said. "If anyone has problems with the amount of playing time he's getting, I'd prefer that he come to me and talk about it rather than disrupting the team's well-deserved victory celebration."

He was looking squarely at me as he spoke.

For a couple of seconds I just sat there, not wanting to turn the matter into a public forum. But what the hell, everyone in the place knew what was going on and who he was talking to. And so I responded.

"Art, I *have* come to you. I've told you that I want out. I've asked you to get me out of here. I've told you that I hate this fucking place."

When I was finished, you could have heard a pin drop.

The last thing I wanted was a confrontation with Art Shell in full view of the team and coaches. I knew he was caught in the middle. But it seemed to me he'd chosen sides. Unfortunately, he wasn't on mine.

The sum total of my contribution in the weeks to come would be in short-yardage situations. And even those were coming fewer and farther between. For all practical purposes, I was no longer a part of the team.

I finally decided it was time to play Al's game.

Throughout my career I had always attempted to be cooperative with the media. If they wanted to talk about the game, I felt a responsibility to answer their questions as honestly as possible. But even as the questions about my lack of playing time became more and more frequent, I had declined to discuss it, stubbornly holding out hope that somehow the problem could be resolved privately.

In time I became convinced it would never be.

On several occasions, Al Michaels, the play-by-play man for ABC's *Monday Night Football*, had approached me to see if I was interested in talking about my situation. He would ask it in a half-joking manner and my response was always to laugh it off. But as a friend and occasional off-season chess rival, Al knew me pretty well. He was aware of how frustrated I had become.

Al never pushed the issue, but continued to bring it up now and then. Finally, he phoned me at home one evening after reading a Jim Murray column in the *Los Angeles Times*, which questioned what Murray rightfully perceived as a standoff between Davis and me.

"You ready to talk yet?" Michaels asked.

I think I surprised him when I told him I might be, but wanted to think about it for a day or two. He told me that if I did decide to do an interview, ABC would be interested in airing it during halftime of our upcoming game against the Dolphins.

I called him back a day or so later and told him I was ready to do it.

Normally, when ABC does an interview for its Monday night game, it is taped on Sunday evening in a TV studio or hotel room in the city where the game is being played. Al suggested that since his Brentwood home was only five blocks away from mine, we do it there before leaving for Miami.

When I arrived on Saturday afternoon, a camera crew had already set up in his living room. For a few minutes we talked about the questions he had in mind to ask. "Any second thoughts?" he finally asked.

"No, I'm ready."

The interview lasted maybe a half hour. From it, Michaels

and his producer would edit it down to the few minutes that would actually air.

For the first time I was candid about my situation. Responding to Michaels's questions, I admitted that my relationship with Al Davis had been, at best, acrimonious for quite some time. Now, I believed, he was trying to ruin my career, destroy my marketability, and kill any chance I might have of ever one day being elected to the Hall of Fame. The decision whether or not I played rested with Davis, not Art Shell. Yes, I told him, I was frustrated and badly wanted the opportunity to play somewhere else.

As soon as the cameras and lights went off, there was dead silence among those who had been involved in the filming. Even Al didn't say anything for several seconds.

It was only after we left the room and walked toward the kitchen that he spoke. "You know," he said, "this is going to create quite a stir." I sensed he had some concern that my comments might have a far more damaging effect on my career than I realized. He suggested I go home and think about the things we'd discussed and call him if there was anything I had reservations about.

I phoned him around ten and assured him I was comfortable with everything I'd said. He told me he would be back in touch to read me the transcript of the portion of the interview that was to be aired.

"And you know," he said, "out of fairness we've got to give Davis the opportunity to respond."

Despite what he called the explosive nature of the interview, it had been determined that there would be no pre-game publicity about it. Al said that ABC executives were concerned that my going public might somehow have a negative effect on the way the Raiders played, and the last thing *Monday Night Football* needed was to be blamed for having an impact on the outcome of a game.

What he would do, he said, was contact both Davis and Art Shell on Monday afternoon, tell them about the interview, and give each an opportunity to respond. Then, at some point during the first quarter, they would mention what was coming up at halftime.

I said nothing about it to any of my teammates.

At mid-afternoon on Monday, Michaels called Davis in his hotel suite and read him the transcript of what would be airing nationwide six hours later. Davis was speechless for several seconds, then told Michaels, "Aw, shit. He's such a fucking liar."

He was told that the interview would air and ABC was ready to allow him equal time to respond. The options offered him were to do a live response following my interview, do a taped response at the hotel or in the broadcast booth before the game, verbally respond but not go on camera, give a written response, or do nothing.

"Let me call you back," he told Michaels.

Art was equally upset but said he had no interest in getting into a war of words. He declined to be interviewed.

As the clock ticked toward halftime, I finally turned to Steve Smith and Lionel Washington, who were seated beside me on the bench. "Well," I said, "in a few minutes the shit's going to really hit the fan."

Neither had the slightest idea what I was talking about.

I was surprised how calm I felt about the matter. There were no regrets, no reservations. Actually, I had begun to feel a surprising sense of relief after doing the interview. With the decision to file the suit, and now the soon-to-be public airing of my grievances, I felt I had sent the loudest and clearest message I could that there was no way I would return to the Raiders for another season.

As the game ended, Al Michaels wrapped up the telecast by saying, "And so the Dolphins hand the Raiders their eighth loss of the season . . . and the long-silent Marcus Allen has spoken."

In the brief written response Davis had decided to make, he dismissed what I had said as the words of "a disgruntled aging veteran."

That Miami defeated us, 20–7, seemed of little interest to the media. As photographers and television cameramen tried to position themselves near our bench during the third quarter to get pictures of me, Al LoCasale, Davis's executive assistant, was doing a bizarre dance in an attempt to block their way and make certain I spoke to no one.

His efforts were unnecessary. I had said all I intended to say about the matter.

In the locker room afterward, Al Davis vanished into the off-limits area of the training room before the media was allowed inside. There would be no further comment from him.

On the flight home, I sat silently tapping thoughts into a laptop computer that Kathryn had bought for me. The trip back to the West Coast was one of the quietest I could ever remember. Few players were talking. And none were talking to me. It was as if everyone feared that by giving even the slightest signal of support to me, he might also find himself in Davis's doghouse as well. I felt like Typhoid Marcus.

And it made me sad to know that my teammates were trapped in a situation that made it necessary for them to apply such caution and put such distance between our friendships.

The following week it was easier to understand. Davis, who had refused to make any additional public comment on my situation, was telling others in the front office that he was strongly considering a defamation-of-character lawsuit against Michaels and ABC for what he called "a fuckin' ambush." He summoned Art Shell into his office and told him that as the head coach it was his obligation to respond.

Art, who I'm sure had hoped such a chore would never become a part of his job description, soon found himself being interviewed by CBS's Jim Gray, one of the few network announcers who had seemingly maintained a close friendship with Davis.

On national television Shell struck back in the name of the Raiders organization, insisting to Gray that I was a liar.

Had those bitter words come directly from Al Davis, not spoken by a man I had so long respected as a teammate and coach, I would have been neither surprised nor upset. But hearing them from Art Shell sent me into a funk that lasted for days.

I couldn't wait for the final two weeks of the season to pass. I had no enthusiasm for the games ahead, nothing left to give even if called upon. For me, the season was already over.

San Diego defeated us handily the following week, setting up the season finale in Washington on the day after Christmas.

TERRY ROBISKIE: *I've been on the sidelines for some strange games during my life, but I've never experienced anything like that cold afternoon in Redskins Stadium. We went into it 6–9 and out of the play-offs, and the coaching staff was wondering how in the hell we'd be able to get the team motivated to end the year on a positive note.*

It started when Greg Townsend, one of our defensive ends, told a reporter that the team was going to dedicate the game to Marcus. I've never seen anything like it. Guys were out there all day, playing their asses off and coming to the sidelines with tears streaming down their cheeks. I've never seen so many players crying during a game; never seen a team feeling such pain and frustration.

Marcus Allen played very sparingly, going in on short-yardage downs now and then. Still, he sparked a late come-back that enabled us to win, 21–20. And all I could think was that I couldn't believe his days with the Raiders were over. Hell, I felt like crying, too.

I did. On that final day of my career with the Los Angeles Raiders, a great sense of irony swept over me. Throughout the season, I'd never felt so removed from the players on the team. Yet on that afternoon in Washington, despite all that had transpired, despite the fact that I had played no real role in the victory, I'd never felt closer to my teammates.

I was greatly moved when I later learned that the members of the team had voted to give me the ''commitment to excellence'' award that went annually to the player judged the most inspirational on the squad. (Actually, I was the co-winner since there had been a tie in the voting between Terry McDaniels and me, something I found a bit unusual since there were an odd number of players on the team to cast ballots.)

I had received the award on four previous occasions during my Raiders career, but this particular time the honor was even more special. In my judgment, it stood as the loudest and most important statement made about me during the traumatic season.

PART III

The name of peace is sweet
and the thing itself is good,
but between peace and
slavery there is a great
difference.

—Cicero

nineteen

Home Shopping

And so, after eleven seasons as a member of the Raiders, it had finally ended. On one hand, I felt as if the weight of the world was lifted from my shoulders. I was liberated, free, and finally had reason to look optimistically to the future. On the other, I felt no small measure of sadness over leaving behind friends and teammates I had been so close to over the years.

There also was some apprehension. I was a thirty-three-year-old running back about whom there were questions. Playing in a position where the average NFL career lasts something like five years, I'd long since gone beyond the life expectancy. I felt great, I'd taken good care of myself, and I was physically sound. But there would be those who wondered if I could still play.

Certainly, I'd had little opportunity to prove myself in those last years with the Raiders. I could loudly proclaim my fitness from the highest mountaintop and *Monday Night Football*, yet I knew there would still be those around the league who assumed that my limited play was nothing more than a coaching decision, based on the fact that I no longer had the ability or desire to compete at the professional level.

Thus I began the process of seeking a new playing home with a mixture of excitement and concern. The latter disappeared quickly when Ed Hookstratten phoned with a list of teams around the league that were looking for a running back and were eager to talk with me. I narrowed the list of five:

Seattle, Washington, Miami, Kansas City, and the New York Giants.

In my mind, I'd already picked the team I wanted to play for but said nothing to Ed. Rather, I took his advice: Look at them all, weigh everything, then let him negotiate to see who was willing to pay top dollar. So off I went, feeling a bit like a high school recruit again.

My first visit was to the Seahawks, where Tom Flores had resumed his coaching career. I'd played well for Tom during his tenure as coach of the Raiders and felt certain that he, better than most, would understand the circumstances of my limited playing time in recent years. He'd seen Al Davis in action from a much closer vantage point than I'd ever enjoyed.

I've always loved the city of Seattle, and the day of my visit there was one that should have been printed on a postcard. There were blue, cloudless skies, a cool breeze blowing off the ocean, and everything appeared so pristine. It wouldn't be a bad place to call home.

More important, the Seahawks were a first-class organization and one that had a real chance to soon develop into a championship contender. And in addition to being a very good coach, Flores was a straight-shooter. He had an excellent running back in Chris Warren and was candid when he explained that he felt Warren would be difficult to displace from the starting lineup.

The only thing I wanted to hear was that I would be given a fair chance to win the starting job. Flores assured me everyone is given that opportunity with the Seahawks. On the other hand, he was honest. What he badly needed was a third-down specialist, someone who could fill the role of a receiver out of the back field.

Would I be interested in that kind of job? I told him I'd have to think about it.

Next stop, Kansas City. For no reason other than the fact that I just simply wasn't able to visualize myself as a player for the Chiefs, I'd placed them last on my list of possibilities. I knew the organization was outstanding and had a great deal of respect for their coach, Marty Schottenheimer, both when he'd been in Cleveland and since he'd come to the Chiefs. I saw or heard nothing that diminished my admiration for the Chiefs, but I still couldn't see myself in their uniform.

But after a couple of days in K.C., I made a mental note that it could be a wonderful place to live. While offering all the benefits of a metropolitan area, it had the warm, friendly feel of a small town. And there seemed to be a great relationship between the community and the Chiefs.

And Marty quickly put to rest my concerns that he might doubt my ability to play. In fact, he'd done that several weeks earlier when we'd had an opportunity to visit at the Frank Sinatra golf tournament.

For some time I'd been aware of a story that had evidently originated with Al Davis. Supposedly he'd once received a phone call from Marty, who had shared with Davis his belief that I was a first-class troublemaker. Prompting the call, I was told, was something that had happened at the Pro Bowl following the 1987 season. What I had thought was a joke, keeping in spirit with the fun the season-ending game is supposed to be, had become a cause of concern to me.

For reasons I've never understood, the AFC team seemed always to take the game far more seriously than the players from the NFC. And the year Schottenheimer and his Cleveland staff coached us was no exception. While the NFC spent the week leading up to the game working out in only shorts and helmets, we went at it in full pads. Our practices were longer and far more intense. While we knocked heads on one end of the practice field, the NFC players played grab-ass on the other. They seemed to be having a lot more fun.

One afternoon as we returned to the locker room, I overheard Hanford Dixon, the Cleveland Browns defensive back, complaining. He'd worked hard all season, he said, was battered and bruised, and had hoped his visit to Hawaii would be a fun-filled reward for all his efforts. He asked why we should be put through such rigors for an all-star game people would forget the moment the final gun sounded.

So I made an offhand suggestion. What if we all just showed up on the practice field the following day wearing only shorts and helmets as the NFC players were certain to again do? "What will they do?" I asked. "Bring in a scab team to replace us?"

Dixon took the ball and ran with it. "Will you do it?" he asked me.

"Hell, yes!"

With that he began circulating among the players, promoting the idea, collecting support. The next afternoon we all stood on the field, our pads left in our lockers, awaiting the arrival of Marty and his coaches.

When he came onto the field, it was obvious that he was surprised. But not missing a beat, he began nodding his approval. "Good," he said with a smile. "Very good. Like I said, we need to start slacking off some so we'll be fresh and ready to play."

It had really been no big thing; no feelings got hurt, no insurrection was threatened. Still, the story suggested to me sometime later was that Schottenheimer had privately been fire-breathing livid and phoned Davis to tell him what a jerk I was.

As we had breakfast one morning during the Sinatra tournament, I decided to ask him about it. "It never happened," he assured me. "In the first place, I thought the whole thing was pretty funny. And, second, I didn't know you were the brains behind the scheme. No, I never called Al."

As I left Kansas City, I promised Schottenheimer that we would stay in touch.

Deep down, I doubt there is any professional athlete who hasn't fantasized about playing for one of the New York teams. Not only is New York considered the media center of the sports universe, but the subsidiary benefits of playing there can be endless. While I could not see making it my long-term home, the idea of experiencing the pace and excitement of New York was intriguing.

For that reason I felt an additional pump of adrenaline as I met with Giants head coach Dan Reeves. I'd been a great admirer of his for a long time, going back to my childhood days when he'd played running back on some of the first great Dallas Cowboys teams. Then there had been his remarkable success with the Denver Broncos before moving to New York.

We got along well and the trip was enjoyable, but I was disappointed to learn that what Reeves was in the market for was someone to serve as a backup.

On the other hand, Washington Redskins coach Richie Pettibone said he was always looking for ways to make his lineup better. He'd make certain that I got the opportunity to compete for the starting job. At the same time, he needed some assurance that I would be willing to function in the role of a third-down back in the event I wasn't a starter.

For a couple of days I saw the city, visited with a number of the players and the coaching staff, met the fabled team owner, Jack Kent Cooke, and considered what for me was one of the biggest pluses the Redskins had to offer. Their home games were played on grass and the prospect of having a minimum of eight games a season away from the rock-hard artificial surfaces that dominated the league sounded great.

Before leaving I told Pettibone that I felt I could deal with the idea of playing a limited role if it came to that. But deep down I knew that to accept a backup spot, when what I really wanted was to win a starting job, was not altogether truthful.

Still, I was trying to remain open-minded, to put all vanity and ego aside and make a decision that was best for my future.

I privately believed that future was in Miami as a member of Don Shula's Dolphins. It would be the best of all worlds, playing for one of the most legendary coaches in the history of the game on a team that was directed by a quarterback like Dan Marino. I felt I would fit well into the offense they ran, liked their personnel, and the idea of living and playing in warm weather. Their modern, new facilities and the fact that Florida has no state taxes were additional bonuses.

I had purposely scheduled my visit to Miami last, feeling that it would take little persuasion to convince me to become a Dolphin for the remainder of my playing career. Everything I saw there impressed me. Coach Shula, rather than dwell on the X's and O's of football, suggested we attend a Florida Marlins game.

I returned to California eager to learn what my agent had heard. Ed started with the bad news.

Part of the routine procedure when visiting clubs as a prospective player is a physical examination by team doctors at each stop. "The Dolphins," Ed told me, "are concerned about your knee."

I had had a couple of knee injuries while playing for the Raiders, but I had been able to rehabilitate without the need for surgery and had never had a long-term problem. When told that I'd easily passed the exams of every other team, I was even more perplexed—and disappointed.

Ed translated for me: What the Dolphins were saying was that they didn't have the money necessary to sign me.

The contract offer made by the Redskins was loaded with incentive clauses. To earn the salary I felt I deserved, I'd have to accomplish a laundry list of things, like starting a certain number of games, gaining a certain number of yards, catching a certain number of passes, etc. If I failed to reach the levels spelled out in their offer, I would find myself playing for an amount that was considerably below the figure I had in mind.

Which left Seattle, New York, and Kansas City.

Throughout the process, Marty Schottenheimer had been the only one of the coaches who stayed in touch. In his calls to me there was no pressure, no sound of urgency, just a reminder that he was interested in having me in Kansas City. By the way, he would casually mention, did I tell you that plans are under way to convert Arrowhead Stadium to a grass field in another year?

Then, a couple of weeks later, he called with yet another interesting tidbit. "You'll be hearing about it soon," he said, "but I wanted you to know that we've made a deal to get Joe Montana from the 49ers."

He didn't have to tell me what the acquisition of the man I considered the greatest quarterback playing the game would do to the Kansas City offense. I felt certain they were already rewriting their playbook to take full advantage of his passing abilities. The Chiefs, who had been a grind-it-up-the-middle and occasional throw-deep kind of team, were about to open the throttle.

Shortly after the deal was announced, Joe called. "Hey, Marcus, we need to talk."

Still stubbornly determined to consider all my options, the last thing I needed was for Joe Montana to begin twisting my arm. "Joe," I said, "it's great to hear from you. Look, buddy, I'm on another line. Let me call you right back."

I never returned the call. Yet I found myself adding to the list of positives about the Chiefs. Their offensive coordinator, Paul Hackett, had been an assistant at USC who I had liked and admired. And I'd been impressed with Jimmy Raye, the team's running back coach. And the job I aspired to was wide open since the previous year's starters were gone. Barry Word had gone to the Vikings and Christian Okoya was still suffering the effects of a severe knee injury.

Not lost on me was the fact that the contract offered by the Chiefs was better than anyone else had made.

Soon I was flying back to the Midwest to attend a press conference at which I was introduced as a new member of the Kansas City Chiefs.

There are things in life that can only be described as serendipitous. For all the planning and weighing and effort you might put into the decision-making process, there are elements that go well beyond your control. Sometimes, simply put, a person just finds himself in the right place at the right time.

Kansas City was my place and time.

There was only one other matter to attend to before taking leave of Los Angeles. On June 26, two weeks after I'd become a Kansas City Chief, Kathryn and I were married. She had asked O.J. if we could have the ceremony at his Brentwood home and he had immediately set about making arrangements.

Kathryn and I exchanged vows under the canopy of two big trees in O.J.'s yard. There was wonderful music and great food. As I looked around the beautifully decorated grounds that evening, feeling better than I had in years, many of my old Raiders teammates were there. Most, it occurred to me, were in Al Davis's doghouse for one reason or another.

• • •

These days I think very little about my conflicts with Al Davis unless someone brings up the matter. Yet as I look back on it all, I find the whole rule-by-fear mentality that he used to drive the Raiders really sad.

Somewhere along the way, Davis lost track of where the man ends and the myth begins. I feel sorry for the guy. But I also learned from him.

There was a time when I was a very vengeful person. If someone gave me a cheap shot, I didn't rest until I got him back, whether it was on the next play, the next game, or the next season. I remember a time when I was still playing for the Raiders that a Seattle defender grabbed me by the face mask and forced me to bite completely through my upper lip. I swore I'd get him. But it was near the end of the year, so I had to wait a whole season. When the Seahawks released him during the off-season, I remember being bitterly disappointed because I had been so looking forward to kicking his ass the next time we played.

For a long time I felt that way about Al Davis. I hated him, not only for what he'd done to me, but for the way he treated virtually everyone in the Raiders organization. During my first couple of years with Kansas City, I literally dreamed of going into Los Angeles and having great games and then looking up at him in his owner's suite and shooting him the finger.

But that's history now.

Do I have any regrets about doing the *Monday Night* interview that brought our problems into the open? None at all. The time had come for me to speak out, and I have no apologies to make for that. All I did was tell the truth, using the same ploy Al Davis had used. I went on national television on a Monday night when the largest audience possible would be listening to what I had to say. I just played his game.

What caused our problem was not the fact that I'd won the Heisman Trophy or was the Super Bowl MVP, or even that I enjoyed a certain degree of popularity in Los Angeles. The problem was that I stepped outside Al's box of control. I refused to be intimidated by him. I saw how he dealt with people in a manner that smacked of slavery and wanted no part of it. I'd seen so many casualties during my years with the Raiders, watched loyal, hardworking people have their lives turned upside-down by his cruel, angry whims. That people could be so afraid of him and his constant threat of retribution became very troubling to me.

And so I became the guy who stood up and said, "Hey, the emperor has no clothes."

When this book is published, I fully expect some of those who witnessed many of the events I've recalled to suddenly develop amnesia rather than risk Al's wrath. Rest assured, he will call out orders to someone in his organization, telling them to follow in the footsteps of Art Shell and assure the public that everything I've written is lies. Another prediction: Doing the interview will be Jim Gray.

Remember the fable about the frog and the scorpion? The scorpion begs the frog to allow him to ride his back to safety across a swollen river. The wary frog makes known his concern that the scorpion, once safely across, might sting him. But the scorpion pleads and promises he'll do no such thing. Then, just as the trusting frog swims him to safety, the scorpion buries his poisonous stinger into the frog's back. Shocked and hurt, the frog looks up at the scorpion and asks, "Why?"

The scorpion only smiles and replies, "It's just my nature."

Al Davis is the same way. His history is filled with proof.

Several years ago, Dr. Rob Huizenga, the former Raiders team doctor, authored a very good book, titled *You're Okay, It's Just a Bruise,* in which he addressed the disregard that Davis and the Raiders organization had for athletes who were injured. In carefully documented detail he told of players being pressured to take painkilling shots so they could play, and of the seriousness of injuries being hidden from individuals. Al was furious after the book's publication and went to longtime team trainer, George Anderson, and told him to go on television and say that Huizenga's book was nothing but lies.

You have to understand that Anderson—whom I dearly love—had been with the Raiders organization for thirty-five years and was planning to retire at the end of that year. Also, his wife had battled cancer and was in remission thanks to a rare treatment that Dr. Huizenga had researched and recommended to her.

So when George explained to his wife what Davis had ordered him to do, she begged him not to. She strongly felt that Dr. Huizenga had saved her life and that certainly bought him more loyalty than any her husband might owe Al Davis.

George refused to carry Davis's message to the media.

Al was furious, telling Anderson that "he'd never been a real Raider and never would be." And with that he told him that as soon as the season ended he never wanted to see him again. One of the most loyal workers in the Raiders organization was banished for stepping outside that box of control.

I'll once again be the "cancer," the "disgruntled aging veteran," the "selfish" ex-Raider. He might even try to revive the story he supposedly passed along to a coach in the league a few years ago: that I was into drugs when I was in Los Angeles.

Looking back on it all, I wish the things that occurred between Al Davis and me had never happened. But in retrospect, it was an experience that taught me a great deal about myself and the resiliency of the human spirit; about the ability to overcome and continue moving ahead.

In that regard, I suppose I owe Al Davis a debt of gratitude.

twenty

Comeback

JIMMY RAYE: *I was hoping we were going to get Marcus, but was really concerned that he might decide to go to Seattle because he'd played so well for Tom Flores when they were together with the Raiders.*

I knew that the fact that he'd played little in two, two and a half years, wouldn't concern Flores. And it didn't bother me. I knew Marcus Allen's background; knew the kind of man he was and the kind of attitude he brought to the game. All I needed to know was that he was physically fit. And all that business about him being a "cancer" was completely contrary to everything I'd heard from people whose opinions I valued. John Robinson had been a good friend of mine for a long time. So was Jim Jackson, the USC running-back coach when Marcus was there. They had nothing but good things to say about the guy.

To me, a person's background is very important. I liked everything I'd heard about Marcus Allen.

I was on vacation in Irvine when he finally signed with us and I immediately called the office and had them send me a copy of the new playbook we had just put together. Then I got in touch with Marcus. Every day he would drive out from Los Angeles and we would meet in a room at the Irvine Hyatt to go over the plays and the new terminology he needed to learn. What first impressed me was the fact that he antici-

pated just about everything I was going to say. He was always a step ahead of my explanations.

After meeting for a couple of hours, we would drive over to Irvine High School, where I'd put up cones and trash cans, anything I could find to use as dummies, and we'd run through the plays. My son would come along to snap the ball and Marcus would bring an old high school buddy of his. Sometimes Rodney Peete, the Detroit Lions quarterback who lived nearby, would come give us a hand with the passing game.

Marcus was like a new colt. Like a rookie, not a thirty-three-year-old veteran who had seen and done it all. I loved his enthusiasm.

But then we got to training camp and for the first few days I had my doubts. He was in excellent shape, but he kept slipping down coming out of his breaks. You could see that he knew what he wanted to do, but his mind seemed to be a half-step ahead of his body. I found myself wondering what in the hell we'd done.

Then, all of a sudden, it came back to him. After a week of drills, he was sharp, looking like the Marcus Allen we'd hoped he would be. It was all just a matter of him getting the rust off and putting those years of inactivity behind him. As soon as he got his football legs back, I knew he was going to make us all look really smart.

The guy reminds me a lot of Kareem Abdul-Jabbar. His body and his age don't match. If Marcus wanted to, I think he could be an effective running back in the NFL until he's forty years old.

As I think back on those first few days of training camp, it was good for him that Joe Montana had come in at the same time. Joe got all the media attention, allowing Marcus to get through the rough spots without anyone really noticing. I guarantee you, if the reporters had been paying attention to him in that first week, there would have been all kinds of Marcus-Allen-is-washed-up stories.

By the time the reporters did begin paying attention to him, he was back on his game. He and Montana were a great *match; it was like they communicated telepathically. And the team responded to him immediately.*

No, sir, Marcus Allen wasn't along for the ride. Marcus Allen was going to be *the ride.*

Like so many athletes, I am a creature of habit and no small amount of superstition. I find great comfort in the familiarity of a routine. On game days when we're playing at home, I make certain to take the exact same route to the stadium, singing along with the likes of Luther Vandross, Lionel Richie, Jeffrey Osborne, or Bryan McKnight as I drive. Music has always been a big part of my mental preparation for a game. I don't believe there is a more powerful motivator in the world than music, particularly when you allow yourself to personalize the lyrics.

If I were coaching a team, I'd make every player memorize the lyrics of the song "The Impossible Dream." What a powerful and inspirational message it has. I think it would serve well as our national anthem.

Inspirational writings also help me to get into the proper frame of mind. William J. Bennett's *The Book of Virtues*, a collection of beautifully written essays and poems, is a virtual treasure chest of positive messages and one of my favorites. A few minutes rereading Ella Wheeler Wilcox's poem "Will," or Edgar Guest's "Can't," before leaving for the stadium is time well spent.

Before home games, Kathryn and I say our prayers together before I leave, then talk for a few minutes. The conversation always ends the same. I'm not even sure how it first began, but she will say, "Make lots of touchdowns and run with the speed of light and the grace of God."

When we're on the road, I phone her before I leave the hotel and we have the same conversation.

In fifteen years, I've become familiar with every stadium in the league, yet I still like to go out early, before any fans arrive, and walk the field, checking for any wet spots, any areas where the footing might be the least bit hazardous. And I like to visualize how things will be in a few hours when the stands are full and the excitement is building.

It's all part of an attempt to gain whatever slight edge I can, an effort to get myself into the proper frame of mind.

In the locker room, I'll get comfortable in front of my locker and read the paper or the articles in the *Game Day* program. But I make a concerted effort to avoid looking over any statistics that are published. I don't want to know where I rank among the other backs in the league or who has the best yards-per-carry average. When I'm getting mentally prepared for a game, statistics don't interest me in the least.

And the last thing I want to see in my locker as I begin to dress is anything new. I hate it when a pair of shoes finally wears out and I have to break in new ones. Or when a shoulder pad breaks and the equipment manager brings me a replacement. I like worn, comfortable things. If my game jersey has a hole in it, I'd much rather they sew it up than give me a new one. Granted, a football uniform is designed for things more important than comfort; still, I like for everything to feel as good as possible. And in that regard, to me old is better.

If you've got a favorite old sweatshirt or a pair of sneakers at home, you know what I'm talking about.

And I like to travel as light as possible. My choice of shoulder pads is much smaller than the ones many of today's backs prefer. I don't like taping on extra padding to protect shins and forearms.

I recall telling Eric Dickerson when he came to the Raiders that next to him I looked damn near naked when I went out on the field. Eric wore the biggest shoulder pads I'd ever seen. By the time he was completely suited up, he looked like he'd ordered up a full set of body armor, including goggles to protect his eyes, neck roll, shin pads, thigh pads, and knee pads. If someone had designed pads to go on pads, Eric, I'm convinced, would have been first in line to buy them. I always marveled that he was able to move as swiftly as he did while carrying all that extra weight.

I suppose when you've spent your entire athletic life hearing that you aren't fast enough, you streamline the load in every way possible. Over the years I've even whittled away at the knee pads I wear to a point where they're now about the size of silver dollars.

Once on the field, I don't want to talk to anyone, even friends or family who might be at the game. Years ago, while still with the Raiders, a couple of old college buddies came out to a game and I stood around with them for a few minutes before we got into our warmup routine. Then, during the game, I fumbled the ball all over the place. I really stunk and was convinced that it was because I'd allowed my concentration to be diverted from my preparation for the game. For the same reason, I don't like to sign autographs when I'm on the field.

At the stadium, I like to retreat into my own little trying-to-get-ready world and put everyone and everything not directly related to the game out of mind. The exception, of course, is Kathryn. The last thing I do before kickoff is locate her in the stands and blow her a kiss.

Not all players prepare for a game in the same manner. I've known guys who appear downright nonchalant about the whole thing right up to kickoff, yet are able to play remarkably well once the bell rings. I've known guys so nervous in the last half hour before game time that they're running back and forth to the rest room to throw up. Yet when they get on the field, they're calm and ready to play.

Everyone prepares in his own way. For me, a high degree of intensity is essential. I like for the adrenaline to be flowing because it helps me to focus. I want my physical and mental energies at the highest possible level when the time finally arrives to play. It is a fine line that I force myself to walk. I don't want to be so keyed up, so anxious, that I'm no longer in control. On the other hand, I want to be prepared to go full-out from the opening gun.

It is a state of mind that is not easily put aside once a game is over. Win or lose, good performance or bad, I find it difficult to immediately erase the game from my thoughts.

On the nights after we've played, I often sit alone, watching television or listening to music into the wee hours. Sleep doesn't come easy. Marty Schottenheimer has always had what he calls his "twelve o'clock rule." By that time, he says, we should forget about the game, whether we won or lost. There is nothing that can be done to change the outcome, so the thing to do is begin looking ahead to the next one. It's a good rule. But I have a helluva time obeying it.

For me, unwinding is difficult.

KATHRYN ALLEN: *When Marcus does finally come to bed after a game, he runs in his sleep. He has all these involuntary muscle movements, kicking away the covers, flinching, twisting, calling out. As soon as it starts, I'm wide awake, watching him.*

I've tried shaking him awake but it doesn't do much good. As soon as he falls back to sleep, he's off and running again.

Occasionally, I'll lean over and whisper "touchdown" in his ear, thinking maybe he'll believe he's scored and be able to relax. But it's never worked.

It felt great to again be excited and enthusiastic about playing. The atmosphere in Kansas City was remarkable. I immediately sensed a single-minded determination among the players and coaches to do whatever was necessary to become an outstanding team. And the fan support was unbelievable. It had been a long wait, but I felt I'd found the ideal place to finish out whatever remained of my career.

All the little traditions and superstitions I'd so long adhered to took on new meaning. I felt the old excitement returning and looked forward to proving that I could still make a contribution.

Kathryn put it best. Before our move to Kansas City, she had no idea that the game of football was supposed to be fun.

Among those who would make the 1993 season so enjoyable was Joe Montana. At age thirty-six he had accomplished every goal a professional quarterback could dream of. Four times he'd led San Francisco to Super Bowl titles, three times being named the game's Most Valuable Player. His passing records, the lengthy list of come-from-behind victories he had engineered, his determination to overcome a variety of serious injuries, had earned him the admiration of everyone who ever watched him play.

All of which would have been enough for most players. No one would have thought less of him had he opted to remain in San Francisco for a couple more seasons, pocketing a big salary while watching from the sidelines as Steve Young took over the role of quarterbacking the 49ers. Joe Montana, already assured a direct pass into the Hall of Fame, could have played out the last days of his career as a backup. Many veteran quarterbacks do.

But he had another ending in mind. Joe wanted to go out in a final blaze of glory, facing one more challenge. He didn't want to watch; he wanted to play—and win. That's how he'd been since his days at Notre Dame. And when the Chiefs not only promised him that opportunity but said they would redesign their offense to fit his talents, he had asked that the 49ers trade him.

What I liked most about him had very little to do with the fact that he had thrown for 40,000 yards during his career, or that he'd won every major honor available to a pro football player. What most impressed me was that Joe Montana was one of those rare athletes who simply refuses to lose. No player I've been associated with had his talent for finding a way to win even when nothing seemed to be going right. As long as there was time on the clock, Joe was confident that he could get the job done.

That was the attitude the Chiefs, who hadn't won a divisional title since 1971, badly needed.

There are times when a gut feeling is your best measuring device. Though confident that I could still perform at a high level, that my career was far from over, there was no real way to see into the future and know for certain that things would take a positive course in Kansas City. So, yes, there were questions.

Though no one mentioned it, I knew full well that there were players on the Chiefs who wondered how management and the coaching staff could rest so much hope on a thirty-three-year-old running back. And I knew there were those on the team who had a personal dislike for me. I played well against the Chiefs during my Raiders career and knew there would be fence-mending to do. Neil Smith, the Chiefs' great defensive end, and I had gotten into a fight almost every time we'd played against each other. He was, I was convinced, a grade-A asshole. And he had made it perfectly clear he felt the same about me.

Historically, the Raiders had dominated the Chiefs and there was no love lost between the two teams. Old grudges die hard and I knew I would be viewed as the enemy by a sizable number of my teammates.

Yet all I wanted was a chance to make a fresh start, to put a lot of old history aside and, like Montana, fit in. It was easier than I would have ever imagined.

Neil Smith was one of the first to welcome me to the team. "I've never liked your sorry ass," he grinned, "but I've always respected you. I guess that's something we can build on." Linebacker Derrick Thomas said basically the same thing, and we soon became good friends.

They made it clear that they had great expectations of me, and I liked that.

The chemistry I encountered was exactly what I'd spent my entire professional career searching for. There were no mind games being played by coaches and the front office. Everyone, from owner Lamar Hunt and general manager Carl Peterson, to the secretaries and locker room attendants seemed to enjoy their work, free of the paranoias in the Raiders organization. What was in place in Kansas City, I quickly realized, was what business analysts refer to as a "horizontal" approach to management. The people work together, each complementing the other, sharing not only the load but the credit when it came due.

If the NFL did in fact have its utopia, I'd found it.

In short order I began to feel accepted. A security guard who had worked for the Chiefs for years approached me one afternoon following a pre-season practice and asked if I had a minute. "Look," he said, "there's something I want to tell you. See, the truth is, before you got here I'd heard that you were a real prick, a prima donna. And, quite honestly, I figured that it was true. I just wanted you to know I was wrong—and to wish you luck this season.''

That meant a great deal to me.

The positive vibes I was feeling came not only from the organization, coaches, and teammates. There was within the Kansas City community a spirit and unity that I found remarkable. I've long believed that few things unite people from all walks of life more quickly than a bonded interest in sports. K.C. was a textbook example. When we returned from a pre-season game against New England at three in the morning, several hundred people were waiting at the airport, all dressed in Chiefs red, cheering as if we'd just won the Super Bowl. I felt like I was back at USC.

Marty Schottenheimer had been honest with me. Before I signed with the Chiefs, he had only promised that I would get an opportunity to play and compete for a starting job. As the season opener approached, he explained to me that while I would be seeing a good deal of playing time, he and the staff felt the starting job should go to Harvey Williams, a talented runner with every physical attribute necessary to become an outstanding player.

Thus, for the first eight games, my role was to platoon with Williams despite the fact it was fast becoming obvious to me that Harvey and Schottenheimer were rarely in agreement on things ranging from practice routines to game plans. For all his talent, Harvey had not been able to get past that headstrong attitude that shortens so many careers.

On several occasions I talked with him, trying to explain the need to work within the system and not allow small grievances to become major confrontations.

In the ego-driven world of professional sports, the advice of elders is not always welcomed. There is an inbred paranoia among some that creates a fear that the player who has been around is not offering genuine help but instead playing some kind of psychological game whose only purpose is to ensure his own longevity. Then, unfortunately, there are those who simply know it all and wouldn't take a suggestion from God himself.

I decided to bide my time, privately convinced that the day was not far off when I would be the Chiefs' starting running back.

And while I felt all the ingredients were in place for us to have an exceptional season, we got a wake-up call early in the year. After opening with a win against Tampa Bay, we visited the Houston Astrodome, where the Oilers cleaned our clock. Montana had injured his thumb late in the Tampa Bay game and watched from the sidelines as our offense went nowhere. Buddy Ryan, the man who had designed the defense that had propelled Chicago to a Super Bowl victory before being hired as head coach of the Eagles, had become Houston's defensive coordinator. And what he'd put together was, to put it mildly, impressive. They beat us 30–0 and were already counting the days until the play-offs got under way.

Schottenheimer is among the best I've ever been around at quickly putting last week's game behind and focusing on the next. To his thinking, there is very little value to dwelling on victory or defeat. In his philosophy, every game is different and must be prepared for from scratch. Which is the origin of his "midnight rule" that insists players and coaches alike forget the past quickly and redirect their energies and focus on the next Sunday.

It works. With Joe back in the lineup, we bounced back with a 15–7 Monday-night win over Denver, during which I came close to a 100-yard game for the first time in years. En route to gaining 91 yards and catching a pass for 10 more, I could feel my rhythm returning.

Then, in the first week in October, we hosted the Raiders. I spent several days leading up to their arrival assuring every reporter who asked that the game had no special meaning for me. It was just another one we badly needed to win. Which, I must confess, was a lot of bull.

The feelings I had as I looked across the field at so many people I'd played with for years was even stranger than I had expected. There were a lot of guys I had long considered family, who I admired and cared for a great deal.

Then there was Al Davis. Before the game he was on the field, doing his customary stroll among his players, stopping to talk with a coach occasionally. And to stare in my direction. During warm-ups, every time I looked in his direction, he was standing, arms folded, just looking at me as if attempting to cast some evil spell. I wanted to yell out to him—*Hey, what the fuck are you staring at?*—but managed to keep my mouth shut.

In a way, it bothered me that I still felt such anger toward the man despite the fact that he no longer had control over my life and career. Wasn't it a senseless waste of energy to harbor such hatred? I'd never been a grudge-keeper in my life and wasn't altogether comfortable with my feelings. But, in all honesty, they were there, so I hoped to be able to use them to my advantage once the game got under way.

I was told beforehand that an edict had come down to the members of the Raiders team and coaching staff before it left California that no one was to speak to me.

The game itself was a dogfight. I carried the ball seventeen times for only 24 yards and couldn't remember being hit harder and more often. At one point during the game I was knocked out of bounds by my old friend Eddie Anderson near the Raiders bench. As I lay on the ground I saw Art Shell looking down at me. He said nothing but gave me a faint smile before I got up and returned to the huddle.

We won 24–9, and I managed to score the 100th touchdown of my professional career. When an announcement went up on the stadium scoreboard immediately afterward, there was a heartwarming roar of approval from the Arrowhead fans. The Kansas City press had made them aware of the differences I'd had with Davis and they enjoyed sharing in the moment of retribution with me.

The poetic justice of the moment didn't escape me.

When games end, it is customary for players from both teams to spend a couple of minutes mingling among friends before heading to the locker rooms. Certainly there were a lot of guys on the Raiders I would have liked to say hello to. But I knew it would not happen as long as Davis sat high above in the visitor's box, keeping watch. Several of my old teammates jogged past me without so much as a handshake, without even looking in my direction. But out of the sides of their mouths they said things like, "Hey, Marcus . . ." and "I'll give you a call when we get back home . . ."

Strange though it was, I understood.

We improved our record to 4–1 with a narrow win over Cincinnati the following week, then went into San Diego to face a Chargers team many had predicted would win our division. This time I placed special significance on the game for a reason far removed from that I'd dealt the Raiders game. Going home, knowing there would be family and friends in the stadium, was always exciting, almost magical, for me. Throughout my career, I'd always played well against San Diego. If you were to check, I bet you'd find that I've scored more touchdowns against the Chargers than any other team in the league.

On that particular Sunday, however, the magic ingredient was Joe Montana.

Though we had played exceptionally well, we trailed 10–7 at the end of the third quarter. In days past, when the Chiefs' offensive philosophy was to live and die by the run, come-from-behind victories had been rare. But with Joe and our new offensive system in place, we were becoming a team that could move the ball quickly in the air. Which is exactly what Montana did.

Watching him work the two-minute passing drill was like looking over the shoulder of an artist as he completes a fine painting. He never gets rattled, never shows concern. There is about him this positive attitude that is unbelievably contagious.

We came back to defeat the Chargers 17–14, in what I would later look on as one of the most important games of the '93 season. With that victory our confidence soared. After that afternoon, every member of the Chiefs knew we had a chance to accomplish something special before the year ended.

And I was having more fun than I'd had in years. In Week 8, as we prepared for a Monday-night meeting with the Green Bay Packers, Schottenheimer told me that the platooning was over and that I would become the starting running back.

Such was the case when we traveled to the West Coast for our second meeting with the Raiders. To say I was excited was a grand exercise in understatement. The idea of going back to the Coliseum, my "home" field since my freshman days at USC, only added to the emotion of the twice-a-year event the entire Chiefs organization referred to as "Raiders Week." But I was not the only one who placed special emphasis on the game. Marty made no secret of his dislike of the Raiders organization "from top to bottom" in team meetings. Though I'm not sure I agree with them, there are those who have followed the Chiefs for years who insist that any season in which Kansas City defeats the Raiders is considered a success, regardless of what happens during the remainder of the year.

This time, a friend told me, even the Raiders cheerleaders had been warned against speaking to me.

Apparently, however, the fans hadn't gotten the message. As I walked onto the field that afternoon there were banners bidding me welcome and calling attention to what one creative sign painter called "Al's Big Mistake." Another offered the suggestion that the Raiders "Trade Davis & Bring Back Marcus." During the pre-game introductions there were cheers and encouraging shouts when my name was called. It was electric. Seeing so many familiar faces—members of the chain crew, security officers, groundskeepers—was an emotional experience. And I had a real sense that most of the 66,000 fans on hand, though diehard Raiders supporters, wanted to see me do well.

I could not have imagined a warmer homecoming. Not only did we win handily—31–20—but I got off a long run and scored a touchdown.

There is an old football axiom that insists a winning team is a happy one. As we steadily moved toward the Western Division championship, we were living proof of the theory. Not only was it a pleasure to go to work each day, but I found myself feeding on the family-style environment the Chiefs organization had established. There were weekly luncheons for the players' wives that Kathryn enjoyed. And the relationship between the team and the community was gratifying. Virtually every member of the squad was involved in some form of charity work. Kathryn and I had begun working with the Ronald McDonald House.

One of the most enjoyable traditions the Chiefs had established was that of having players pass out bags of groceries to needy families during the Thanksgiving season. Martin Bayless and Kevin Ross had been the ones to come up with the idea. The players pitched in to purchase all the ingredients for first-rate turkey dinners, then each received the names of two families to whom he would personally deliver the food. Let me assure you, it is a spirit-lifting experience, one that causes you to pause and put your own life and purpose into perspective.

It was a small thing, to be sure, but the looks on the faces of the people whose doors we appeared at was worth a million dollars.

By the time we closed out the regular season with a win over Seattle, Kansas City was in a college-town frenzy. Shop owners decorated their windows and Chiefs red became the official dress. Being in the play-offs was actually nothing new, but too often it had been only a one-game appearance before elimination. This time there was a strong feeling that we still had a great deal of football left to play.

Against the Pittsburgh Steelers in the first round, it would be our special teams that got the job done. We were trailing late in the game when Keith Cash broke through to block a Steelers punt that Freddie Jones picked up and ran deep into Pittsburgh's end of the field. The stage was set for another of Joe's comeback miracles.

With only two minutes remaining, he threw a fourth down touchdown pass to Tim Barnett that was vintage, a thing of pure beauty, tying the game. We won it in overtime, earning the opportunity to face Houston for the Divisional title.

Buddy Ryan and his Oilers defense were at their trash-talking best in the days preceding the game. Looking back on the shutout they'd registered against us in the second game of the regular season, they were, to put it mildly, confident.

What they were not taking into consideration was that we would be arriving in the Astrodome in good health this time. Montana wouldn't be in street clothes. Our offense had blossomed and our defense had developed into one of the best in the league.

I was ready to bet the farm that we were going to win the game, despite the fact that handicappers had made us a decided underdog.

On that Saturday afternoon it seemed there were as many Chiefs fans in the stands as there were Oilers followers. And the roar, which never seemed to subside, became deafening in the fourth quarter as Joe threw for three touchdowns to put us into a one-point lead. Then, with time running out, I scored from 20 yards out to put the game away.

We were one game away from the Super Bowl. But it would end there.

In the AFC championship game against Buffalo, nothing went right. Montana was pounded into the frozen turf of Rich Stadium, suffering a concussion that sent him to the sidelines early. Our defense, prepared for the passing game that the Bills were certain to use, found itself facing a running attack that it had little success stopping. We were soundly beaten, 30–13, in a game that was over long before the scoreboard clock ran out.

There is a unique kind of disappointment that is attached to coming so close to a goal yet missing. The frustration is heightened, the questions linger. In a word, the feeling is terrible.

As we returned home that night, the team charter taxied to a remote hangar at the far end of the airport where only family members were waiting to greet us. On this cold, dismal night there was no triumphant return, no cause for welcoming fans.

But as we drove from the airport, along a service road leading to the interstate, thousands of people stood in the freezing temperatures, waving and cheering. The welcome stretched for over two miles. I'd seen nothing like it—not even the downtown Los Angeles parade after the Raiders' Super Bowl victory. I felt badly for having let these people down. On the other hand, it was wonderful to be playing in a place where there was such genuine support for the team.

The championship game aside, it had been a great season. If there were doubts that I was still capable of playing, they were set to rest. I'd led the team in rushing, had scored twelve touchdowns, and was selected by my teammates as the Chiefs' Most Valuable Player. I was also invited to play in the Pro Bowl for the first time in six years. Also named to the AFC team were teammates Joe Montana, John Alt, Neil Smith, and Derrick Thomas.

Then had come word that *Pro Football Weekly* had named me the NFL's Comeback Player of the Year, an honor generally reserved for someone who had returned to the game after suffering a serious injury of some sort. I wasn't sure I deserved it, but it did put a loud exclamation point to the end of my first season as a Chief.

Football was again a joy. And I found myself looking ahead to the next season far earlier than I had in years.

twenty-one

Nightmare in Brentwood

When I was younger, there was never a break in my training schedule. As soon as one season ended, I'd begin conditioning myself for the next. Then, as the aches and pains began taking a bit longer to heal, it finally occurred to me that rest, not exercise, was what my body needed.

Thus, when the season ended, I vowed to do nothing more physically exerting than swinging a golf club for at least a couple of months.

In time, though, I heard the call back to work. By early summer I was driving out to the UCLA track daily, going through a demanding regimen designed for me by former USC long jumper Henry Hines. In addition to doing many of the same things Jim Bush had had me doing years earlier, Henry added such painful novelties as doing repeat 220- and 440-yard sprints and lapping the track with someone riding on my back. I'd often run into such internationally known Olympic stars as pentathlon and long-jump gold medalist Jackie Joyner-Kersee, 100-meter champion Gail Devers, and quarter-miler Quincy Watts. I enjoyed getting to know them and watched their fluid grace with no small degree of awe. But when they would invite me to run sprints with them, I quickly declined.

I've got absolutely nothing against women, you understand, but the last thing I needed was to have Gail or Jackie showing me up. I chose instead to prepare for the upcoming season at my own non-world-record pace.

With training camp just a month away, an invitation came to spend a week with friends in the Cayman Islands. Mike Ornstein, no longer working with the Raiders, had become an agent and promoter, and he and ESPN had come up with the idea of doing a TV show that would be a one-hour mixture of travelogue, football, and outdoor programming. They were going to call it *The NFL Super Bowl of Marlin Fishing*.

I had no illusions that my fishing talents had earned me an invitation. At the same time, I had serious doubts that Junior Seau, Sean Jones, or Tim Brown were exactly deep-sea fishing experts either.

Kathryn and I had taken a 10:30 P.M. red-eye flight out of Los Angeles on Sunday, changed planes in Miami, and reached the Caymans just as a glorious sunrise was spreading over the Caribbean. With jet lag certain to set in, we chose not to attempt an early-morning nap and instead began taking advantage of our tropical surroundings immediately.

Kathryn and several other wives went to the beach. Tim, Mike, and I headed for the golf course.

An hour later a nightmare unlike anything I could ever have imagined began.

The assistant pro found me on the course and told me that I had an emergency phone call from my sister-in-law. The stress he placed on the word *emergency* immediately signaled to me that it wasn't something that could wait.

"There's a phone in the pro-shop office you can use," he said.

As he drove me in his golf cart, taking the shortest route across the manicured emerald fairways, my mind raced with dreaded possibilities. Debbie, Kathryn's younger sister, had agreed to house-sit for the week, and I was certain she wouldn't call unless there was something terribly wrong. Had the house caught fire? Could there be something wrong with my parents?

It was the same kind of feeling that sweeps over you when you're awakened by a phone call at three in the morning. Whatever Debbie had to tell me, I instinctively knew, I wasn't going to want to hear.

Ushered into a small office, I picked up the phone and

heard her strained voice. "Marcus," she said, "I have some terrible news. It's Nicole. She's dead."

As if it was taking every bit of strength she had, she continued before allowing me time to respond. "She was murdered, Marcus. Somebody killed her. O.J.'s been trying to reach you."

"Where is he?"

"I'm not sure. He called from a plane; he said he was on his way back from Chicago," she said. "He was crying."

I felt as though I were suddenly paralyzed. For several seconds I struggled to grasp what she had said, but with little luck. She had to be wrong. There had to be some horrible mistake.

Holding the receiver to my ear, I couldn't form the words to ask the questions that were racing through my mind. What could have happened? Was O.J. going to be okay?

Debbie broke the silence, her voice a whisper, almost apologetic. "Marcus," she said, "the television is saying that O.J. might have done it."

And with that statement the pain I was feeling escalated to a new level.

Leaving the golf course, I walked toward the hotel in search of Kathryn. I had just entered the courtyard as she was returning from the beach with Junior Seau's wife, Gina.

She smiled and waved. "That was a fast eighteen holes."

"I have some bad news. Nicole's dead." I still couldn't believe the words I was hearing myself speak. Kathryn shook her head in disbelief and began to cry. I grabbed her just as her knees began to buckle.

The remainder of the morning was an ugly dream. I tried O.J.'s house and got no answer. I phoned Al Cowlings and got a recording. I called the number of Orenthal Enterprises, O.J.'s office, and was surprised to learn that Bob Kardashian, one of O.J.'s closest friends, was there. He said all he knew was that the police had taken O.J. to Parker Center (which was just down the street from where he was sitting) for questioning. Cursing the three-hour time difference, I continued with little success to get in touch with anyone back home who could shed light on what might have happened. Kathryn turned the television on to CNN and we began getting reports. Not only had Nicole been murdered in front of her Brentwood town house, but a waiter from the Mezzaluna restaurant had also been killed.

When I finally reached O.J. at his home, the anguish in his voice was like nothing I'd ever heard. "Oh, my God," he kept saying over and over. "Oh, my God . . . oh, my God . . ."

I didn't know what to say. "You going to be okay, man? Is there anything I can do?"

The police, he said, were accusing him. "They won't even let me mourn . . . Oh, my God . . ."

He sounded confused, barely coherent. Kathryn got on the phone and asked about the kids. If he needed any help with Sydney and Justin, she said, just let her know.

I told him we would get back as quickly as possible.

"You don't want to come," he said. "Please don't. The media's going nuts. Everything's crazy. You guys just stay there. I'll see you later."

I agonized over the idea of remaining in a tropical paradise while someone who I felt needed my help was so far away, suffering so terribly.

Later, Ed and Jon Hookstratten phoned. They had anticipated that I would want to fly back to L.A. as soon as possible. "You've got to do whatever you feel is right," Ed said, "but I want you to listen to me for a minute. You have no idea what a media frenzy is taking place here. There's nothing you can do to help anything or anybody right now. All you're going to get is a lot of microphones shoved in your face and have people asking if you think O.J. could have done this. My advice is that you stay there, complete your vacation, and then come on back and see how things are."

Kathryn urged me to listen to him.

And so for the next few days I went through the motions as the fishing competition was filmed. My heart wasn't in the project. All I wanted to do was watch the television and see what new developments might have occurred.

It was on Friday, the day after Nicole's funeral, that we

got word that an arrest warrant had been issued for O.J. and that he and A.C. had disappeared. Bob Kardashian stood before a bank of microphones and television cameras and read a letter that Juice had written and given to him.

I stared silently at the familiar face on the screen, speechless as I listened to what I was certain was a suicide letter. Kathryn moved to sit next to me as I began shaking my head.

Just seconds later Kardashian came to a point in the letter that was addressed to me: "Marcus, you've got a great lady in Kathryn. Don't mess it up. . . ."

I wasn't sure what he meant, but I was convinced that he had killed himself.

As if reading my thoughts, Kathyrn made a comforting observation: "If they haven't found A.C., that means they're somewhere together. You know that A.C. will take care of O.J." She suggested they might have left the country.

Moments later, Ed Hookstratten phoned again. The Los Angeles police, he said, wanted permission to search our house. "They're going to do it one way or the other," he explained. "Either with your permission or a search warrant. They just want to see if O.J.'s there."

I told him to contact my sister-in-law and let her know they were coming.

KATHRYN ALLEN: *Marcus has a remarkable ability to hold his emotions in check, to not let others know when something is really troubling him. But for the first time since I'd known him, he wasn't able to hide the pain he was feeling. He was quiet and withdrawn, staying to himself as much as possible. The sadness in his face was heartbreaking.*

He was on the phone constantly with A.C., asking how O.J. was; if there was anything he could do. I think he was hoping someone would tell him to get back to Los Angeles so he might do something—anything—to somehow make the terrible situation better. But there was nothing that anyone could do. A.C. told him the same thing O.J. had: Stay away.

On Friday, after the filming was completed, we were all to be guests at a dinner hosted by the Cayman Islands Minister of Tourism. I was in no mood for it, but at everyone's urging finally agreed to go.

We were dressed and preparing to leave the hotel when CNN came on with a bulletin. A.C. and O.J., a reporter announced, had been seen in a white Ford Bronco on the Santa Monica Freeway. Soon there were helicopter camera shots of the Bronco, followed by a constantly growing convoy of police cars.

A.C. was in telephone contact with the police, frantically urging them to pull back. O.J., he said, was in the backseat with a Smith & Wesson .357 magnum pointed at his head. Newscasters were speculating that their destination was the grave site of Nicole.

I glanced across the room at Ornstein and our eyes met for only a second. We didn't speak but both knew immediately where O.J.'s gun had come from. For Christmas back in 1989, Mike had gone to Earl Paysinger, a lieutenant with the Los Angeles Police Department who occasionally worked as Al Davis's personal security guard, and asked his help with purchasing gifts for Terry Robiskie, Bo Jackson, O.J., and myself. Orny had given each of us a blue-steel Smith & Wesson .357 magnum handgun.

I was certain that O.J. was planning to end his life and repeatedly dialed the numbers of his and Al's cell phones. But I couldn't get through.

There was nothing to do but sit and watch the surreal event play out. My friend Jim Hill, the Channel 2 sportscaster, came on and pleaded with O.J. to give himself up, to stop and think of all the people who cared deeply for him. Then the concerned face of Al Michaels filled the screen, and he began to eloquently explain the lifelong relationship between A.C. and O.J. His description of A.C. as a "gentle giant" was right on the money. It was good to hear the observations from someone who actually knew O.J. and A.C.

It was a strange feeling to be sitting in a hotel room, thousands of miles away, seeing so many familiar faces and recognizable places.

Only when A.C. drove the Bronco through the gate at Rockingham did I begin to relax, suddenly aware of the tension that had knotted every muscle in my body. I dialed the number of O.J.'s home and someone identifying himself as a police officer answered. O.J. was fine, he said, but he couldn't come to the phone. And, finally, I could no longer hold back the tears. As Orny and his wife, Kristi, excused themselves, I sat on the edge of the bed and wept uncontrollably, allowing a week's worth of emotion to pour out.

In time I looked up at Kathryn. "You know," I told her, "if we had gone home, I probably would have been in that Bronco with them."

She, too, was crying. "I know," she said.

Mixed with the disbelief I was feeling came a flood of suddenly bittersweet memories. I thought back to that day when I was still a high school kid, in New York to receive the Hertz Number One Award. I had been filled with boyish awe when I first met O.J. I'd asked him to telephone my mother, bashfully explaining how thrilled she would be to have him say hello. He'd quickly obliged.

In time our friendship had begun as he followed my career at USC, always quick to offer encouragement. He'd been on the dais at the Heisman presentation, gracious with praise for the season I'd had. This man I'd first known only as one of the greatest running backs in the history of the game who had played a part in my decision to attend Southern Cal, and had pointed me in the direction of an agent once my collegiate days were over.

Over the years there had been numerous stories in the press that suggested I had adopted him as my mentor, the person I looked to for guidance and advice. When sportswriters had referred to me as "Little O.J." during the early stages of my college career, I'd been at first amused by the comparison, then put off. I wanted only to be myself, to make my own way. For all the admiration I had for O.J. as an athlete and business success, I'd never tried to pattern myself after him.

There was only one O.J. Simpson and he was my friend, not my father figure, not my mentor. We hung out, watched ball games, played tennis and golf, and enjoyed each other's company. We'd even become partners in a thoroughbred we named Reiterate. I had come up with the name after a speaking engagement he and I had attended together. Talking with a group of youngsters, O.J. had gotten hung up on the word *reiterate*, using it a number of times to a group who, I felt reasonably sure, were too young to understand its meaning. Afterward I kidded him about it and it became a standing joke, like so many other things between us over the years.

In time I'd also grown close to A.C. We even enrolled in *tae kwon do* classes together, played some hoops now and then, and occasionally went to dinner or to a club together.

Those had been fun days. I'd been welcomed into a circle of friends who I enjoyed being around. And during that time I'd never seen the O.J. Simpson that was being castigated by the media. The O.J. I knew was gracious and caring and one of the warmest and funniest guys I'd ever been around.

And there was Nicole, this vibrant, lovely woman who had come into Juice's life. I'd liked her from the first time he introduced us. She, too, was funny and also headstrong and intelligent. She was good for O.J. And a friend to me. When I'd moved into my first apartment after signing with the Raiders, Nicole had volunteered to serve as my decorator.

Despite the problems that would cloud the later stages of their marriage, she and O.J. had been drawn together like powerful magnets.

She had been a wonderful mother to their children and a friend to everyone who was a part of O.J.'s life. It's interesting, the things you remember about a person after they're gone. Nicole loved holidays like no one I'd ever been around. She delighted in decorating and hosting parties, and always greeted each arriving guest with a small, carefully wrapped gift.

And now she was gone and O.J. was being accused of the unthinkable. It was more than I could grasp.

I was still numb as we returned to Los Angeles, my thoughts a muddle of questions, disbelief, and memories that continued flooding back. How could people's lives change so swiftly? That Nicole could be gone seemed impossible. That O.J., always so happy and upbeat, friends with the world, could be in such pain, locked away and suspected of murder, was something I could not even begin to comprehend. What I was feeling was indescribable, heightened by the frustration of not being able to do anything that would help life to return to the normalcy we'd all so taken for granted.

I finally got in touch with A.C., learning that he was staying at the home of O.J.'s business manager, Wayne Hughes. He'd gone there to avoid the members of the media who had been staked out at his house around the clock since the tragedy occurred. If anyone had answers to the questions that were eating away at me, A.C. would. He and O.J. had been like brothers all their lives. One of the kindest, most caring people I've ever known, A.C. was the kind of person who would do anything within his power for a friend. I remember a time when a buddy of his was in a financial bind and had mentioned his problem to A.C. A.C. didn't have the money but he borrowed it and gave it to him. Kathryn always described him as the textbook example of a caregiver.

He seemed in shock when I saw him at Hughes's house. He looked as if he had aged twenty years. The whole thing was crazy, he said. Impossible. How could they think that Juice had anything to do with the horrible tragedy that had occurred in front of Nicole's house?

"How's he doing?" I asked.

"Not good," A.C. told me. The stories that were circulating, spreading like some out-of-control grass fire, had become increasingly absurd with each passing day. In addition to the speculation that O.J. was responsible for the death of Nicole and Ron Goldman, the young Mezzaluna waiter, there was even the suggestion that A.C. might also have been somehow involved.

The whole matter sounded like a bad dream that continued to get worse. I wanted to see O.J.

Before I could do that, however, Cathy Randa, O.J.'s secretary, telephoned to say that a meeting was being planned by attorney Robert Shapiro, who was representing O.J., and he wanted everyone mentioned in the letter Kardashian had read to be present. "Juice is in terrible shape," she said, "and he needs a show of support from his friends."

• • •

Kathryn and I arrived at Shapiro's Fox Tower office late on a Saturday afternoon and were quickly ushered into a large meeting room. Cathy was already there, along with Juice's agent Skip Taft, Wayne Hughes, and Robert Kardashian. In time, the group would include Allen Schwartz, Joe Stellini, Thomas McCollum, and Joe Kolkowitz. And Vince Evans, my former Raiders teammate, joined us at a large table.

Shapiro immediately took charge, assuring us that he was in control of the situation, and began briefing us on the legal strategy he'd already begun planning. He impressed me, not only with his businesslike demeanor, but with his obvious conviction that his new client had been unjustly accused. He introduced us to Bill Pavelic, who would serve as his chief investigator. "We're going to press hard for a speedy trial so we can get O.J. home as quickly as possible," he told us.

Then he warned us that we could all anticipate being barraged by the media. "I would urge each of you to say nothing. Absolutely nothing, not even 'No comment.' Even if you think you have something to say that you feel might be beneficial to O.J., rest assured it will get twisted. If you get to a point where you feel you have to respond to a reporter's question, please talk to us first."

O.J.'s greatest need at the moment, Shapiro pointed out, was to know he had the love and support of his friends. "We're going to get him on the speakerphone in a few minutes," he said, "so everyone can say hello. I urge that you be very positive and upbeat when you're speaking with him."

Moments later the meeting took on a dreamlike quality as my friend's voice came over a speakerphone that had been placed in the middle of the table.

At first O.J. sounded strong and confident as Shapiro talked with him, telling him who was assembled. Then everyone took his turn: "Hey, Juice, we love you . . . Hang in there, pal . . . Hi, O.J., I'm praying for you, buddy . . . This'll all be over soon . . . Stay strong . . . We're with you . . ."

As the first few people spoke, O.J.'s response was almost cheerful. But with each passing acknowledgment, his voice seemed to weaken, becoming more distant and distraught. By the time my turn came to say hello, his depression was easily detected.

There was so much I wanted to say, but I couldn't find the words. "Hey, Juice," I finally said. "It's Marcus. I'm praying for your liberation. You've got to hang in there . . . I love you."

His reply was a whisper. "I appreciate it," he said. "I appreciate all of you."

A cold hush settled over the room when the conversation finally ended. It was as if the last bit of energy had been drained from each of us. I fought unsuccessfully to hold my emotions in check. Rising from my seat, I realized that my legs felt weak. I turned toward a window, buried my hands in my pockets, and looked out onto a world that suddenly seemed unreal to me. And I began to cry.

Before the meeting broke up, Alan Austin took charge, suggesting that we immediately begin a series of visits to O.J. "He's got to have our constant support," Alan said, "so we need to have someone there as often as possible." He pointed out that we would be allowed to visit for two hours at a time and began mapping out a schedule.

Kathryn and I went to see him the next day.

Forewarned that the media was camping out at the entrance to the Los Angeles County Jail, recording the comings and goings of anyone they thought might be visiting O.J., I let Kathryn off a block from our destination and told her to go in alone. I would wait five minutes and follow her. By doing so, we were able to slip past the unsuspecting reporters.

So that we might visit in a room generally reserved for attorney-client conferences, Shapiro had placed our names on a list of potential witnesses. Still, the standard jail procedures were observed. We sat in a waiting room where we filled out questionnaires and were told to place everything in our pockets into an assigned locker. Then we were searched before being escorted through a series of hydraulically barred doors. The slamming of each one echoed loudly through the corridor, causing my heart to beat faster. It was as if we were suddenly playing roles in a bad B movie.

Finally seated in front of a shield of Plexiglas, I quickly realized I was unprepared for what was to come. Wearing a jail jumpsuit and looking tired and disheveled, O.J. was escorted into the room. The handcuffs he was wearing were removed, but the waist chain to which they had been attached remained as he took a chair across from us and smiled.

To this day I don't remember a great deal about the conversation. Kathryn and I said very little and instead just listened as O.J. talked about Nicole, how much he loved her, and about his concern for his children. Repeatedly, he insisted that he had nothing to do with their mother's death.

I'd never seen him as he was that day. The O.J. Simpson I'd known for fifteen years had always been carefree and energetic, full of life and enthusiasm for everything and everyone around him. And now he was being accused of something so horrific that it defied imagination, was being portrayed in the press as a person I'd never known—a dark and sinister person who stared at the world from the cover of *Time* magazine.

Try though I did, I could not bring myself to even believe we were sitting there, separated by glass, unable even to touch. I wanted to somehow wake from the nightmare and return to the way things were, the way things should be. And as badly as I wanted that, I could only imagine the pain that my friend was enduring.

Before we left we all placed our hands against the Plexiglas and prayed.

As we left the jail, I got my first glimpse of what Shapiro had warned us about. Cameras and microphones were pointed at us as we walked out, everyone wanting to know what O.J. might have said, how he looked, whether we thought he was guilty of the crime he'd been charged with.

I took Shapiro's advice and said nothing.

It was the last time I saw O.J. in person. Pre-season training camp was about to begin in Kansas City, and for the first time in my life I found myself looking on football as a means of escape. The twice-daily workouts, the meetings, the focus, and the tiring routine of preparing for another season, I hoped, would help to blur the ugly images and troubling thoughts of what had happened.

Kathryn, who would remain in California until training camp ended, went with A.C. for one more visit with O.J., and they regularly called to keep me informed of what was going on. They became my only source of information as I made a concerted effort to watch no television and not read any newspapers.

Still, it was impossible to isolate myself from the constant flow of speculation and rumor, the ugly gossip and distasteful jokes that swirled around the case. Reporters, who generally visited training camp to ask questions about the upcoming season, were suddenly interested in nothing but my relationship with O.J. I told Bob Moore, the Chiefs' director of publicity, to make it clear to everyone that I would have no response to any questions that didn't directly concern football.

Still, I quickly realized that there was no way anyone associated with O.J. could expect to avoid being drawn into the story.

One evening as I spoke with Kathryn, she told me that my name had been mentioned on one of the nationally syndicated tabloid television shows. A woman named Jill Shively told a *Hard Copy* reporter that she had been driving her Volkswagen along San Vicente Boulevard on the night of the murders and had very nearly had an accident when a fast-moving white vehicle drove in front of her at the Bundy intersection. To avoid a collision, both drivers had come to a halt and, according to her story, the other driver began to curse and shout at her, demanding that she move her car.

As she related her story, she told the reporter that she had at first thought the other driver was me.

Then, she said, she realized the voice of the man yelling at her to move out of the way was that of O.J. She had taken down a license-plate number that reportedly matched that of O.J.'s Bronco.

It would get worse.

• • •

As the 1994 season got under way, expectations were high. Because the Chiefs had reached the AFC championship game the previous season, the obvious goal was to move things up one more notch and get to the Super Bowl. And while O.J.'s troubles continued to weigh on me, I focused on what I had to do to help make that happen.

We opened with three straight victories, including a win over Montana's old 49ers. It amused me to hear Joe assuring the media throughout the week leading up to the game that it had no added significance for him. It was just another game. I'd told the same white lies myself in weeks leading up to games against the Raiders. I knew damn well that Joe badly wanted to show his buddies on the 49ers that he still had it.

The smile on his face after we beat San Francisco 24–17 was the real proof of how important the game had been to him.

The fact that the season was off to such an impressive start lifted my spirits greatly, to the point where I was not really looking forward to an open date the following Sunday. We were on a roll and I wanted to keep the momentum building. Also, staying busy and focusing on game preparation had been the godsend I badly needed to put O.J.'s problems out of mind.

Even as I began to dread the brief layoff, Fox TV came to the rescue, asking if I would like to do color commentary on the telecast of the Detroit–Tampa Bay game. They said I would be only the third active player ever to do so. While I had no experience and many reservations, it was an opportunity I couldn't refuse.

When not in team meetings or on the practice field, I did my homework. I studied the rosters and depth charts of the Lions and Buccaneers, read news clippings and press guides that the network sent to me, and called my friend Al Michaels for any advice he might have to offer.

By the time I traveled to Tampa Bay on Saturday to sit in on meetings with coaches and talk to players, I was feeling pretty good about my preparation. On game day, though, I became a basket case, far more nervous than I'd ever been when I was playing.

Sitting high in the broadcast booth, I had difficulties with the telestrator and with communications from the statistician and the spotter. During the early stages of the broadcast I don't think I did much of anything that would convince the viewers at home that I was an old hand at what I was doing. The truth is, I was intimidated by all the technical bells and whistles that are part of a football telecast.

As the game progressed I became more comfortable. The final scorecard: not a great debut, but an overall good job. All in all, it was a great experience, and I left the booth sure that I'd like to one day return to give it another try.

For now, it was time to get back to the business I was more comfortable with.

In our fourth game of the season we experienced one of those afternoons for which there is absolutely no rhyme or reason. It wasn't the first time I had seen it happen, nor would it be the last. But against the Los Angeles Rams we could do nothing right. Our offense never got out of low gear. The defense got shoved all over the field. The Rams scored on fluke plays. The harder we tried, the worse we got. And we lost 16–0.

Normally there are obvious reasons for such a showing: a poor week of preparation, injuries to key personnel, playing against a team that is simply better. None applied to the Rams loss, however. We had practiced well, had been building momentum through the early weeks of the season, and were confident that we were the better team. But, as unscientific as it might sound, it was just one of those days when we'd all have been better off calling in sick.

The glumness I was feeling over the loss did not improve when I received a call from Christopher Darden, a prosecutor in the Los Angeles County District Attorney's office, saying that he wanted to come to Kansas City and ask me some questions.

He was involved in a grand jury investigation of A.C.'s role in the now-infamous Bronco chase, trying to determine whether charges should be filed. Certain that A.C.'s only concern at the time had been to protect O.J.—and save his life—I looked forward to telling them of the unique relationship between my two friends. A.C., as Kathryn had repeatedly said, was doing nothing but being a loyal friend, playing his familiar role as caregiver. And that violated no laws.

I agreed to meet Darden at the Sheraton Suites in downtown Kansas City after a midweek practice.

Accompanied by detectives from the Los Angeles Police Department, the assistant district attorney was pleasant, almost apologetic. "We realize that you had nothing to do with any of this," he said, "but we have to do our jobs."

He had only a few questions, he said.

"Can you tell us where you were when you heard about the deaths of Nicole Simpson and Ron Goldman?"

I explained the trip to the Cayman Islands and the phone call from Kathryn's sister.

"And who have you spoken with about the matter?"

Reasonably certain that he already knew the answer, I told him of the conversations I'd had with A.C. and O.J. and the meeting Kathryn and I had attended in Shapiro's office. I was beginning to wonder why he'd traveled all the way to Kansas City to ask such questions. And I decided it best to be very careful about what I said.

He asked about my relationship with O.J. and I tried to explain our friendship, pointing out that I'd seen him only occasionally in the years since I'd met my wife. I had played golf with him now and then and we'd see each other at the holiday get-togethers that Nicole enjoyed hosting.

Then, after a pause, he asked a question that came flying out of deep left field: "Did you have an affair with Nicole?"

Stunned by the question, I said, "No, I didn't."

"Do you know a woman named Faye Resnick?"

Puzzled, I explained that I knew her only as one of Nicole's friends. What the hell did Faye Resnick have to do with the investigation?

"Mr. Allen," Darden said, "that's all I have. We appreciate your cooperation. Again, I hope you understand that we're just doing our jobs." With that he asked if I would suggest a good place they might go for dinner.

The entire interview had lasted no more than fifteen minutes.

In a sense it was just the beginning of a new kind of nightmare. While I had received an inordinate amount of sports-page publicity throughout my playing career, I'd never experienced anything like what lay ahead.

I was about to become grist for the tabloid mill.

It soon became clear to me what Faye Resnick's involvement was. With the help of a writer for the *National Enquirer*, she had written a book in which she claimed that I had been romantically involved with Nicole.

Two weeks later we were in Denver for a Monday-night game. As I stepped off the bus to enter Mile High Stadium, a female reporter stuck a microphone in my face and asked, "Did you sleep with Nicole?"

Furious, I stared at her for a second but chose not to respond.

Later, on the field, Frank Gifford walked up to me during pre-game warm-ups. The smile that was normally on his face was absent as he shook my hand. "The shit has hit the fan," he said. The *New York Post*, he explained, had published a front-page story saying that I had been involved in a lengthy affair with Nicole after she and O.J. had divorced.

It had been a topic of discussion on the morning network show his wife and Regis Philbin hosted. It was a show I knew Kathryn religiously watched.

No game I've ever participated in was as difficult as that one against the Broncos. Though I played well and we won in Denver for the first time in years, I was absolutely numb, my thoughts on how Kathryn might be dealing with the ugly rumor that refused to go away. Just the night before, I'd called her to wish her happy birthday. Now I felt a million miles away at a time when I wanted badly to be at home, assuring her that all this would somehow soon pass.

The only real consolation I felt was in the knowledge that she was a strong person and that we'd both worked diligently to make our marriage a solid one.

Everyone's strength would be tested in the weeks to come as the supermarket tabloids jumped on the bandwagon.

One ran a story that said Nicole had been deeply in love

and that she had "begged me to marry her." Another wrote that I had attempted suicide by overdosing on drugs. According to the story, Kathryn had found me lying on the floor, unconscious, and only after having second thoughts had phoned my mother to ask what she should do. The incident, according to the article, had taken place in San Diego—at the time I was in Kansas City getting ready for the season.

An Oregon state trooper told the media of seeing Nicole and me together the previous summer when he'd pulled a car over for speeding. There was only the slightest grain of truth to what he had say. Kathryn and I had joined a group that included A.C., Ronnie Lott and his wife, and Steve Smith and his wife, on a fly-fishing vacation. We were in a convoy on the highway when either Ronnie or Steve was pulled over for speeding. We had all stopped and tried to convince the officer everyone had been driving within the speed limit. The woman he had seen me with was my wife.

Every time I felt things had reached the ultimate in absurdity, something else would happen. Members of the tabloid press tried every ruse to gain entrance into the building where we lived—insisting to security guards they were close friends, trying to deliver flowers, or posing as plumbers or electricians—making us virtual prisoners in our own home.

Once, while flying home from a business trip, a woman seated next to me struck up a conversation, introducing the man sitting next to her as her husband. As we talked, she mentioned that we had several friends in common, including Ed Hookstratten.

It made no real impression on me at the time, but her husband spent an inordinate amount of time with his back turned to us, talking on the in-flight phone. It also seemed strange to me that as soon as we landed he left his wife behind and was the first off the plane.

Only when I walked into the terminal did I figure out what the phone conversations had been about. He had alerted a TV crew that I would be arriving. They got their footage, but no response to their questions.

Faye Resnick began spreading a story that we'd bumped

into each other shortly after a book she'd written was published and that I'd somehow threatened her.

Holding to the advice to say nothing was becoming increasingly difficult.

ED HOOKSTRATTEN: *In building their defense, Simpson's lawyers obviously felt it would be beneficial if they could show that their client had not been jealous of Nicole and any relationships she might have had after they divorced. That's where all this crap about Marcus came into play.*

Johnny Cochran called me about it and said that Lee [F. Lee Bailey] felt pretty strongly about the Marcus-Nicole rumors. He started telling me some of the stories that Bailey was passing around: One had Marcus and Nicole at some bar, her sitting on his lap. They were supposedly drinking margaritas and shooting pool. That was absurd. I know for a fact that Marcus doesn't drink, and I doubt seriously that he's much of a pool player. I told Cochran and Shapiro that involving Marcus was a bullshit deal.

What angered me was the fact that all this was making Marcus and Kathryn into two more victims in this awful mess.

Frankly, I think Marcus had become more than a little weary of the whole public notion that O.J. Simpson was his mentor and adviser. All that had begun way back when Marcus was still at USC, when the press was constantly making comparisons between the two. Frankly, I think O.J. liked it and had continued to perpetuate it. But Marcus had long since grown up and was his own man, fully capable of making his own decisions.

I know how difficult it was for him, but I tried to explain to Marcus that nothing he could say would be of any real benefit to anyone—himself or O.J. One of the hardest things in the world to do when people are hurling false allegations at you is to remain silent. But I urged him to think of himself and his family; to stay above it all.

By the time we played the Raiders in the eighth game of the season, I was doing everything short of wearing a different jersey number to stay out of the public eye. And to complicate matters, I suffered strained ligaments in my knee when I collided with a Raiders defender toward the end of the game.

Like anyone who has ever played the game, I have a frightening concern when it comes to knee injuries. There had been those incidents with the Raiders when I'd been considerably younger and they had concerned me just as much then. When you feel that initial pain, the first thing that flashes through your mind is that it could be all over, even before you have any idea how serious it might be.

The way I've always tried to combat such thoughts is to rely on something John Robinson taught us when I was playing at USC: Never let the other guys know you're hurt. Never show pain until you're back on the sidelines. With that in mind, I've always been something of a frustration to team doctors who come on to the field to check on me after an injury. I'll curse them, yelling for them to get the fuck away and let me get up. It may not be the wisest philosophy, but I've always felt it important that I walk from the field after any injury.

On that afternoon I did manage to walk to the bench, comfortable in the knowledge that I'd again played well against my old team and we had the game under control. But the damage was such that I would be forced to sit out our next three games.

Not only did I feel I was letting the team down by my absence, but the escape I so badly wanted was taken from me. There are few things in football worse than standing on the sidelines, dressed in street clothes, when your team is playing. Unable to make any kind of contribution, you feel totally isolated despite the fact that you are standing in the middle of things. You feel you're in the way, not at all a part of what's taking place. And regardless of how long you've played, a kind of paranoia creeps in as you deal with thoughts that the player replacing you might do something magnificent and steal away your job. I hated not playing.

We lost two of the three games I missed. And then lost two more.

Suddenly, with only two games remaining, we were 7–7, and in danger of not even making it into the play-offs.

It was time for me to speak out—at least to my teammates.
During a meeting to discuss the problems we were having, I
heard a number of what I viewed as lame excuses for the
position we were in. It was mentioned that some of the players were affected by the distractions and pressures of outside
business concerns. I've always been vocal in such meetings,
and on this particular occasion I really went off. I'd kept my
feelings about the O.J. matter private until then. But as I got
up to speak I could feel my temperature rising. No one in the
room had more distraction and pressure than what I was dealing with, I assured them, and I damn sure felt like I was still
focusing on the season and doing my job. And if I could do
it, everyone else in the room could.

We closed out the season with a 31–9 victory over the
Oilers, then beat the Raiders, 19–9.

Wearing a knee brace, I carried the ball thirty-two times
against my old teammates for 132 yards.

It is interesting how certain teams seem to develop something
akin to a mastery over others of close or equal talent. When
I was with the Raiders, for instance, we had been able to
dominate the Denver Broncos and the Miami Dolphins, despite the fact that they were routinely among the best in the
league. Kansas City, on the other hand, had enjoyed little
success against either team. Why? If I knew, Coach Schottenheimer would have me on his coaching staff rather than
playing for him.

In the first round of the play-offs, our luck against Miami
didn't improve. It was another of those days during which
nothing went right. Joe threw interceptions. I fumbled. Our
defense couldn't find a way to stop Dan Marino. And our
season ended with a 27–17 defeat.

At 9–7, we'd fallen far short of what we had hoped the
year would be. Yet with a couple of exceptions, our losses
had been ones of strange happenings and fluke plays that
generally come around only a few times in a season. We'd
endured enough to last us well into the next century.

In the twenty-seven years I've been involved in athletics,
I've never learned to completely accept defeat. Unrealistic

though it might be, I have gone into every game, every season, expecting nothing but victory. Which, I suppose, makes me a bad loser. As I looked back on the season, I didn't separate it into games won and games lost. The battles we had won meant little. We had lost the war.

But mixed with the disappointment was a feeling of confidence that we had the talent to make another run for the Super Bowl when the next season rolled around.

I knew, however, that we would have to do it without Joe Montana. We had become good friends—Kathryn and I had spent Thanksgiving with the Montanas—and I could tell by the way he had begun to talk that he wasn't going to come back for another year. He had given everything to the game for so many years and had begun to think more and more about spending time with his family, away from the spotlight's glare. The toll taken by the game, he confided, was more mental than physical. I understood what he was saying.

We—players and fans alike—want an athlete like him to play forever. But, as Joe understood, the best two-minute drill in the world couldn't continue to win against Father Time. On one hand, I was saddened when he announced his retirement. Like everyone else, I selfishly wanted him back on the field the next fall, working his indescribable magic. At the same time, I was happy for him; aware of how eagerly he looked forward to enjoying a quieter, more normal life. No one deserved it more.

I was beginning to contemplate some of the same things myself.

For the first time in my athletic career I found myself resentful of the media and its mean-spirited invasion of my private life, and of the quick-to-judge attitude of people I didn't know and who didn't know me. It bothered me a great deal to realize the delight some seemed to derive from the pain of others; how some people took from you whatever they wanted—a sensational headline, an item of untrue gossip—and went on with their lives, never considering the effect they had on others.

I had finally begun to realize that life in the public eye was indeed a double-edged sword. I felt trapped in a situation that

I could find no good way to fight my way out of. If I spoke out, there would be those who wouldn't believe me. If I remained silent, they would read whatever they wished into that. Yet there was no place to hide from the opinions. There were those quick to believe my friend guilty, others who adamantly insisted there was no way he could have done something so unspeakably terrible. In time it began to destroy friendships as people were worn down by the constant barrage of questions and loss of their own privacy. A.C. and I no longer see each other, despite sharing a common grief that will bond us forever.

The nightmare was endless. There were hateful catcalls in a few stadiums during the season, and tasteless questions had been posed to Kathryn by women she hardly even knew. I received a couple of death threats in the mail, one claiming that Ron Shipp, a Los Angeles police officer and good friend of O.J's, and I had somehow conspired to "set Simpson up."

I was attending some of the Super Bowl functions when defense attorney Cochran made his opening statement, pointing out that O.J. had never been the meanly jealous person portrayed by the prosecution. He then launched into the tiresome scenario about Nicole and me and the fact that O.J. had made his home available to Kathryn and me for our wedding. The following day, a man I can only describe as a skinhead walked up behind me, took a swing at me and asked, "How was she?"

One of the tabloid television shows had even purchased a video of our 1993 wedding from the photographer we'd hired, and aired it. Then had come word that O.J.'s lawyers were pressing to have me subpoenaed as a witness.

What good could they possibly think I might do them? Ed Hookstratten contacted Shapiro and told him I would return to California only if ordered to do so by the court.

Amidst all the legal mumbo jumbo and gamesmanship, I found myself wondering if the insanity would ever end. There seemed to be no safe place to hide.

On the few business trips I was required to make, I'd begun checking into hotels under the name "Roy Green," borrowing from my friend who had been an outstanding two-way performer for the Cardinals during their days in St. Louis. Backdoor entrances and service elevators became quite familiar to me.

Weary of it all, Kathryn and I made plans for a weekend visit to the Phoenix home of our friend Charles Barkley. To do so, I enlisted the help of Ray Zacovitch, an ex–Secret Service agent who had served as bodyguard to five Presidents before his retirement. He assured me he could get us out of town without anyone knowing.

The whole thing was like a scene out of a *Mission: Impossible* episode. Ray pulled into the parking garage and Kathryn sat in front with him while I got into the backseat and lay on the floorboard during the drive to the airport. En route, he radioed ahead to security officers at the terminal to tell them we were approaching and then escorted us onto the plane.

Such treatment was not only foreign to me but distasteful. I've never felt comfortable with limos or even having someone carry my bags into a hotel. And suddenly, out of sheer necessity, I was being treated like some privileged, self-important character.

In Phoenix, my hopes of a couple of quiet rounds of golf with Charles fell by the wayside when we found him recovering from recent knee surgery. So we spent a leisurely weekend in his home, doing little more than enjoying the peace and quiet his sanctuary afforded.

It wasn't long before the tabloids wove a completely fictional account of our visit. This time the story was that Kathryn and I had gotten into a violent argument, with me hitting her and Charles breaking us up before things had gotten completely out of hand. The article suggested that Kathryn would soon be filing for divorce.

Aside from its complete falsehood, the most troubling aspect of it was that it quoted "a close Allen family member" as the source of the absurdity. Rest assured, the source of that story was not a member of my immediate family.

The matter of my becoming a witness in O.J.'s trial came to a head when F. Lee Bailey arrived in Kansas City in June while we were in the middle of an off-season minicamp. He filed papers at the Jackson County Circuit Court, including one signed by Los Angeles trial judge Lance Ito stating that I was a material witness in the Simpson case, expected to testify sometime in July.

I sat in the courtroom with Jon Hookstratten, who had flown in from Los Angeles, and Kansas City attorney Paul Sheppars, listening as Bailey forcefully argued that I had testimony that was absolutely vital to his defense team's case. I watched in silence as he displayed the kind of aloof confidence one from the big city so often displays when visiting what he considers the hinterland.

Meanwhile, Jon and Paul only reminded the court that I had already been interviewed by representatives of the Los Angeles police and district attorney's office, and had told them that I had not been involved in an affair with Nicole Simpson.

I was relieved when the judge announced that he found no merit to the visiting attorney's claim and ruled against my extradition. Bailey went back to Los Angeles, and I went back to the business of being a football player, pleased that the matter was over.

Which shows you what little I knew of the tenacity of lawyers.

twenty-two

Coming to Grips

Just as the '94 season was one of disappointment and bizarre misfortune, 1995 quickly developed into one in which the Chiefs could do little wrong. With Montana gone, another expatriate 49er, Steve Bono, took over as quarterback.

And my role changed.

Greg Hill, the team's number-one draft choice the year before, was a running back with great promise. He had played well as a rookie, starting in my place during the three weeks I was sidelined with the knee injury. Clearly, he figured prominently in the team's future. Not only did I admire his talent and work ethic, but I liked him personally. A Texan like my dad, he was outgoing and inquisitive. Greg wasn't one of those rookies who comes into the league convinced he knows it all.

Both Jimmy Raye and Schottenheimer had told me that Greg would be seeing more playing time. The plan was for us to play almost equally. "You're the starter," Jimmy explained, "but we've got to get him on the field, too. We've got to get him ready."

Truth? I didn't exactly do cartwheels at the news. No one I know in this league wants to share his job. And I've always been a firm believer in the theory that the longer a running back is in the game and the more times he carries the ball, the more effective he will be. The idea of alternating series or even quarters is in direct opposition to that theory.

On the other hand, there is something to be said for having

what amounts to a fresh and rested back in the game at all times. That was the basis for the decision, and I chose not to take it personally. I was still the starter and liked the idea of helping to mold the guy who would one day take over my position.

As you age, you become a bit more of a realist. I no longer believed I would play forever.

Actually, I had to admire Greg's attitude toward the matter. I'm sure he wanted badly to be on the field full-time, recognized as the starting running back he was certain to one day be. And I admire that kind of thinking. If he doesn't feel that way, he has no business in the game. But he hid well any impatience he might be feeling. We became a pretty damn good tandem.

The plan was an unqualified success. For the first time ever, the Kansas City Chiefs would lead the entire NFL in rushing.

And our defense was extraordinary.

Again we opened with three straight wins, including a 23–17 victory over the Raiders. In the fourth week we lost at Cleveland, but then went on a seven-game winning streak that gave rise to a degree of excitement in Kansas City that was amazing. The atmosphere was like that you generally encounter in a college town whose team is having a kick-ass season.

And I was becoming increasingly comfortable with the idea of alternating with Greg. It was working well for both of us, as he was thriving in the additional playing time. And I felt good about the small part I was playing in his development. The coaches had not devised a strict schedule of when I would be on the field or when Hill would come in for me. It was more of a "feel" thing. If I was on a hot streak, I stayed in; same with Greg. No one was counting the number of plays.

Against the Broncos, for instance, I was running well despite the fact that we were playing in one of Denver's worst snowstorms of the year. I carried twenty-one times for 121 yards and got the 100th rushing touchdown of my career. On that day, Greg carried only ten times for 27 yards. But against

Seattle earlier in the year he'd been the real force in our attack, gaining 109 yards.

I'm sure opposing defenses did not look forward to playing against our one-two punch.

While I was happy in the confined world of NFL football, much of the nation was, of course, fixated on the Simpson trial, which droned on endlessly. I had made up my mind to ignore it, to remain focused, but it was impossible. There was nowhere you could go and not hear conversation about the day's televised testimony—at restaurants, standing in line for a movie, at the checkout stand in the grocery store. The tragedy that had already marked so many lives had become a sordid and sad industry, fueling TV ratings, newspaper and magazine sales, and mesmerizing the public like no news event in modern history. And it was destroying friendships like a plague sweeping down from the Los Angeles County Courthouse. Those who supported O.J. quickly found themselves ostracized by that part of the public that believed him guilty and was prone to a guilt-by-association way of thinking. To those supportive of Simpson, anyone who did not embrace their feelings was immediately branded a fairweather friend or, worse, a traitor.

There were those who placed me in the latter category. And while it bothered me, I had to wonder what they thought I might do that could magically turn public favor in O.J.'s direction. God knows I had labored over the question for months, only to come up with the same unsatisfactory answer: nothing.

The acquittal verdict did nothing to calm the public furor over the case. It seemed to resolve little in the minds of those who had already reached their own decisions. I viewed a nation divided and felt a new kind of sadness sweep over me.

And what did I think? I'd long since made up my mind that I would refuse to judge. And to this day there is but one certainty I can share: I am and forever will be tortured by the loss of two people who were my friends; one murdered, one now forced to live a lifetime being blamed for the tragedy.

While the whole matter continued to pain me greatly, I had

Despite the distractions, I was feeling good about my play and the direction in which the team was heading.

Against the Raiders I carried twenty-one times for 124 yards and a touchdown and we won, 29–23, with a late comeback. And during the course of the afternoon I reached a career milestone I was very proud of, becoming the first player in NFL history to gain 10,000 yards rushing and 5,000 receiving.

I don't have to tell you that it was an accomplishment that received scarce mention that day in the Oakland Coliseum, to which the Raiders had returned. In my mind's eye, I could see Al Davis boiling. And, while I had been warmly welcomed by those in the stands, there were, as usual, a few oddballs who seemed determined to spoil things for everyone, throwing flashlight batteries in the direction of players on the field.

Still, I judged it a banner day. The reception I'd received from the fans, the post-game congratulations of my teammates, and the fact that we'd won was plenty for me.

To the O.J.-obsessed media, though, I would have nothing to say. Instead, I slipped away to the game officials' dressing room to shower and change; then I was taken to the airport by car rather than trying to make my way through the cameras and microphones that waited outside near the team buses.

For the first time, my home state was a place I wanted to get away from as quickly and quietly as possible.

Finally, I wearied of the cloak-and-dagger routine that I'd been playing for weeks. I was tired of being held prisoner in my own home, of acting like some two-bit crook on the run from the law. And it was not right that the Chiefs organization and my teammates had to go to such lengths to protect me. I wanted to end it.

And so one morning, as I looked out the bedroom window and saw the familiar car that seemed rarely to leave its place just outside our building, I decided the game was over. I went to my car and drove up adjacent to its occupant, rolled down my window, and extended my hand.

The surprised process server hurriedly reached into the

pocket of his jacket and handed me the subpoena requiring me to give a deposition to defense lawyers in O.J.'s upcoming civil case. "Sorry," the man said as I rolled up my window.

I was surprised at the sudden relief I felt in knowing that the days of looking over my shoulder and making backdoor entries were over.

Months later I would give the deposition, which, incidentally, would never be used in the civil trial.

We ended the regular season 13–3 and champions of our division. Despite sharing time with Greg, I had rushed for 890 yards—my best since joining the Chiefs. Combined with Greg's 667, the running-back position had accounted for 1,557 yards. The two-back experiment had clearly paid off.

As the wild-card week of play-offs neared, I received a call from ABC, asking if I would like to come to New York and work in the studio with Robin Roberts and Chicago coach Dave Wannstedt. Apparently my debut in the broadcast industry the previous season hadn't scared everyone off. Again I jumped at the opportunity.

Even as I watched and made comments on the wild-card games being played, I could feel the adrenaline surging as I thought ahead to our participation in the play-offs. Not since the days of the Raiders team that had won the Super Bowl had I been more convinced that I was part of a team that had the capability to win it all. While our offense had become more run-oriented with Montana's departure, it was still solid. Bono had stepped up and done his job well. However, it was our defense that would see us through the play-offs. With people like Neil Smith, Derrick Thomas, Dale Carter, Tim Grunhard, Tracy Simien, Tracy Rogers, and Dan Saleamua playing better than I'd ever seen them play, I felt sure we were going to prove the old adage that insists that it is defense that wins championships.

Such would not be the case. On a numbingly cold day in Arrowhead Stadium, the Indianapolis Colts abruptly ended our season with a 10–7 victory. Our running game got us into field goal range repeatedly, but Lin Elliott, our kicker, couldn't get the ball through the uprights. I felt badly for him, knowing that he had taken it upon himself to shoulder the blame for the loss.

I tried to remind him of the close games he'd helped us win during the course of the regular season; that if we'd scored the touchdowns we should have, the decision would never have fallen to him. Nothing anyone said really helped. It never does in the immediate aftermath of such a loss.

For all except that one team that manages to make it through the play-offs and win the Super Bowl, the end of a football season comes so abruptly that you feel like you've just suffered whiplash. Since the opening of training camp in July, you've raced from one week to another like a runaway train. Then it suddenly collides into a wall of steel. And it's over. No more practice, no more meetings, no more game plans to study. There is no way to prepare for it.

That night as I drove home, there was a hush over Kansas City unlike any I'd ever experienced. Streets were empty, no traffic. It was as if the Rapture had suddenly occurred and God had reached down and taken everyone. I had lingered in the dressing room longer than usual, tired, disappointed, and not wanting to accept the reality that the season was over.

I knew I would not sleep. Long after Kathryn had gone to bed, I would still be staring at the television or listening to music, replaying the game until I had set every missed opportunity, every failure to memory. Coach Schottenheimer's "midnight rule" would not be in effect.

In time perspective would salve the immediate disappointment. I would come to realize that the pluses of the recent season had far outweighed the minuses. I would feel better about the year I'd had; about the fact that my teammates had again voted me the Chiefs' Most Valuable Player.

And while the hurt and pain of old friends still lingered, I could feel some consolation in the fact that I'd come to grips with the responsibilities I owed my wife and family. I had done what I felt necessary to avoid the maelstrom that had sucked so many into an ugliness I shall never completely understand.

As I look back over two decades of wins and losses, it occurs to me that the thing that makes sports unique is the fact that it offers only highs and lows. There is no definable measurement for anything in-between. You win and celebrate the great feeling of accomplishment that accompanies it. You lose, and everything goes pitch-black until you get another shot, next week or next season.

I'd been in each position many times before. And would be again—until that inner voice I was not yet ready to acknowledge whispered that it was time to call it a career.

twenty-three

Touchdown Number 112 and Final Thoughts

No matter how careful the planning or how high the hopes, it is impossible to forecast the future in sports. Oddsmakers never cease to amaze me with their bold predictions that Team A is certain to win over Team B by X number of points. Theirs is the perfect example of a faulty science. In pro football there are simply too many variables, too much of a human element involved, to ever be absolutely sure that one team will beat another. In this era of league-office orchestrated parity, the tired old "any given Sunday" cliché applies more than ever.

For all the optimism I've applied to my job over the years, I have never gone into a game 100 percent certain that we would win. I've always felt that those teams with a healthy fear that they might lose are the ones most likely to avoid it.

In 1996, even before the first pre-season practice, the Chiefs were the pick of many to win the AFC. The experts were predicting that we would ultimately face Green Bay in the Super Bowl. I'll save you the O. Henry ending and note that things didn't work out. The unpredictables crashed down around our heads—injuries, an unstable quarterback situation—and we finished the year at 9–7, not even making the play-offs.

And while the season was disappointing, it was not without its moments. The media began making a big deal of the fact that I was closing in on several NFL career records, including the rushing touchdown mark of former Chicago Bears running back Walter Payton.

The anticipation supplied me with all the motivation I needed. In the off-season I had spent a lot of time contemplating my future. The end of my career was getting close—one more year, maybe two—and I looked at having my name in the record books as a nice way to make my exit.

It would also afford me an opportunity to express my gratitude to the people of Kansas City who had made the last years of my career so enjoyable. In my mind I began visualizing a scenario where I would get the record on a warm, sunlit Sunday afternoon in Arrowhead Stadium.

My vision was no better than that of the oddsmakers.

For a while it seemed everything was falling nicely into place. I got a couple of touchdowns in the third game of the year in Seattle, then another the following week in Denver. By the end of October I had scored three more. With a three-game homestretch coming up, I needed only one to tie Payton.

I was a little surprised by the excitement I was beginning to feel. The Chiefs, I found out, were already making big plans to celebrate touchdown number 112 when it finally came. The game would be halted briefly while the public-address announcer acknowledged the historic moment. "I'm not going to ruin the surprise," Bob Moore, our PR man told me, "but, rest assured, it will be memorable."

And I didn't get close to the end zone. Worse, we lost two of the three.

While I had badly wanted to set the record at home, I have to admit that the day on which it finally came was highly appropriate.

Playing against Detroit in the Silverdome on Thanksgiving Day, before a national television audience, I finally tied the record with a one-yard run in the first quarter.

Soon thereafter all thoughts of the record attempt went by the wayside as we found ourselves in a knock-down-drag-out battle with the Lions. With just over eight minutes remaining in the game, they were ahead, 24–21.

Only forty-six seconds were left when Rich Gannon, quarterbacking in place of Steve Bono, handed-off to me on a second down play at the Detroit one. I went up and over—and into the end zone.

Describing the moment is difficult. Naturally, there was elation, not only because I'd finally broken the record but also over the fact that we'd managed to come from behind and win the game. And there was a certain amount of relief. The pursuit had gone on for thirteen weeks.

Only later, during the post-game interviews, would I have the chance to put the accomplishment into some kind of perspective. I made no secret of the pride I felt. At the same time, I had no illusions about any long tenure in the record book. Emmitt Smith, the talented Dallas Cowboys running back, was only four touchdowns behind me and gaining fast. With several good years still in front of him, he was almost a cinch to eventually go well beyond any mark I might put up.

I was, I told reporters, pleased to be borrowing the record for a while.

Two weeks later, during pre-game ceremonies in Arrowhead, I got a big thrill when Walter Payton narrated a tribute to me that was shown on the stadium video screen. It was one of the nicest moments I'd ever experienced.

A few sportswriters even suggested that I should forget thoughts of soon retiring and set my mind to improving on the record for several years to come.

Had members of the media seen me a few weeks earlier, they would have likely advised that I forget records and steal away to a rocking chair.

Returning to the condo after practice, I was hit by a sudden back spasm unlike any I'd ever felt. In pain and unable to even stand straight, I lay on the floor, hoping that it would soon go away. But it only got worse, to the point where I realized I wasn't even going to be able to get up from the floor and into bed without help from someone.

Kathryn had left a few days before on a brief trip to California. I lay there for almost an hour, trying to figure out what to do about my situation. Sure that the problem was temporary, I didn't want to contact a team doctor or trainer for fear they might make me sit out a game or two.

Finally I came up with a plan. I managed to crawl over to the coffee table, where I'd left the cellular phone, and I placed a call to Kathryn in California. Already feeling a little embarrassed about the whole thing, I asked her to phone one of our neighbors and have a security officer let them in. "Tell them it isn't serious," I said. "But I need some help getting into bed."

The proof that Kathryn had become a full-fledged football player's wife, familiar with the difference between serious injury and the routine aches and pains of the game, came in the muffled laughter I heard.

I did ultimately tell the trainer I'd experienced some "tightness" in my back and was allowed to skip practice for a couple of days. But by week's end I was ready to get back to work.

I've now begun my last season of football, as excited about what the season holds as ever. And while I'm still playing because I believe I can continue to perform at a high level, I know that won't always be the case. Once the 1997 season is over, I'm calling it quits. One of the most important lessons anyone who plays this game has to learn is that you can't go on forever, that the time comes to move on to something else. I'm ready for that.

Actually, I find myself thinking less of the end and more of some new beginning that awaits me. What's next? I'm not really sure.

I've played football all of my life. It has been my passion and my calling. Now I'm looking for some new calling. All I know for certain is that I have a responsibility to do something meaningful with the rest of my life and that I'll always be dealing with people, likely in some educational capacity.

As I've mentioned, professional athletes have been given a rare platform, and each of us needs to use it to make some kind of positive impact on the lives of others. If, for example, there's a way I can help focus more attention on the need for blacks to be given opportunities for head-coaching jobs and management positions, I want to get involved.

Sports just may provide the arena in which we as a nation can one day resolve our differences. It is far from perfect, but in my opinion it is the most color-blind segment of today's society. And I think there are lessons to be learned from that. I can honestly say that I've never felt people were at all concerned with whether I was black or white when I made a good run or caught a pass or scored a touchdown. I was simply Marcus Allen, and I've enjoyed that. I'd like everyone— of all colors, from all walks of life—to experience that feeling.

Once the hectic schedule of NFL life is behind us, Kathryn and I hope to begin our own family. And as we talk about it, she always brings one familiar question into the conversation: If we have a son, will I encourage him to get involved in sports, to aspire to become a professional athlete like his old man?

I hope when the time comes, I can handle it in the same way my own father did. He never pushed, only encouraged. The decisions were left to me.

What I will tell my child is the same thing I've told a lot of youngsters. The last thing I want to do is shatter anyone's dreams. I think it is necessary to nurture and encourage them. At the same time it is important to understand the realities of the world. The odds that any high school athlete will one day play at the professional level are something like 10,000 to 1. Even for the exceptionally talented there are no guarantees.

But, rather than dismiss the dreams, I think it important that we point out and encourage alternatives. We have to make kids aware of the value of education. Only with it can they be guaranteed success in life.

You've heard the old line that says a person is successful if somewhere along the way he is able to touch one life in some positive fashion. To me that's a pretty poor percentage. I think we should all aspire to do things on a grander scale.

I've tried to do that. But the truth is my balance sheet is far too one-sided at this point. The game has given me a great deal.

It is difficult to explain except to say that it has been much more to me than touchdowns and records, trophies and pay-checks. It has offered me a wonderful learning experience. The journey has been the most rewarding thing. That and the relationships I've enjoyed. The people who have come into my life as a result of my involvement in athletics stand out in my mind far more than any particular game or awards banquet.

I like to think I've been a part of the evolutionary process of sports. To those pioneers I've mentioned, I owe a great deal for the opportunities that have been afforded me. They left a legacy, a standard, a tradition that I've tried to carry on. It has been my responsibility to play the game the best I could. I feel I've done that. And now the time is nearing for me to pass that responsibility on to someone else.

And I hope he recognizes the fact that sports are an un-believably powerful force in our society. Not only is it good to those who play the games, but to the fans who live vicar-iously through their favorite teams and athletes. I'm glad I had the opportunity to be a part of that. And to grow and mature along the way.

In telling my story, I've attempted an honest look at what the athletic world in which I've lived is all about. I've attempted to show that it is not always as glamorous and free-spirited as the public is led to believe. At one point, I considered including a list of those fellow NFL players who have passed away during the years I've been playing. I found myself re-flecting on friends and rivals whose lives were cut short by plane crashes, automobile accidents, gunshots, and drug over-doses and finally dismissed the idea. The list was far too long.

At the same time, I've tried to show that its impact on history will never compare with the social issues that bombard us on the nightly news. Regardless of the importance players, coaches, and people in the front offices assign it every Sunday afternoon or Monday night, it is only a game.

The only pressure I've ever felt was that which I placed on myself. The truth is, everyone deals with pressure, so to suggest that it is unique to athletics is unfair to everyone who gets up and goes to work every day, expected to meet his quota or bill a certain number of hours. The pressures I've been exposed to have been minor. Real pressure is the homeless guy trying to find something to eat, hoping to make it through one more day, or the guy sitting in a foxhole somewhere with artillery exploding all around him. Pressure is the father working two jobs to keep his family fed. So when I hear or read that some athlete has done something remarkable, overcoming a great amount of pressure to do so, I'm not really that impressed.

Economically, the game has been very good to me. Since the day I became a pro ballplayer, I've been in the upper income-tax bracket and it has enabled me and my family to live a very good life. For that I have no apologies.

I'm delighted every time I see a player sign a new contract for more money. Knowing how all the front-office mind games are played and aware of the kind of money franchises make these days, I want every player, regardless of his sport, to get as much as he can..

Still, I wish the general public had a better understanding of what we do and of the short time frame during which we're able to earn the kinds of salaries we do. It is difficult for some to realize that professional sports is just another giant, moneymaking business.

The only real concern I have about the economics of the game today is that the profits being made by the league and the owners are so much greater than the money the players are getting. I think it unfair, for instance, when NFL Properties gets more compensation for a television commercial than the players who actually do the work, just because the NFL has licensed the uniform or insignia they're wearing. And I wonder at the logic in the fact that the league should be the one to profit when a facsimile of a player's jersey is purchased. It has, for instance, been Detroit's Barry Sanders who has made number 20 marketable, not the NFL. So why shouldn't Sanders be the beneficiary of his efforts? I'd also like to see the league promoting more players for roles in commercials and endorsements. I'm sure the argument would be that product manufacturers want only the high-profile, "name" players. But it seems to me that with an energetic promotional effort, more players could be elevated to that status and the rewards spread more equally.

I worry, too, about the young players who are making a great deal of money and seem to believe it will go on forever. I see so many guys living beyond their means, not thinking ahead to the day when there won't be a multimillion-dollar contract to sign or bonus checks to cash. They, like so many of the fans, haven't come to the realization that they are in a business, not just playing a game. But the quicker they understand that, the better off they'll be.

Despite all my concerns, I've always admired the sheer beauty of football. That may sound like a strange way to describe a sport that is built on the principle that the guy who knocks the other down the most is probably going to win. But the game is so much more if you just stop and look at it. It takes grace and style, as well as speed and strength. It teaches hard lessons about success and failure, joy and disappointment. And when played well, it has a poetry all its own.

That's the part of the game I've always loved. What I've disliked are the same things I've always found abhorrent in life: bigotry, mediocrity, and injustice.

In recent years there have been a few players who have received a great deal of bad publicity and it has, at least to some degree, been a reflection on all of us. On one hand, the media are very good at perpetuating this bigger-than-life image of today's sports celebrities. Then, they are just as quick to rub his nose in it when he falls from grace. The public needs to understand that even though we play football and are on television every Sunday afternoon, we're still human, with all the flaws that society has to offer. In a perfect world, there would be no stories of athletes being arrested for DWI or spousal abuse or involvement with drugs. But that will never be the case. We can only hope that such behavior is the rare exception rather than the rule. At the same time, I find myself wishing that the good is not exaggerated out of proportion. The media attention attached to my quest for that record-breaking touchdown last year became embarrassing. And when I finally got it, there were far too few public pats on the backs of those who helped get me in position to score.

Perhaps we would all be better served if the praise—and the blame—were spread more evenly.

I recognize that the mystique of pro football has been built around a macho, superhuman image. And because of it we are asked to believe we're invincible when, in reality, we're just as fragile as the next guy.

Our quarterback Rich Gannon put things into perspective last year after having an exceptional game. While the members of the media were huddled around him, asking that he relive every pass he'd completed, eager to make him the hero of the day, he explained that in the big picture he was no different than he'd been when he was on the sidelines as a backup. Regardless of what he'd done on the field, he still had to go home that evening and change the baby's diapers.

I've always thought of myself as a pretty regular guy. But I realize there are those who see me differently. A few years ago, while playing in the pro-am at the Bob Hope Desert Classic, I was spraying the ball all over the course, really hacking away. Finally, one of my playing partners said, "Hey, it's good to see you're just one of us."

Except for a few hours on Sunday afternoons, that's what I've always been.

Postscript

I can tell you that ending a playing career, even when you think you've planned it quite well, does not come easy.

Through the annual agonies of training camp I made it from one day to the next, comforted by the knowledge that it was an exercise I'd never have to face again. And as we moved toward the season I kept reminding myself that Marty had publicly announced during the summer that Greg Hill was going to be the Chiefs' starting running back when the 1997 season began. I knew what that meant, I knew the role I would be playing. In addition to being ready to contribute whenever called on—most likely on third downs and short yardage situations—I would be there to do whatever I could to aid Greg in his transition. That, I was sure I could handle and, in fact, looked forward to serving as mentor to someone who I sincerely wanted to see succeed. That Greg was getting his well-deserved chance was part of pro football's natural progression. I'd been around long enough to understand that everyone who plays the game reaches a point where he eventually comes face-to-face with his own athletic mortality. Fortunate enough to play sixteen seasons, I'd already beaten the odds.

In a manner of speaking, I was going to be ending my career with Kansas City just as it had begun, back when I'd started out as the team's No. 2 running back. And while I still prepared for the season the only way I've ever known—getting myself physically and mentally ready to be on the field for 25–30 carries a game—I knew it was not something that was likely to happen. Some of my teammates even suggested it would be the most enjoyable year I'd ever experienced. With limited playing time there would be far fewer bumps and bruises to suffer through. Not spending all week trying to work out the soreness from the previous Sunday's game wouldn't be all bad. In fact, it all sounded pretty good. Aware that it would soon end, I planned to enjoy being around my teammates, the travel to rival cities, and the excitement of the new season. If I was to get one last look, I wanted to be keenly aware of every aspect of life in the NFL.

All of which is to say I felt quite confident that I had properly prepared myself for what would be the most unusual year of my NFL career.

I was kidding myself. Big time.

By the end of our opener against Denver I was miserable, feeling an emptiness unlike any I'd ever experienced as an athlete. That a season of high expectations got off to a losing start—the Broncos defeated us 28–14—was bad enough. The fact I'd done little but stand and watch only compounded the disappointment. It is not ego speaking when I say that despite the fact Hill played well, I couldn't help but believe I might have made some kind of difference had I not spent all my time pacing the sidelines with helmet in hand. Competitive instincts insist that one always believe that he can positively affect the outcome. Doing so, however, is all but impossible when one's entire contribution amounts to touching the football three times.

Understand, I wasn't upset with Marty or Jimmy Raye or Greg. I had gone into the game fully aware of the plan. I just wasn't prepared for the anxious feelings I experienced as things progressed. If that was what the final year of my career was going to be like, I thought to myself, the next fifteen weeks were going to be torture.

Compounding my frustration was the fact that I was absolutely convinced we had a team capable of accomplishing something special. From the early days of camp there had been a very positive feeling in the air about our chances to be a vastly improved team. For several years the Kansas City reputation had been founded on our talented defense which had proven again and again that it was capable of shutting down the most explosive of offenses. The Chiefs' offense, meanwhile, had gained the reputation of being solid but somewhat methodical. We could put enough points on the scoreboard to win, but lacked the reputation of a fast-striking, high-scoring unit. That, everyone sensed, was going to change with the presence of newcomers Elvis Grbac and Andre Rison.

Elvis had, like Joe Montana and then Steve Bono, come to Kansas City from the 49ers and he brought with him a fiery eagerness to win that quickly spread throughout the team. It was soon clear that he was the offensive leader we badly needed. There had, on the other hand, been some eyebrows lifted when it was first announced that Rison was joining us. Recognized as a wide receiver with excellent speed and great hands, he had a lengthy history of not fitting in with the teams he'd previously played for. In Atlanta, Cleveland, Jacksonville and Green Bay, things hadn't worked out for a variety of reasons which the press boiled down to the notion that Andre seemed to be a square peg trying to fit into a round hole. There were those, I'm sure, who wondered if the Chiefs hadn't bought themselves trouble when they signed him. Despite the fact he'd been a four-time Pro Bowler, a pre-season rating published by *Sports Illustrated* had not included Rison among its list of the 90 top wide receivers in the game. Some privately wondered about Marty's let-bygones-be-bygones philosophy when he decided to sign a guy who liked to call himself ''Bad Moon'' Rison.

What we got, in fact, was a big-play performer who dramatically changed the complexion of our offense. With Andre in the lineup, we suddenly had the long-ball, fast-strike threat that had been so long absent. And he quickly proved to be one of the most unselfish players on the team. Unlike some wide receivers who spend a great deal of time in the huddle lobbying for the ball, always trying to convince the quarterback they can get open on every play, Andre would lend constant encouragement to the other receivers as our season progressed. Aware that he was likely to draw double coverage in obvious passing situations, he would urge others to do whatever they had to do to get open. It was quickly apparent to me and everyone else on the team that what drove Andre Rison was winning, not individual statistics. And in that regard, he fit in nicely—even if he did put me in my place during one of the first conversations we had after his arrival. "You know," he told me, "when I was a kid I tried to model myself after you. You were the player I wanted to grow up to be." I didn't know whether to give him a grandfatherly pat on the head or pop him in the nose.

It didn't take long for Andre to prove his worth.

Our second game of the season was a Monday-night visit to Oakland. Though I knew it wasn't likely that I would see a great deal of playing time, the press seized on the opportunity to revisit my history with the Raiders and Al Davis, and point out that I would be making my swan-song appearance in a place I'd once called home. Needless to say, it got my adrenaline pumping.

On that evening, as is always the case with Monday Night Football, there was a four-star carnival atmosphere. Despite a crippling mass transit strike which made getting to the game difficult for many, the Coliseum was filled long before time for the kickoff. Out early for pre-game warmups, I had a chance to say quick hellos to a few old Raiders teammates like Tim Brown and Chester McGlockton and was asked by photographers to pose for a picture with actress Bo Derek, and the ABC Monday Night Football crew, Frank Gifford, Al Michaels, and Dan Dierdorf.

Though they had lost their opener to the Oilers in overtime, there was a new optimism surrounding the Raiders as they had opened the season with yet another new head coach— Joe Bugel—and a new quarterback—former Atlanta Falcon Jeff George. Al Davis, the media, and Oakland fans seemed convinced they would provide the needed talent and direction to return the team to championship level.

For a time, it appeared as though that optimism was justified as they took a 7–0 lead in the opening quarter. Pete Stoyanovich soon got us untracked with a 23-yard field goal, then Elvis hit Kimble Anders for a touchdown that put us into the lead.

Oakland pulled into a tie with a field goal as only 63 seconds remained in the second quarter. Then, with time ticking away, Grbac connected with Rison on a 43-yard pass that set up another Stoyanovich field goal with just two seconds remaining before intermission.

The traditional Chiefs–Raiders seesaw battle was holding to form.

Though we led 13–10 at halftime, nothing had come easy. And the issue was far from settled.

In the third quarter, George immediately brought the Raiders fans to their feet. He quickly drove Oakland to a touchdown, covering 76 yards in just three plays. Soon thereafter they added a field goal and suddenly it was 20–13. Our offense finally got a drive going and, as we moved deep into the Raiders' end of the field I got a chance to do my part, going in on a short-yardage situation—and fumbled the ball.

Less than a minute later, George threw his second touchdown pass of the night to Dudley. They added a field goal to go up 27–13. I stood on the sidelines in agony, convinced that I had let the game slip away from us.

But it was far from over. As has so often been the case, our defense stepped up to add a badly needed spark. Darren Anderson picked off a George pass and ran it back 55 yards for a touchdown. Marty decided to attempt a two-point conversion that would pull us to within three points but Grbac's throw to Rison was knocked away.

With time running down, we had to have a touchdown to win.

With only 1:01 remaining in the game, the defense forced an Oakland punt, giving our offense one final chance. It was what Grbac and everyone else on our bench had been screaming for.

From our own 20, Elvis connected with Lake Dawson for 21 yards, then got 20 more on a pass to Brett Perryman. Then, with no time-outs left and only 11 seconds remaining, Grbac got great protection and launched a 33-yard touchdown pass to Rison deep in the corner of the Raiders' end zone, putting us ahead 28–27 as the final seconds ticked away.

Had it not been for the lack of speed I'd become so famous for over the length of my playing career, I would have been the first Chiefs player to reach Andre and hug his neck. I had to be satisfied with joining the mob scene in the end zone as we celebrated the come-from-behind victory. I sought out every player on the team to personally thank him for the part he had played in getting me off the hook.

In retrospect, that victory fueled a fire that would burn brightly for the Chiefs for the remainder of the season. Our confidence, shaken by the opening loss to Denver, had been jump-started. For the night Elvis had completed 21 of 35 passes for 312 yards. Andre had caught eight for 162. Numbers like that, we knew, would win a lot of ball games.

My contribution? I did catch one of Grbac's passes for a 14-yard gain during our first touchdown drive. I ran the ball only three times for 13 yards. And there was that damned fumble which, in the locker room afterwards, I jokingly told sportswriters had only added to the drama of the game.

On that night I was too happy to concern myself with the minimal role I'd played. Just being a part, however small, of a victory like that offered the kind of satisfaction every athlete strives for. There were those who, in hindsight, would suggest that the loss ripped the heart out of the Raiders and set the tone for what would ultimately be the worst season in the franchise's recent history, prompting Davis to go searching for yet another coach at season's end. For the Chiefs, on the other hand, it was just the beginning.

That night, as I walked out of the Coliseum, I had a grin on my face that dynamite couldn't have blown away. And I had a souvenir I would forever cherish.

In the dressing room, after things had finally quieted, a much-deserving Andre Rison was presented the game ball. As the cheers celebrating his heroics echoed through the room, he walked over to where I was standing. ''I know how important this game was to you,'' he said. The following week, when he was a guest on my TV show, he walked into the studio and handed me the game ball. ''I want you to have this,'' he said.

Speaking of the TV show, I had begun to feel a little uncomfortable hosting it in light of the limited contribution I was making to the team. It had been far more fun when I could talk first hand about something that went on in the huddle or during the course of a particular play in which I was involved. A segment dreamed up by the producer when we first starting doing the show was really going to become a problem. He had titled it "Marcus Moments," and the idea was to show tape of some play I was involved in while I explained it to the audience. With my playing time, I feared, the Marcus Moments were going to be very short and not too sweet.

The win over the Raiders set us off on a four-game winning streak. With a boldness that reminded me of Joe Montana when he was quarterbacking the Chiefs, Grbac attacked the opposing defenses with a mixture of short, medium and long passes, moving the ball around from wideouts to tight ends to running backs. We won over Buffalo, Seattle, and Carolina before losing to Miami in a game where our running attack was shut down.

I'd seen considerable playing time against the Seahawks, carrying the ball 19 times for 78 yards, but had seen limited action against Miami. Jimmy Raye and Marty were both aware of the difficulty I was having with my inactivity and made it a point to constantly urge me to "be ready." "It's a long season," Raye began constantly reminding me.

One I feared at times would seem endless. In wins over San Diego and St. Louis the following weeks, I played some but far less than I wanted. All I could do was remind myself that I was, in fact, playing on borrowed time and give Greg as much encouragement as possible.

It isn't the kind of thing that shows up on any stats sheet, but one of my primary objectives was to make Greg aware of the importance of jealously holding on to the opportunity he'd been given. Now that you've got the starting job, I repeatedly told him, you have to do everything in your power to keep it. Don't let anyone take it away from you.

Of course, I was, in effect, preaching against myself; urging him to make sure that my butt stayed on the bench. Strange though it might seem, that was part of my job. During one game after a good run, Greg waved toward the bench, indicating that he needed a breather. It is a relatively new tradition which, in my estimation, is being exercised all too often by players these days.

As I ran onto the field to replace him, I stopped him before he got to the bench and yelled at him. ''Are you crazy?'' I said. ''If you want this job, you've got to stay out here until they drag you off.'' With that I urged him to get back into the game as quickly as possible. A play later he was back in the huddle.

Any player who says he doesn't fantasize about doing something exceptional during the course of a Monday night football game is simply not being truthful. Not only do you have the undivided attention of the country's NFL fans but you know that players from all other teams in the league are tuned in. To those who thought our first Monday-night win—the last minute, one-point victory over the Raiders—was a fluke, we were eager to prove ourselves.

In the early going of our meeting with the AFC Central-leading Pittsburgh Steelers, however, we didn't do a lot that was likely to earn us high praise. Kordell Stewart got the Steelers off to a 10–0 lead in the first quarter as he connected on a 44-yard touchdown pass to Courtney Hawkins, then drove his team into range for a 27-yard field goal as the first period ended.

But in the second quarter the defense settled in and our offense began to move the ball. Stoyanovich narrowed the Steelers' margin with field goals from 35 and 44 yards early in the quarter. Just minutes after the second field goal, Jerome Woods gave us a big lift when he stepped in front of a Stewart pass, picked it off, and returned it 17 yards to the Steelers' 45.

Four plays later we were at the 14 and a dream came true for me when I heard Grbac call the play. Every week, it seemed, we practiced it. We talked of how it was certain to work against whatever defense we were scheduled to face in an upcoming game. And we never seemed to get around to using it.

But finally the time had come. Elvis took the ball and handed it to me as if a sweep to the right was taking form. After a couple of steps, however, I stopped, planted, and threw a pass to Danan Hughes who was in the end zone, four yards behind any Steelers defender. Arrowhead turned into a thunder of cheers as we took a 13–10 lead.

It was the first touchdown pass I'd thrown since the 1991 season and only the fifth of my career. But I don't recall one that ever felt better.

Though the score would never change, we dominated the game throughout the second half, failing to score only because of a couple of fumbles at crucial times. Early in the fourth we had advanced to the Steelers four-yard-line and needed less than a yard for a first down. I went up the middle and was near the goal line when I felt the ball slip away. No first down; Pittsburgh's ball. Later, during another productive drive, Kimble fumbled the ball away.

And so it was left to our defense to finally get the job done. Derrick Thomas, Anthony Davis and Woods were unbelievable as they completely shut down a Steelers offense that had earned a reputation as a highly productive second-half team. Pittsburgh's outstanding running back, Jerome Bettis, who had run for 36 yards in the first quarter alone, added only 35 to his total in the next three periods. Stewart's passing game was wrecked by the constant pressure through the scoreless second half.

While the win improved our record to 7–2, there was little post-game celebration. Victory had come at a high—and frightening—price. At one point in the third quarter the game was delayed for ten minutes while Ted Popson lay motionless on the field after taking a blow to the chin from the Steelers' Donnell Woolford. Everyone's immediate concern was that he had suffered some kind of neck injury. Only after the game did we learn that he'd received a mild concussion.

Then, in the fourth quarter, Grbac left the field with what was later determined to be a broken left clavicle that was certain to sideline him for quite some time.

Rich Gannon, who had come in to help us control the ball and run the final few minutes off the clock, had suddenly inherited the role of starting quarterback.

In today's game, where players seem to be bigger, faster and more aggressive with each new season, there is no one more vulnerable to injury than a quarterback. All you have to do is chart a season and see how many are forced to the sidelines with concussions, shoulder separations, broken fingers, you name it. So, while it is a rule that is unspoken, every team in the league prepares for that eventuality when it has to go with its backup quarterback at some point during the season.

While Grbac had brought new excitement and firepower to our offense, there was absolutely no thought among the Kansas City players that the team would go south in his absence. Rich Gannon, we knew, had the talent and credentials to keep the ball rolling. He'd come on as a starter last year on Thanksgiving Day to help us get a win over Detroit. In his career with the Minnesota Vikings, and now the Chiefs, he'd started 42 NFL games. Which is to say he knew the drill. And, while there was a feeling that we would all need to step everything up a notch in Elvis's absence, there was unanimous agreement that Rich could get the job done.

And, except for one dismal Sunday, he did so with flying colors.

Traveling to Jacksonville after the short week of preparation following our Monday-night game, we fell behind 24–3 in the first half and never got back into it. Despite the fact our defense held the Jaguars scoreless in the third and fourth quarters, we couldn't get our offense into high gear, and lost 24–10. Aside from a 30-yard run in the third quarter which caused the public address announcer to make note of the fact that I'd become the seventh player in NFL history to surpass 12,000 yards rushing, I did little to aid the cause. My only other carry was for a three-yard gain. By day's end the media was suggesting that with Grbac indefinitely out and a rematch with division leader Denver coming up, our season was quickly going to turn into a huge disappointment.

The rumors of our demise were greatly exaggerated.

The proof came in Arrowhead Stadium the following week in a game I'd been looking forward to. As the season had progressed, Greg Hill had begun to experience a series of frustrations that visit all running backs at one point or another in their career. His rhythm seemed off. His cuts were not as sharp. He was getting to the hole a split second too late.

Though working as hard as he'd been all year, his production had dramatically decreased. While never specifically saying that I was going to be called on more, Jimmy Raye had begun asking a question that was music to my ears: "How many plays can you go?" My answer, of course, was that I was ready to carry the ball as often as it was given to me.

Against the Broncos, I finally went back to work, carrying the ball 16 times for 43 yards, and it felt great.

It was one of those typical KC-Denver dogfights, with John Elway having one of his typically remarkable days and Broncos running back Terrell Davis, another San Diego Lincoln High alumnus, putting on an impressive show as he went over 100 yards for the ninth time of the season.

Denver jumped out to an early lead but late in the first half Tamarick Vanover returned a kickoff 77 yards to put us in position to get back into the game. With just over four minutes left in the first half, I scored from the six to cut the Bronco lead to 13–7. Then, with 1:08 left in the half, Gannon hit Danan Hughes on a five-yard scoring pass and we went into the locker room with a 14–13 intermission lead.

No defense in the world is going to completely shut down a John Elway–driven offense, but ours put on a remarkable show in the second half. Davis, who had broken for good gains early in the game, got only 19 yards on 15 carries in the final 30 minutes. And Donnie Edwards's recovery of an Elway fumble at the Denver 36 set a drive in motion that ended when I got in from a yard out midway through the third.

But a 21–13 deficit is the kind of situation Elway lives for. I've long since quit counting the number of come-from-behind victories he's engineered in his career. For a time it looked as if he'd added to that list. By the end of the third quarter, he'd moved the Broncos into field-goal range twice, narrowing the margin to 21–19.

And then, with just a minute left to play, he did it again, moving his team 59 yards in six plays before our defense again held. Still, Jason Elam connected on a 34-yard field goal that gave them a one-point lead.

In our huddle, Rich Gannon was a picture of poise. "We're gonna get it back," he said. Seconds later he hit me with a perfect pass that was good for an 18-yard gain, then threw to Andre for 12. Spiking the ball to preserve the few seconds remaining, he then threw again to Rison for 10, moving the ball to the Denver 37.

With time for only one more play, Marty sent Stoyanovich in to attempt a 54-yard field goal. An eerie silence fell over the stadium as our offense moved into position. Then, as the ball narrowly cleared the crossbar, giving us the 24–22 victory, the place went absolutely crazy.

There is no rush greater than winning one like that, nothing that builds a team's confidence more dramatically than coming back to win over a championship-caliber team. This one beat the comeback win over the Raiders earlier in the season by light years.

At home that night, I sat up long after Kathryn had gone to bed, replaying the game, savoring its importance—and the fact that I had been on the field long enough to feel I had made a measurable contribution. The post-game aches felt good to me. Being tired and drained, physically and emotionally, was like a visit from an old friend. And a thought that had been playing in my mind began to take serious shape: I was still physically capable of helping the team. Football was fun again and one more year remained on my contract. The idea of calling it a career at season's end was no longer set in stone. I found myself thinking that the announcement of my intent to retire might have been premature.

But there was the current season to tend to before thinking too seriously about another.

Back in the race for the AFC West title, we kept our momentum going with a 19–14 win over Seattle that was a sterling tribute to our defense. Again they allowed the opposition no points in the second half and came up with big plays at critical times. In the final minute of the fourth quarter, for instance, Warren Moon drove the Seahawks to our 10. On a fourth down passing attempt to score the go-ahead touchdown, Moon was hit by a blitzing Reggie Tongue and fumbled the ball away to Dan Williams.

It wasn't until the next day that I learned that the first-quarter touchdown I'd scored against Seattle was my forty-first as a Chief, moving me ahead of Christian Okoye in the Kansas City record books. I had become the first player in NFL history to lead two teams—the Chiefs and Raiders—in rushing touchdowns.

Though winning, there was a feeling among our offensive players that we had fallen back into the pattern of placing too much pressure on our defense. We weren't scoring at the pace we'd hoped to, just putting enough points on the board to get by. Meanwhile, the defense had played remarkably well against such explosive quarterbacks as Pittsburgh's Kordell Stewart, Denver's Elway, and Seattle's Moon.

Next up, San Francisco's brilliant Steve Young. It was going to be essential that the Chiefs' offense do its part.

Through the first twelve weeks of the season we'd won big on occasion, our defense had played with remarkable consistency, we'd come from behind, and we'd shown that we could win with Gannon standing in for Grbac. We'd made a variety of statements that spoke to the character and talent of the Chiefs. None, however, was as loud and profound as the statement we made against the 49ers when they visited Kansas City.

We started fast, jumping out to a 28–6 halftime lead, and never slowed. By day's end we had scored a 44–9 win that I'm sure raised the eyebrows of everyone in the league. San Francisco, in fact, managed only three field goals during a day when everything went our way.

Gannon threw for three touchdowns and I got the chance to throw another from the halfback option. I scored a touchdown from a yard out following Tommy Thompson's return of a blocked San Francisco punt. Rison got back to his normal self, catching TD passes of six and 29 yards. And in addition to holding the 49ers' offense at bay, the defense, which had not given up a second-half touchdown in eight weeks, got in on the scoring as well. Donnie Edwards and Joe Phillips tackled San Fran's Terry Kirby in the end zone for a safety and Mark McMillian returned as interception 12 yards for a score.

It was one of those magical Sundays when everything we did was right, when every player was in sync, when the game plan worked perfectly. It was one of those days when the Chiefs showed the rest of the NFL what we were made of.

And we continued at that high level for the next two weeks, breezing past a devastated Raiders team, 30–0, then beating San Diego, 29–7. By winning over the Chargers in San Diego, we were only a game away from assuring ourselves home field advantage in the play-offs and there was growing media speculation about our making one more trip there. My hometown was to be the host of the Super Bowl and already I was thinking of how much fun it would be to wind up the season there. Though not superstitious, I did mention to Kathryn that there might be something prophetic in the fact that the upcoming championship game would be the 32nd Super Bowl, the same as my jersey number. Toss in the fact that it was home, and everything seemed in place. "It's got to be," I told her.

As we prepared to close out the regular season against New Orleans, the attention turned to our quarterback situation. Though Rich had performed quite well, Grbac was again healthy, leading to a great deal of media speculation about what Marty's decision would be. Did he continue with Gannon or return the starting job to Grbac? I can honestly say the players took no sides. We believed in them both; we believed in ourselves.

Schottenheimer decided to use the Saints game as a test for Grbac, returning him to his job after six weeks of inactivity. That Elvis was rusty was no surprise—he completed just five of 14 in three quarters of playing time—but there were signs of his old spark nonetheless. By the time he gave way to Gannon late in the game we were in control of things, thanks in no small part to a dazzling show put on by punt returner Vanover. He took one back 82 yards for a touchdown in the second quarter, then added a 48-yarder to the Saints eight in the fourth to set up my three-yard scoring run. And, less than two minutes later Gannon threw a TD pass to Ted Popson to put the issue to rest. It was one of those games you're just glad to have behind you, played in mud, rain and a cold that seemed to knife through you. The touchdown I scored on that dismal afternoon had no special meaning at the time. Only later would I look back on it as the last one of my career.

At 13–3, we were the AFC West champions, had home field

advantage, and had a week off to get ready to play the Denver Broncos again.

Two more games and we'd be in the Super Bowl. That's all I could think of in those endless days of preparation for our January 4 date with the Broncos. All year we'd fought not only for the home field advantage in the playoffs but the off-week at the end of the regular season, when wild-card teams played for the right to stay alive. We'd wanted that extra rest, time for nicks to heal and fine-tuning of the game plan. But there is a downside: The waiting, wanting to get on with the business of getting on the road to the NFL championship, becomes a battle in itself. I saw it in the locker room every day as we sat through meetings and on the practice field as everyone wanted time to pass more quickly. There was an eagerness unlike any I'd ever seen displayed by a Kansas City team; a confidence that this was the magical season when all was going to go as planned.

Not that we didn't view the prospect of facing Denver for the third time as a monumental challenge. No one need tell us they, too, were confident. I knew Denver coach Mike Shanahan had always felt his team matched up well against the Chiefs. Over the years he had felt comfortable in the Broncos' ability to hold our offense to relatively low scores, thus giving Elway a chance to work his wonders even if they trailed late in the game. And, while we'd split in the first two meetings, both games had played into Mike's philosophy. If we were to advance in the playoffs, we were going to have to put points on the board. We knew we could not count on our defense alone to get us to the AFC Championship.

They did their part.

Through the first half, Denver was able to put together only one sustained drive, moving 65 yards on eight plays before Terrell Davis scored on a one-yard run early in the second quarter. And while our offense struggled through the first half, the 7–0 halftime deficit was hardly cause to be discouraged. We had, after all, been a "second-half team" all year. I was fully convinced we were going to win the game, so much so that at intermission I approached the trainer with a request I'd sparingly made during my career. I'd twisted my ankle in a pileup late in the second quarter, and was concerned that it might slow me later in the game if I didn't get a shot that would kill or at least mask the pain.

As the second half got underway, Grbac began connecting on passes, moving us into field-goal range ten minutes deep into the third quarter. Stoyanovich's 20-yarder narrowed Denver's lead to four. Then, in another sudden burst, our offense moved 65 yards in just four plays before Elvis connected with Gonzalez for a 12-yard touchdown that put us into the lead.

It wasn't to last long, however, as Elway and Davis combined to move Denver to the go-ahead touchdown early in the fourth. Terrell, who would rush for 101 yards in the afternoon, scored from a yard out.

And then the defenses took over. For most of the final quarter there was a ferocity being displayed that was something to see. Elway, constantly pressured, would manage only ten completions all day for 170 yards. Elvis, meanwhile, was sacked four times by blitzing Denver defenders. The fact that I carried 12 times for just 37 yards says something about how well they shut down our running game.

Still, in the long shadow moments of the game, we had a chance. In a season of miracles, we had the opportunity to fashion one more. Of the 24 completions Elvis would have during the game, seven came on our final drive. With the clock ticking away the last minute and no time-outs remaining, we'd moved to the Denver 20, facing fourth and short yardage.

And then communications broke down—literally. The roar of the crowd was suddenly deafening, making it impossible for Grbac to hear the play being radioed to him from the press box. As precious seconds ticked off, lineman Dave Szott began yelling, "We need a play." Receiver Lake Dawson chimed in, "What's the play? We gotta go." On our sidelines, coaches and players were screaming at the top of their voices, urging us to get into position.

In the pressbox, offensive coordinator Paul Hackett was desperately trying to relay a message for Elvis to throw a quick sideline pass that would allow the receiver to get out of bounds after getting the first down. But it was no use. Turning to a fellow coach, a frantic and frustrated Hackett said, "He can't hear the play."

And so, with precious seconds wasted, Elvis called a play of his own choosing, taking the only option left to him.

The entire season had come down to one play called with only 20 seconds remaining.

Sending Lake Dawson into the deep left corner of the end zone, Grbac lofted the ball in his direction despite the fact that he'd drawn double coverage. So often during the course of the season Lake had outjumped the defenders to make remarkable catches, but this time the ball was batted away as the Arrowhead crowd went suddenly silent. The ball went over to Denver.

All that remained was for Elway to take one more snap, go to a knee, and let the final seconds tick away. Final score: Denver 14, Kansas City 10. As I stood there, watching our season come to an end, helpless to do anything about it, it was as if my heart stopped beating for a moment. The irony of things having come full circle did not escape me. Weeks earlier, in the season opening loss to the Broncos, I had stood on the sidelines, feeling that I'd not done my part to avoid the defeat. And there I was, in the season finale, feeling much the same.

And so it ended, all the season's high points and triumphs suddenly clouded by one narrow defeat. That, I suppose, is the hardest lesson an NFL player ever has to learn. Success is measured not by sixteen weeks of effort, not by glittering statistics or headline-making individual performances, but, rather, what the scoreboard reads in the last game. In team sports there is no consolation prize. For the Broncos, there would be another day, the AFC Championship, then victory in the Super Bowl.

For the rest of us there would only be next year.

Despite the disappointment, I found myself thinking ahead to another year as I drove home with Kathryn. This time I had vowed not to allow myself to sink into morose self-pity. Second-guessing would be useless and futile. I had no intention of sitting alone into the wee hours, pondering what might have been. We had given it our best shot, fallen short, and all I wanted was for the pain to go away quickly.

• • •

Though I had not said so publicly, I had all but decided that I would play one more season. The year had been enjoyable, I loved the chemistry of the team Marty had assembled, and— bottom line—I still felt I could run with the best of them.

But it was important that I be certain, so I spent the next couple of months thinking about it and trying to get my golf game back into shape. Meanwhile the NFL rumor mill, which never sleeps, had my future figured out. One day I'd hear that I was going to be back in training camp for the '98 season to play out the final year of my contract. The next day someone had heard from reliable sources that I was hanging it up. Then there were the speculations that I would give up the game to pursue a career as a network television sportscaster. The latter idea was certainly something I'd always hoped might be in my future, but I had no real reason to believe it was going to happen immediately.

Then, while I was playing in Bryant Gumbel's charity golf tournament in Orlando, I received a call from CBS, asking if I would be interested in coming to New York for an audition. Obviously thrilled to be back in the business of televising NFL games, they were assembling their broadcast teams and studio hosts for the upcoming season. I knew my agent had been talking with them about the possibility of me being among those they were considering. I was flattered by the invitation and immediately agreed to be in the New York studios the following week.

There are probably those who will tell you that if I was offered a position by CBS, all thoughts of playing another year would quickly fly out the window. Such was far from the case. In fact, I looked upon the audition as an experience that might be an advantage to me at some future date. I'd made no secret of the fact that it was a profession I one day hoped to get the opportunity to pursue, but only when the time was right—and when I was actually offered a job.

So, I went to New York for the experience. As far as I was concerned, I was still a football player, looking ahead to yet another shot at making it to the Super Bowl.

Jim Nantz, one of the CBS sportscasters who I'd long admired, met me upon my arrival and explained that what they were looking for was a staff for their pre-game and halftime in-studio show, which he would host. He explained that what we would do was tape a simulated show, complete with some interviews, inside tips (I thought it a bit ironic that he asked me to do a demonstration of how to protect the ball to avoid fumbling), and thoughts on match-ups of games that we would pretend were about to be played.

The whole process lasted no longer than an hour. Aside from fumbling the telestrater a time or two, I felt I'd done well. Nantz was complimentary and said he hoped things worked out. While I knew he would have input, the final decision would not be his. Aware that I was likely only one of several who had and would be invited to such auditions, I left feeling good about my chances of being offered a job. I thanked Jim and was on my way back home to work on my golf game.

A week or so later, I was in Las Vegas where I had an opportunity to play golf with Marty Schottenheimer at Shadow Creek. Nothing was mentioned about football as we played, but that evening as we had dinner he finally asked if I'd made a decision about returning for another season. He said he'd heard the rumors that I was moving into television. I explained that there had been no offers and that it was my intention to play if he felt I could benefit the team.

The next day the Chiefs publicity department issued a release stating that I had made the decision to return for my seventeenth NFL season. To my thinking, the issue of my immediate future was settled.

Then Ed Hookstratten phoned to say CBS had made an offer and that he had begun full-fledged negotiations. "But," he warned, "you can't tell anyone but Kathryn. This could take a while and we don't want a lot of rumors flying around."

For a time I kept my silence, but something as exciting as a change of careers is a hard secret to keep. I phoned my parents to tell them what was going on, swearing them to secrecy. Their reaction was one I had not anticipated. On one hand they were thrilled at the new opportunity that awaited me; on the other I was aware of a certain degree of sadness in their voices. The excitement of spending weekends in Kansas City, attending games in which I played, was coming to an end. In a manner of speaking, an exciting part of their lives was coming to an end as well. And I had to let at least one of my old buddies know. Ronnie Lott, who had already made the successful transition from the playing field to the studio, was the only other person I told until the negotiations were over.

During that time I gave serious thought to what leaving the game would mean, making mental lists of pluses and minuses, and one thing finally jumped out at me. Throughout my career I'd always prepared for opponents during the off-season by visualizing every member of the defense we would face over the course of the year. I always felt I knew what every player I was going up against would do in certain situations. But, truthfully, those images hadn't been as strong of late. To me, it was as much a disadvantage as losing a step of speed.

And the idea of walking away from the game instead of limping just made sense. When Ed phoned to say the deal was done, my decision was already made.

Then came the hard part. I called Marty. He told me he was disappointed but said he felt I was probably making the right decision. Jimmy Raye, who had just taken over the offensive coordinator's job vacated by Paul Hackett, wasn't so understanding at first. "You can't do this to me," he said. "I need you." Soon, though, we were laughing, talking of old times, friends for life. "You'll do well," he finally said, "but we're going to miss you."

And I them.

Later I spoke with team president Carl Petersen to make him aware of my decision. He asked if it was based on the financial terms of my contract and I assured him that was not the case. "I've always been told that if you make an important decision," he offered, "it's a good idea to sleep on it for twenty-four hours and be sure you feel the same way when you wake up."

"Carl," I said, "I think the time is right." He pressed the issue no further.

The press conference organized by the Chiefs wasn't easy. Marty was there and said a few words, getting teary-eyed in the process. Jimmy Raye told those in attendance that he had never thought this day would come. When it came my time to step to the mike and say a few words I looked out into the audience and saw the faces of a number of my teammates, coaches, trainers, and front office people who had been so much a part of my life in Kansas City. At that moment it finally hit home that I was leaving a life and a group of people I cared for dearly.

I tried to keep it brief, to share with those on hand my love for the game and my appreciation for what it had meant to me; to verbalize the special feeling I had for Kansas City and its people. I tried to thank everyone who had helped my career along, knowing all the while that I was leaving people out who should be mentioned. But the words and thoughts weren't coming nearly as easily as I had thought they would. And yes, I cried. "I feel like the luckiest guy alive," I said. "So few people get to live what they always wanted to do. I have. Football has been my field of dreams."

Never in my life have I felt such a confusing mixture of sadness—for what I was leaving behind—and excitement—for what lay ahead.

That evening, Carl Petersen and his wife invited Kathryn and me to dinner—and yet another emotional experience I'd not expected. As we took our seats in the restaurant, everyone there rose, called out my name, and offered up a toast.

It was one of the warmest, kindest gestures I've ever experienced.

And so I leave the game with more than my share of fond memories, fully aware that whatever I provided it can never compare to what it gave to me. The sudden stop to a routine that I've followed throughout my adult life won't be an easy adjustment. Now, several months after making my decision to retire, I still find myself thinking of those things I'll no longer do: the off-season conditioning program and training camp, getting to the stadium before most of my teammates on game day, the jogs around the field, the team chapel services, standing in the tunnel, high-fiving everyone on the team as we prepared to take the field. I'll miss the camaraderie and the competition. I'm glad that I'll be able to remain close to it, even if in a network studio, alongside new CBS teammates Nantz, Brent Jones, and former 49ers coach George Seifert, instead of on the field.

I look forward to the new challenge.

APPENDIX

COLLEGE DAYS

In 1981, Marcus Allen's senior year at the University of Southern California, he set or tied twelve NCAA records en route to winning the Heisman Trophy. The list included:

Most yards gained, regular season. 2,342

Highest per-game rushing average. 212.9

Most games 200 yards or more rushing 8

Most consecutive 200-yard games 5

Most yards rushing in four consecutive games. 926

Most yards rushing in five consecutive games. 1,136

Most rushes, season 403

Most all-purpose running plays, season. 432

Most all-purpose yards, season. .2,559

Highest per-carry rushing average, season. 5.81

Most yards, two successive seasons 3,905

Most 100-yard games, season (shared by 5) 11

Source: USC Sports Information Department

IN THE PROS

ALLEN'S GAME-BY-GAME STATISTICS

1982—Los Angeles Raiders

Date		Opp.	No.	Yds.	Avg.	TD	No.	Yds.	Avg.	TD
				Rushing				**Receiving**		
9/12	@	San Francisco	23	116	5.0	1	4	64	16.0	0
9/19	@	Atlanta	12	56	4.7	1	4	39	9.8	1
11/22		San Diego	18	87	4.8	2	5	37	7.4	0
11/28	@	Cincinnati	8	0	0.0	0	6	54	9.0	0
12/5		Seattle	24	156	6.5	2	2	14	7.0	0
12/12	@	Kansas City	18	47	2.6	0	1	1	1.0	0
12/18		L.A. Rams	25	93	3.7	3	8	61	7.6	0
12/26		Denver	12	16	1.3	0	5	91	18.2	2
1/2	@	San Diego	20	126	6.3	2	3	40	13.3	0
Playoffs										
1/8		Cleveland	17	72	4.2	2	6	75	12.5	0
1/15		N.Y. Jets	15	36	2.4	1	6	37	6.2	0

1983—Los Angeles Raiders

Date		Opp.	No.	Yds.	Avg.	TD	No.	Yds.	Avg.	TD
				Rushing				**Receiving**		
9/4	@	Cincinnati	17	47	2.8	2	3	19	6.3	0
9/11		Houston	17	96	5.6	0	4	29	7.3	0
9/19		Miami	22	105	4.8	0	1	10	10.0	0
9/25	@	Denver	15	45	3.0	0	4	20	5.0	0
10/2	@	Washington				*Did Not Play*				
10/9		Kansas City	21	53	2.5	0	6	58	9.7	0
10/16	@	Seattle	18	86	4.8	0	5	25	5.0	1
10/23	@	Dallas	15	55	3.7	0	7	67	9.6	0
10/30		Seattle	13	30	2.3	1	8	104	13.0	0
11/6	@	Kansas City	21	64	3.0	1	3	31	10.3	0
11/13		Denver	18	84	4.7	1	6	49	8.2	0
11/20	@	Buffalo	26	89	3.4	1	8	68	8.5	0
11/27		N.Y. Giants	13	64	4.9	1	4	19	4.8	0
12/1	@	San Diego	16	38	2.4	0	1	7	7.0	0
12/11		St. Louis	18	86	4.8	0	3	15	11.7	1
12/18		San Diego	16	72	4.5	2	5	49	9.8	0
Playoffs										
1/1		Pittsburgh	13	121	9.3	2	5	38	7.6	0
1/8		Seattle	25	154	6.2	0	7	62	8.9	1
1/22		Wash. (SB XVIII)	20	191	9.6	2	2	18	9.0	0

1984—Los Angeles Raiders

		Rushing				Receiving			
Date	Opp.	No.	Yds.	Avg.	TD	No.	Yds.	Avg.	TD
9/2	@ Houston	21	81	3.9	1	5	38	7.6	0
9/9	Green Bay	20	81	4.1	1	3	13	4.3	0
9/16	@ Kansas City	22	69	3.1	0	6	46	7.7	0
9/24	San Diego	18	47	2.6	3	6	62	10.3	1
9/30	@ Denver	13	66	5.1	0	4	44	11.0	0
10/7	Seattle	15	40	2.7	1	4	173	43.3	1
10/14	Minnesota	17	54	3.2	1	6	42	7.0	0
10/21	@ San Diego	19	107	5.6	0	5	40	8.0	1
10/28	Denver	16	70	4.4	1	6	63	10.5	1
11/4	@ Chicago	15	42	2.8	0	4	53	13.3	0
11/12	@ Seattle	15	57	3.8	2	5	37	7.4	0
11/18	Kansas City	16	95	5.9	0	3	21	7.0	0
11/25	Indianapolis	18	110	6.1	0	1	9	9.0	0
12/2	@ Miami	20	155	7.8	3	1	10	10.0	0
12/10	@ Detroit	17	56	3.3	0	3	93	3.1	1
12/16	Pittsburgh	13	38	2.9	0	2	14	7.0	0
Playoffs									
12/22	@ Seattle	17	61	3.6	0	5	90	18.0	1

1985—Los Angeles Raiders

		Rushing				Receiving			
Date	Opp.	No.	Yds.	Avg.	TD	No.	Yds.	Avg.	TD
9/8	N.Y. Jets	20	76	3.8	2	2	30	15.0	0
9/12	@ Kansas City	14	59	3.6	0	6	27	4.5	0
9/22	San Francisco	12	59	4.9	0	8	53	6.6	0
9/29	@ New England	21	98	4.7	0	3	30	10.0	0
10/6	Kansas City	29	126	4.3	0	3	24	8.0	0
10/13	New Orleans	28	107	3.8	2	3	51	17.0	0
10/20	@ Cleveland	20	81	4.1	0	3	41	13.7	1
10/28	San Diego	30	111	3.7	3	3	24	8.0	0
11/3	@ Seattle	19	101	5.3	0	5	49	9.8	0
11/10	@ San Diego	28	119	4.3	1	5	30	6.0	0
11/17	Cincinnati	31	135	4.4	0	6	54	9.0	1
11/24	Denver	24	173	7.2	1	4	49	12.3	0
12/1	@ Atlanta	29	156	5.6	0	2	42	21.0	1
12/8	@ Denver	25	135	5.4	1	5	21	4.2	0
12/15	Seattle	27	109	4.0	1	1	5	5.0	0
12/23	@ L.A. Rams	24	123	5.1	0	8	25	3.1	0
Playoffs									
1/5	New England	22	121	5.5	1	3	8	2.7	0

1986—Los Angeles Raiders

Date	Opp.	Rushing				Receiving			
		No.	Yds.	Avg.	TD	No.	Yds.	Avg.	TD
9/7	@ Denver	24	102	4.3	1	6	102	17.0	1
9/14	@ Washington	23	104	4.5	0	5	33	6.6	0
9/21	N.Y. Giants	15	40	2.7	0	5	86	17.2	0
9/28	San Diego	Did Not Play / Ankle							
10/5	@ Kansas City	Did Not Play / Ankle							
10/12	Seattle	6	11	1.8	0	1	11	11.0	0
10/19	@ Miami	21	96	4.6	2	3	20	6.7	1
10/26	@ Houston	Did Not Play / Hamstring							
11/2	Denver	22	71	3.2	0	4	19	4.8	0
11/9	@ Dallas	7	29	4.1	0	1	5	5.0	0
11/16	Cleveland	13	56	4.3	0	1	3	3.0	0
11/20	@ San Diego	21	88	4.2	1	4	19	4.8	0
11/30	Philadelphia	24	59	2.5	0	5	91	18.2	0
12/8	@ Seattle	9	12	1.3	0	2	14	7.0	0
12/14	Kansas City	13	60	4.6	1	6	38	6.3	0
12/21	Indianapolis	10	31	3.1	0	3	12	4.0	0

1987—Los Angeles Raiders

Date	Opp.	Rushing				Receiving			
		No.	Yds.	Avg.	TD	No.	Yds.	Avg.	TD
9/13	@ Green Bay	33	136	4.1	1	2	0	0.0	0
9/20	Detroit	22	79	3.6	1	3	6	2.0	0
10/25	Seattle	11	29	2.6	0	3	14	4.7	0
11/1	@ New England	16	41	2.6	1	5	60	12.0	0
11/8	@ Minnesota	11	50	4.5	0	4	12	3.0	0
11/15	@ San Diego	13	82	6.3	0	3	21	3.0	0
11/22	Denver	11	44	4.0	0	4	60	15.0	0
11/30	@ Seattle	18	76	4.2	0	3	20	6.7	0
12/6	Buffalo	15	47	3.1	1	5	58	11.6	0
12/13	@ Kansas City	18	60	3.3	1	3	53	17.7	0
12/20	Cleveland	14	35	2.5	0	10	84	8.4	0
12/27	Chicago	18	75	4.2	0	6	22	3.7	0

1988—Los Angeles Raiders

Date	Opp.	Rushing				Receiving			
		No.	Yds.	Avg.	TD	No.	Yds.	Avg.	TD
9/4	San Diego	28	88	3.1	2	1	9	9.0	0
9/11	@ Houston	22	70	3.2	2	1	9	9.0	0
9/18	L.A. Rams	14	53	3.8	0	5	54	10.8	1
9/26	@ Denver	22	56	2.5	1	2	16	8.0	0
10/2	Cincinnati	11	53	4.8	0	5	32	6.4	0
10/9				*Did Not Play*					
10/16	@ Kansas City	11	20	1.8	1	1	7	7.0	0
10/23	@ New Orleans	20	102	5.1	0	3	26	8.7	0
10/30	Kansas City	21	70	3.3	1	2	20	10.0	0
11/6	@ San Diego	17	67	3.9	0	0	0	0.0	0
11/13	@ San Francisco	14	58	4.1	0	1	9	9.0	0
11/20	Atlanta	7	18	2.6	0	3	30	10.0	0
11/28	@ Seattle	8	75	9.4	0	1	17	17.0	0
12/4	Denver	13	57	4.4	0	3	25	8.3	0
12/11	@ Buffalo	11	37	3.4	0	3	31	10.3	0
12/18	Seattle	4	7	1.8	0	2	5	2.5	0

1989—Los Angeles Raiders

Date	Opp.	Rushing				Receiving			
		No.	Yds.	Avg.	TD	No.	Yds.	Avg.	TD
9/10	San Diego	13	51	3.9	1	2	−1	−0.5	0
9/17	@ Kansas City	18	58	3.2	0	3	44	14.7	0
9/24	@ Denver	10	45	4.5	0	6	63	10.5	0
10/1	Seattle	11	65	5.9	0	3	31	10.3	0
10/9	@ N.Y. Jets	10	43	4.3	0	4	34	8.5	0
10/15	Kansas City			*Injured Reserve / Knee*					
10/22	@ Philadelphia			*Injured Reserve / Knee*					
10/29	Washington			*Injured Reserve / Knee*					
11/5	Cincinnati			*Injured Reserve / Knee*					
11/12	@ San Diego			*Injured Reserve / Knee*					
11/19	@ Houston			*Injured Reserve / Knee*					
11/26	New England			*Injured Reserve / Knee*					
12/3	Denver			*Injured Reserve / Knee*					
12/10	Phoenix	4	10	2.5	1	1	9	9.0	0
12/17	@ Seattle	1	8	8.0	0	0	0	0.0	0
12/24	@ N.Y. Giants	2	13	6.5	0	1	11	11.0	0

1990—Los Angeles Raiders

		Rushing				Receiving			
Date	Opp.	No.	Yds.	Avg.	TD	No.	Yds.	Avg.	TD
9/9	Denver	8	47	5.9	0	1	12	12.0	0
9/16	@ Seattle	10	35	3.5	0	1	29	29.0	0
9/23	Pittsburgh	11	44	4.0	1	1	2	2.0	0
9/30	Chicago	12	57	4.8	2	0	0	0.0	0
10/7	@ Buffalo	20	71	3.6	1	2	16	8.0	0
10/14	Seattle	12	41	3.4	0	1	11	11.0	0
10/21	@ San Diego	8	45	5.6	0	3	50	16.7	0
11/4	@ Kansas City	7	24	3.4	0	0	0	0.0	0
11/11	Green Bay	5	17	3.4	2	0	0	0.0	0
11/19	@ Miami	19	79	4.2	1	2	22	11.0	0
11/25	Kansas City	15	76	5.1	3	0	0	0.0	0
12/2	@ Denver	11	22	2.0	0	0	0	0.0	0
12/10	@ Detroit	7	18	2.6	1	3	28	9.3	0
12/16	Cincinnati	14	39	2.8	0	0	0	0.0	0
12/22	@ Minnesota	12	37	3.1	0	1	19	19.0	0
12/30	San Diego	8	30	3.8	1	0	0	0.0	0
Playoffs									
1/31	Cincinnati	21	140	6.7	0	1	24	24.0	0
1/20	@ Buffalo	10	26	2.6	0	2	19	9.5	0

1991—Los Angeles Raiders

		Rushing				Receiving			
Date	Opp.	No.	Yds.	Avg.	TD	No.	Yds.	Avg.	TD
9/1	@ Houston	8	17	2.1	0	3	16	5.3	0
9/8	Denver			*Injured Reserve / Knee*					
9/15	Indianapolis			*Injured Reserve / Knee*					
9/22	@ Atlanta			*Injured Reserve / Knee*					
9/29	San Francisco			*Injured Reserve / Knee*					
10/6	San Diego			*Injured Reserve / Knee*					
10/13	@ Seattle			*Injured Reserve / Knee*					
10/20	L.A. Rams			*Injured Reserve / Knee*					
10/28	@ Kansas City			*Injured Reserve / Knee*					
11/10	@ Denver	4	15	3.8	0	0	0	0.0	0
11/17	Seattle	9	54	6.0	0	1	10	10.0	0
11/24	@ Cincinnati	3	19	6.3	1	0	0	0.0	0
12/1	@ San Diego	9	45	5.0	0	2	7	3.5	0
12/8	Buffalo	16	57	3.6	1	3	38	12.7	0
12/16	@ New Orleans	5	25	5.0	0	1	15	15.0	0
12/22	Kansas City	9	55	6.1	0	5	45	9.0	0
Playoffs									
12/28	@ Kansas City	7	39	5.6	0	1	4	4.0	0

1992—Los Angeles Raiders

Date		Opp.	Rushing				Receiving			
			No.	Yds.	Avg.	TD	No.	Yds.	Avg.	TD
9/6	@	Denver	1	4	4.0	0	0	0	0.0	0
9/13	@	Cincinnati	4	22	5.5	1	3	49	16.3	0
9/20		Cleveland	8	52	6.5	0	8	57	7.1	0
9/28	@	Kansas City	6	−3	−0.5	0	1	10	10.0	0
10/11		Buffalo	10	37	3.7	0	1	11	11.0	0
10/18	@	Seattle	10	38	3.8	0	0	0	0.0	0
10/25		Dallas	3	9	3.0	1	0	0	0.0	0
11/8	@	Philadelphia	6	23	3.8	0	1	14	14.0	0
11/15		Seattle	1	3	3.0	0	0	0	0.0	0
11/22		Denver	1	5	5.0	0	2	21	10.5	1
11/29	@	San Diego	4	20	5.0	0	3	34	11.3	0
12/6		Kansas City	5	37	7.4	0	1	8	8.0	0
12/14	@	Miami	1	2	2.0	0	3	23	7.7	0
12/20		San Diego	2	12	6.0	0	1	13	13.0	0
12/26	@	Washington	5	40	8.0	0	4	37	9.3	0

1993—Kansas City Chiefs

Date		Opp.	Rushing				Receiving			
			No.	Yds.	Avg.	TD	No.	Yds.	Avg.	TD
9/5	@	Tampa Bay	13	79	6.1	0	1	12	12.0	1
9/12	@	Houston	6	17	2.8	0	0	0	0.0	0
9/20		Denver	17	91	5.4	0	1	10	10.0	0
10/3		L.A. Raiders	17	24	1.4	1	1	8	8.0	0
10/10		Cincinnati	13	48	3.7	1	1	9	9.0	0
10/17	@	San Diego	13	46	3.5	1	3	30	10.0	1
10/31	@	Miami	4	14	3.5	0	5	36	7.2	0
11/8		Green Bay	17	35	2.1	1	2	15	7.5	0
11/14	@	L.A. Raiders	17	85	5.0	1	1	4	4.0	0
11/21		Chicago	16	78	4.9	2	1	11	11.0	0
11/28		Buffalo	22	74	3.4	0	2	28	14.0	1
12/5	@	Seattle	12	73	6.1	3	4	26	6.5	0
12/12	@	Denver	14	41	2.9	1	1	0	0.0	0
12/19		San Diego	14	16	1.1	1	5	20	4.0	0
12/26	@	Minnesota	4	9	2.3	0	3	15	5.0	0
1/2		Seattle	7	34	4.9	0	3	14	4.7	0
Playoffs										
1/8		Pittsburgh	21	67	3.2	1	4	29	7.3	0
1/16	@	Houston	14	74	5.3	1	1	12	12.0	0
1/23	@	Buffalo	18	50	2.8	1	2	36	18.0	0

1994—Kansas City Chiefs

Date		Opp.	Rushing				Receiving			
			No.	Yds.	Avg.	TD	No.	Yds.	Avg.	TD
9/4	@	New Orleans	17	82	4.8	1	3	16	5.3	0
9/11		San Francisco	20	69	3.5	1	2	45	22.5	0
9/18	@	Atlanta	8	11	1.4	0	3	22	7.3	0
9/25		L.A. Rams	15	59	3.9	0	2	6	3.0	0
10/9	@	San Diego	10	17	1.7	0	9	83	9.2	0
10/17	@	Denver	16	63	3.9	1	5	49	9.8	0
10/23		Seattle	14	77	5.5	1	2	17	8.5	0
10/30	@	Buffalo	8	27	3.4	1	3	18	6.0	0
11/6		L.A. Raiders	15	62	4.1	0	5	30	6.0	0
11/13		San Diego			*Inactive / Knee*					
11/20		Cleveland			*Inactive / Knee*					
11/27	@	Seattle			*Inactive / Knee*					
12/4		Denver	16	49	3.1	1	2	12	6.0	0
12/12	@	Miami	7	19	2.7	1	5	49	9.8	0
12/18		Houston	10	42	4.2	0	1	2	2.0	0
12/24	@	L.A. Raiders	33	132	4.0	0	0	0	0.0	0
Playoffs										
12/31	@	Miami	14	64	4.6	0	5	49	9.8	0

1995—Kansas City Chiefs

Date		Opp.	Rushing				Receiving			
			No.	Yds.	Avg.	TD	No.	Yds.	Avg.	TD
9/3	@	Seattle	4	19	4.8	0	1	11	11.0	0
9/10		N.Y. Giants	19	86	4.5	1	2	−1	−0.5	0
9/17		Oakland	17	53	3.1	0	4	37	9.3	0
9/24	@	Cleveland	1	3	3.0	0	0	0	0.0	0
10/1	@	Arizona	11	62	5.6	0	1	13	13.0	0
10/9		San Diego	14	26	1.9	0	3	14	4.7	0
10/15		New England	13	61	4.7	0	2	10	5.0	0
10/22	@	Denver	21	121	5.8	1	1	−1	−0.5	0
11/5		Washington	9	34	3.8	1	1	9	9.0	0
11/12	@	San Diego	16	63	3.9	1	1	19	19.0	0
11/19		Houston	16	49	3.1	0	1	4	4.0	0
11/23	@	Dallas	3	4	1.3	0	1	11	11.0	0
12/3	@	Oakland	21	124	5.9	1	3	33	11.0	0
12/11	@	Miami	16	88	5.5	0	2	7	3.5	0
12/17		Denver	16	64	4.0	0	4	44	11.0	0
12/24		Seattle	10	43	4.3	0	0	0	0.0	0
Playoffs										
1/7		Indianapolis	21	94	4.5	0	2	21	10.5	0

1996—Kansas City Chiefs

		Rushing				Receiving			
Date	Opp.	No.	Yds.	Avg.	TD	No.	Yds.	Avg.	TD
9/1	@ Houston	6	18	3.0	0	0	0	0.0	0
9/8	Oakland	12	34	2.8	0	1	29	29.0	0
9/15	@ Seattle	12	52	4.3	2	1	10	10.0	0
9/22	Denver	17	55	3.2	1	1	6	6.0	0
9/29	@ San Diego	9	35	3.9	0	6	88	14.6	0
10/7	Pittsburgh	18	69	3.8	1	4	29	7.2	0
10/17	Seattle	14	39	2.8	2	0	0	0.0	0
10/27	@ Denver	7	22	3.1	0	3	29	9.6	0
11/3	@ Minnesota	18	89	4.9	1	1	2	2.0	0
11/10	Green Bay	10	48	4.8	0	0	0	0.0	0
11/17	Chicago	16	64	4.0	0	0	0	0.0	0
11/24	San Diego	6	30	5.0	0	7	60	8.6	0
11/28	@ Detroit	15	73	4.9	2	0	0	0.0	0
12/9	@ Oakland	14	64	4.6	0	1	4	4.0	0
12/15	Indianapolis	12	51	4.3	0	1	7	7.0	0
12/22	@ Buffalo	20	87	3.9	0	1	6	6.0	0

1997—Kansas City Chiefs

		Rushing				Receiving			
Date	Opp.	No.	Yds.	Avg.	TD	No.	Yds.	Avg.	TD
8/31	@ Denver	3	−2	−0.7	0	0	0	0.0	0
9/8	@ Oakland	3	13	4.3	0	1	14	14.0	0
9/14	Buffalo	1	8	8.0	0	0	0	0.0	0
9/21	@ Carolina	9	31	3.4	1	0	0	0.0	0
9/28	Seattle	19	78	4.1	2	2	18	9.0	0
10/5	@ Miami	7	25	3.6	0	2	0	0.0	0
10/16	San Diego	7	29	4.1	1	1	13	13.0	0
10/26	St. Louis	3	7	2.3	1	1	10	10.0	0
11/3	Pittsburgh	10	49	4.9	0	0	0	0.0	0
11/9	@ Jacksonville	3	37	12.3	0	1	7	7.0	0
11/16	Denver	16	43	2.7	2	2	19	9.5	0
11/23	@ Seattle	7	19	2.7	1	0	0	0.0	0
11/30	San Francisco	13	48	3.7	1	0	0	0.0	0
12/7	Oakland	6	26	4.3	0	0	0	0.0	0
12/14	@ San Diego	8	44	5.5	1	0	0	0.0	0
12/21	New Orleans	9	50	5.6	1	1	5	5.0	0
Playoffs									
1/4	Denver	12	37	3.1	0	1	8	8.0	0

Source: Kansas City Chiefs Public Relations Department